Engaging Children in Applied Linguistics Research

Who should speak for children in applied linguistics research? Should it be only adults, or is there room for children's perspectives and views as well? This pioneering book brings children's voices to the forefront and shows that listening to them can open up new possibilities to conduct research 'with' children rather than just 'on' them. It covers a range of possibilities, from simply asking for children's perspectives to increasing levels of active participation, including adult–child partnerships as well as child-led research. Examples taken from the interdisciplinary literature illustrate what is feasible to achieve in different contexts, and both benefits and challenges are discussed alongside the most pressing ethical dilemmas. A new, alternative framework for researching with children is promoted, which invites teachers and researchers to consider a wider range of roles that children can play. It also encourages them to find their own opportunities when it comes to research involving children.

Annamaria Pinter is a professor at the Department of Applied Linguistics, University of Warwick. She is the author of *Teaching Young Language Learners* (2017) and *Children Learning Second Languages* (2011), and she is joint series editor of Early Language Learning in School Contexts by Multilingual Matters.

THE CAMBRIDGE APPLIED LINGUISTICS SERIES

The authority on cutting-edge Applied Linguistics research

Series Editors 2007–present: Carol A. Chapelle and Susan Hunston
        1988–2007: Michael H. Long and Jack C. Richards

For a complete list of titles please visit: www.cambridge.org

Recent titles in this series

Language Aptitude Theory and Practice
Edited by *Zhisheng (Edward) Wen*, *Peter Skehan* and *Richard L. Sparks*

Learning Vocabulary in Another Language
3rd edition *I. S. P. Nation*

Reading in a Second Language
Moving from Theory to Practice 2nd edition *William Grabe* and *Junko Yamashita*

Corpora in Applied Linguistics
2nd edition *Susan Hunston*

The Language of Mental Illness
Corpus Linguistics and the Construction of Mental Illness in the Press *Hazel Price*

Mobile Assisted Language Learning
Concepts, Contexts and Challenges *Glenn Stockwell*

Research Genres across Languages
Multilingual Communication Online *Carmen Pérez-Llantada*

Validity Argument in Language Testing
Case Studies of Validation Research Edited by *Carol A. Chapelle* and *Erik Voss*

Doing English Grammar
Theory, Description and Practice *Roger Berry*

Learner Corpus Research Meets Second Language Acquisition
Bert Le Bruyn and *Magali Paquot*

Second Language Speech Fluency
From Research to Practice *Parvaneh Tavakoli* and *Clare Wright*

Ontologies of English
Conceptualising the Language for Learning, Teaching, and Assessment Edited by *Christopher J. Hall* and *Rachel Wicaksono*

Task-Based Language Teaching
Theory and Practice *Rod Ellis*, *Peter Skehan*, *Shaofeng Li*, *Natsuko Shintani* and *Craig Lambert*

Feedback in Second Language Writing
Contexts and Issues 2nd Edition Edited by *Ken Hyland* and *Fiona Hyland*

Language and Television Series
A Linguistic Approach to TV Dialogue *Monika Bednarek*

Intelligibility, Oral Communication, and the Teaching of Pronunciation
John M. Levis

Multilingual Education
Between Language Learning and Translanguaging Edited by *Jasone Cenoz* and *Durk Gorter*

Learning Vocabulary in Another Language
2nd Edition *I. S. P. Nation*

Narrative Research in Applied Linguistics
Edited by *Gary Barkhuizen*

Teacher Research in Language Teaching
A Critical Analysis *Simon Borg*

Figurative Language, Genre and Register
Alice Deignan, *Jeannette Littlemore* and *Elena Semino*

Exploring ELF
Academic English Shaped by Non-Native Speakers *Anna Mauranen*

Genres across the Disciplines
Student Writing in Higher Education *Hilary Nesi* and *Sheena Gardner*

Disciplinary Identities
Individuality and Community in Academic Discourse *Ken Hyland*

Replication Research in Applied Linguistics
Edited by *Graeme Porte*

The Language of Business Meetings
Michael Handford

Reading in a Second Language
Moving from Theory to Practice *William Grabe*

Modelling and Assessing Vocabulary Knowledge
Edited by *Helmut Daller*, *James Milton* and *Jeanine Treffers-Daller*

Practice in a Second Language
Perspectives from Applied Linguistics and Cognitive Psychology Edited by *Robert M. DeKeyser*

Task-Based Language Education
From Theory to Practice Edited by *Kris van den Branden*

Second Language Needs Analysis
Edited by *Michael H. Long*

Insights into Second Language Reading
A Cross-Linguistic Approach *Keiko Koda*

Research Genres
Exploration and Applications *John M. Swales*

Critical Pedagogies and Language Learning
Edited by *Bonny Norton* and *Kelleen Toohey*

Exploring the Dynamics of Second Language Writing
Edited by *Barbara Kroll*

Understanding Expertise in Teaching
Case Studies of Second Language Teachers *Amy B. M. Tsui*

Criterion-Referenced Language Testing
James Dean Brown and *Thom Hudson*

Corpora in Applied Linguistics
Susan Hunston

Pragmatics in Language Teaching
Edited by *Kenneth R. Rose* and *Gabriele Kasper*

Cognition and Second Language Instruction
Edited by *Peter Robinson*

Research Perspectives on English for Academic Purposes
Edited by *John Flowerdew* and *Matthew Peacock*

Computer Applications in Second Language Acquisition
Foundations for Teaching, Testing and Research *Carol A. Chapelle*

Engaging Children in Applied Linguistics Research

Annamaria Pinter
University of Warwick

CAMBRIDGE
UNIVERSITY PRESS

CAMBRIDGE UNIVERSITY PRESS

Shaftesbury Road, Cambridge CB2 8EA, United Kingdom

One Liberty Plaza, 20th Floor, New York, NY 10006, USA

477 Williamstown Road, Port Melbourne, VIC 3207, Australia

314–321, 3rd Floor, Plot 3, Splendor Forum, Jasola District Centre, New Delhi – 110025, India

103 Penang Road, #05–06/07, Visioncrest Commercial, Singapore 238467

Cambridge University Press is part of Cambridge University Press & Assessment, a department of the University of Cambridge.

We share the University's mission to contribute to society through the pursuit of education, learning and research at the highest international levels of excellence.

www.cambridge.org
Information on this title: www.cambridge.org/9781316518069

DOI: 10.1017/9781009049078

© Annamaria Pinter 2023

This publication is in copyright. Subject to statutory exception and to the provisions of relevant collective licensing agreements, no reproduction of any part may take place without the written permission of Cambridge University Press & Assessment.

First published 2023

A catalogue record for this publication is available from the British Library.

Library of Congress Cataloging-in-Publication Data
Names: Pinter, Annamaria, author.
Title: Engaging children in applied linguistics research / Annamaria Pinter.
Description: Cambridge, United Kingdom ; New York, NY : Cambridge University Press, 2023. | Series: Cambridge applied linguistics
Identifiers: LCCN 2023007607 (print) | LCCN 2023007608 (ebook) | ISBN 9781316518069 (hardback) | ISBN 9781009048873 (paperback) | ISBN 9781009049078 (epub)
Subjects: LCSH: Applied linguistics–Research–Methodology. | Children–Research–Methodology. | Participant observation.
Classification: LCC P129 .P55 2024 (print) | LCC P129 (ebook) | DDC 418.007–dc23/eng/20230313
LC record available at https://lccn.loc.gov/2023007607
LC ebook record available at https://lccn.loc.gov/2023007608

ISBN 978-1-316-51806-9 Hardback
ISBN 978-1-009-04887-3 Paperback

Cambridge University Press & Assessment has no responsibility for the persistence or accuracy of URLs for external or third-party internet websites referred to in this publication and does not guarantee that any content on such websites is, or will remain, accurate or appropriate.

Contents

List of Figures   xi
List of Tables   xii
Series Editors' Preface   xiii

1 Setting the Scene   1
  1.1 Introduction   1
  1.2 A Few Key Premises and Why I Decided to Write This Book   2
  1.3 The Title of the Volume   6
  1.4 Why Is This Book Needed Now?   8
  1.5 The Use of Key Terms   11
  1.6 The Map of the Book   13
  1.7 Conclusion   17

2 *From Traditional to Contemporary Conceptions of Childhood*   18
  2.1 Introduction   18
  2.2 Who Is a Child?   18
  2.3 A Brief Historical Overview of Studying Children   21
  2.4 Developmental Psychology   22
  2.5 The Emergence of the New Sociology of Childhood   23
  2.6 The Social Child: A 'Rights-Bearing' Citizen   28
  2.7 Childhood Studies from the 1990s to Current Times and Children as Future Makers   32
  2.8 Towards a New Framework in Working with Children in Applied Linguistics   34
  2.9 Children as Social Actors in Second Language Education Research   39
  2.10 Conclusion   41

viii Contents

3	*Voice, Agency and Participation*	42
	3.1 Introduction	42
	3.2 The Key Concepts	42
	3.2.1 Voice	43
	3.2.2 Agency	46
	3.2.3 Degrees of Participation	47
	3.3 Using Participatory Methods and Tools	53
	3.4 Types of Participation: Research 'with' and 'by' Children	60
	3.5 The Relationship between Co-Researching (with) and Child-Led Research (by)	68
	3.6 Conclusion	74
4	*Child-Centredness and Democratic School Structures*	75
	4.1 Introduction	75
	4.2 Child-Centredness	76
	4.3 Learner-Centredness in Applied Linguistics	80
	4.4 Self-Determination Theory	82
	4.5 Engagement and Positive Emotional States	83
	4.6 Twenty-First Century Demands and Twenty-First Century Skills: Future-Proofing Education	84
	4.7 From Traditional to Democratic School Structures	86
	4.8 Learner-Centred Education and International Baccalaureate Schools	90
	4.9 Active Self-Directed Learning in Maker Spaces	90
	4.10 School Reform: Learner Consultation in Schools	92
	4.11 UNICEF Schools and Voice-Inclusive Practices in Schools	94
	4.12 Democratic Schools	95
	4.13 The Extended Framework of Researching with Children in Applied Linguistics	97
	4.14 Conclusion	101
5	*Children's Roles and Status in Applied Linguistics Research*	103
	5.1 Introduction	103
	5.2 Influences of Child Development Theories on Child L2 Education	103
	5.3 From a Narrow Focus to a Wide Range of Topics	107
	5.3.1 Areas of Research Activity	109
	5.4 Main Characteristics of SLA Research	110

	5.5	The Selected Set of Studies	112
		5.5.1 Focus/Area of Interest	114
		5.5.2 Age of Participants	114
		5.5.3 About the Contexts of Research	115
	5.6	Studies Positioned on the 'on-about-with-by' Continuum	116
		5.6.1 Research 'on' and 'about' Children	117
		5.6.2 Towards Research 'with' Children	122
	5.7	Conclusion	126
6	*Filling the Gap: What Kind of Research Is Needed?*		127
	6.1	Introduction	127
	6.2	A Move from Studies 'on' and 'about' to 'with' and 'by' Children	128
	6.3	Category 1: Eliciting Children's Views about Important Matters (Examples 1–7)	129
	6.4	Category 2: Children in Active Roles (Examples 8–15)	149
	6.5	Category 3: Child-Led Research (Examples 16 and 17)	164
	6.6	The Focus of Research 'with' and 'by' Children in Applied Linguistics	170
	6.7	Conclusion	172
7	*Ethical Issues and Dilemmas*		173
	7.1	Introduction	173
	7.2	Origins of Research Ethics with Children	173
	7.3	The UNCRC and Rights-Based Research Ethics with Children: A Compromise between Children's and Adults' Rights	174
		7.3.1 A Balance between Protection and Participation Rights	176
	7.4	Codes of Practice Relating to Applied Linguistics	178
	7.5	The Debate about Consent	187
		7.5.1 Challenges with Consent	188
		7.5.2 Practical Difficulties Relating to Wording Consent Forms	192
		7.5.3 Consent across Local and Global Contexts	194
	7.6	Adult Roles in Research	196
	7.7	Challenges in Studies Where Children Play Active Roles	198
	7.8	Conclusion	200

8 *Towards Children's Active Engagement in Applied Linguistics Research* — 201
   8.1 Introduction — 201
   8.2 The Relevance of the Extended Framework for All — 201
   8.3 Bringing Together Arguments for More Active Participation — 204
   8.4 Research in the Vacuum versus Incorporated into School Life — 206
   8.5 Benefits and Challenges of Children's Active Participation — 206
   8.6 Future Directions and Challenges — 209
      8.6.1 The Future of Childhood Studies — 209
      8.6.2 The Unpredictability of the Future — 210
      8.6.3 The Need to Embrace Critical Approaches — 212
   8.7 What Is Needed in Our Field Now? — 213
   8.8 Conclusion — 216

Appendix of Studies — 217
References — 296
Index — 324

Figures

2.1	Key elements in the extended framework of research involving children in second language education	35
2.2	Types of research: 'On', 'about', 'with' and 'by' (on a continuum)	35
3.1	Hart's ladder of participation	49
3.2	Pathways to participation	50
3.3	Lundy's model of participation: Guiding questions	52
3.4	Identity collage created by a multilingual child (Sophie's collage, from Prasad, 2020, p. 919)	58
3.5	The continuum between research 'with' and research 'by' children	69
4.1	The key components of the extended framework	98
5.1	Types of research involving children	113
6.1	Diamond ranking activity template	140
6.2	Empty boxes representing different activities inviting children to place one, two or three beans to evaluate their experiences	141
6.3	Diamond ranking tool (Zandian, 2021)	142
6.4	Possible components of a mosaic	143
6.5	Body map–inspired identity text produced by a Polish–English bilingual EAL learner and a Vietnamese–English bilingual EAL learner in England	147
6.6	Can stories develop our language proficiency? Child questionnaire from Rout (2017)	158
6.7	Example of a questionnaire from child-led research (Pinter, 2019)	167
6.8	Examples of children's data analysis slides from the child-led project (Pinter, 2019)	169
7.1	Extract from Code of Ehtics (BAAL)	180
7.2	Extract from Code of Ehtics (BERA)	181
7.3	ERIC Guidelines	182
7.4	EECERA Guidelines	184
8.1	An example of running multiple child-led research projects in a school (Fielding & Bragg, 2003, p. 42)	207

Tables

1.1	Types of research involving children, adapted from Kellett (2010a) and Mayne and Howitt (2015)	6
1.2	Structure of the book	13
2.1	Traditional conceptions of childhood (adapted from James et al., 1998)	26
2.2	Child roles in research (framework adapted from Mayne & Howitt, 2015 and Christensen & Prout, 2002, p. 480)	39
3.1	An actual CAR project (adapted from Kellett, 2005)	65
4.1	A framework of twenty-first century skills (adapted from Binkley et al., 2012)	85
4.2	Six attributes of autonomy-promoting schools (adapted from Reeve & Assor, 2011)	88
4.3	Framework of pupil consultation (adapted from Flutter & Rudduck, 2004)	93
4.4	Learner feedback: Summary of themes (adapted from Flutter & Rudduck, 2004)	94
4.5	Fielding: Six types of partnerships (with reference to Fielding, 2001, chapter 3; Hart, 1992; Shier, 2001)	97
5.1	Broad areas of child L2 education	111
5.2	Age distribution in the studies in the Appendix	115
6.1	Summary of studies: Increasing levels of active participation	130
6.2	Topics of interest for research with and by children in applied linguistics	171

Series Editors' Preface

Global circumstances including migration, language education policy and recognition for the importance of English as a lingua franca have resulted in growing numbers of children learning a language in addition to their home language. This has led in turn to an increase in research undertaken by applied linguists where young learners are the subjects. Researchers regularly acknowledge the age-relevant practices that inform their investigations, but this often involves only limited modifications to normal research practice. It is reasonable to ask in addition whether research investigating children might better conceive of the subjects differently than as producers of data.

In *Engaging Children in Applied Linguistics Research*, Annamaria Pinter asks this question and responds to it in the affirmative. In particular, Pinter finds much of the research on children as second or foreign language learners lacking relevance for addressing children's needs, priorities, wellbeing and challenges. The purpose of the book is to sketch an alternative vision for conducting research on children as language learners by treating them as partners in research that investigates their acquisition of language. The idea of partnership is signalled by the title, 'engaging children in' rather than 'conducting research on', and the book discusses research projects that exemplify the unique findings that emerge when children are engaged. Pinter presents the philosophical motivation for proposing a shift in research orientation in addition to showing that child second and foreign language education could be better understood if children's perspectives were systematically invited into the design of research.

Engaging Children in Applied Linguistics Research is a welcome addition to the Cambridge Applied Linguistics Series because of the pioneering insights Pinter shares on a topic of central interest to applied linguists. Although the main focus of the book is language acquisition, the issue of involving research participants in the research process has a wider relevance, as does the issue of researching with children. The book will be a key reference as the need for understanding children as second and foreign language learners continues to grow.

Carol A. Chapelle

Susan Hunston

1 Setting the Scene

1.1 Introduction

This introductory chapter will outline the purpose of the volume and explain my personal commitment to the topic. The chapter will also begin to build a case for more diverse and more active roles for children in applied linguistics research.

Even though more and more empirical research has been targeting young language learners in applied linguistics, almost all this research is conceptualised and interpreted via an adult lens without any serious input from children themselves. The main argument of the volume is that such adult-focussed research could be usefully complemented with alternative methods and approaches which would give children the opportunity to engage in research more actively. Opening up a range of new participatory opportunities would bring many benefits to children, teachers and researchers alike. Such research can promote 'the wellbeing and flourishing of children' (Montreuil et al., 2021, p. 12) as well as generating knowledge that is fresh and uniquely different from adult views and representations.

This volume will begin to develop a justification for this argument by discussing evidence emerging from studies across a variety of disciplinary areas in order to incorporate fresh insights into research with children in applied linguistics and to raise awareness about child-focussed research. It is hoped that such cross-fertilisation between distinct bodies of literature relating to different disciplines, such as education, sociology, health care, social work, or climate change education, will lead to sparking new ideas, promoting new debates and inspiring new, creative ways of researching *with* children in applied linguistics.

1.2 A Few Key Premises and Why I Decided to Write This Book

This volume has emerged from my experience of engaging with both the theory and the practice of English as a second and foreign language teaching for young learners for over twenty-five years, as well as from inspirational work I have encountered in other disciplines. As a result of this, I have come to believe that the current, largely traditional approaches in applied linguistics research with children could be usefully expanded and supplemented with alternative approaches that encompass a wider range of roles for children.

I would like to start this book by laying down some premises to justify the content and the shape of the volume.

Premise 1: Children Are Routinely Underestimated by Adults

Let me illustrate this first premise with a story that takes me back more than twenty years to when I was working on my own PhD study. With an interest in task-based language teaching, I set out to design some classic 'spot the differences' tasks for ten-year-old children learning English in a state school in Hungary. The children were almost complete beginners, despite the fact that they had been learning English for two years at the time of the data collection. As an outsider researcher who had no previous connections with the school and the children, I relied on the English teacher's help and the textbook to design the linguistic content of the tasks. When I completed the tasks, the teacher said that the tasks looked too difficult and that the children were not going to be able to use them to interact with each other in English. Naturally, I got deeply worried and began to prepare myself for needing to redesign all my data elicitation tools. However, to my delight, and the English teacher's utter astonishment, when I tried the first set of tasks with the group, the children managed it, skilfully complementing their limited L2 English resources with some miming and code-switching. Over three video-recorded repetitions of practising with the same type of task, they improved both the fluency and the accuracy of their English performance, used gradually less L1, spotted more differences between the pictures, and collaborated more effectively with each other (Pinter, 2006; 2007). The children also seemingly enjoyed interacting with their partners in English. In the lesson breaks many of them created hand-drawn versions of the spot the differences task and carried on playing in pairs to entertain themselves, presumably because they were motivated to do better and better in the repeated task recordings. At the end of the data collection period, when the children were invited to watch their own video-recorded performances in pairs, they commented that they felt proud of their final performances and wanted to carry on. They expressed their regret that the textbook or the teacher never encouraged them to work with similar interactive tasks that required spontaneous rather than scripted language use.

This experience twenty years ago taught me many important lessons, but perhaps the most important one is that we must never underestimate what children can do if they put their minds to something. I also learnt that language learning, or any learning for that matter, is most effective when children enjoy the process, see the point of it, feel motivated to carry on practising even outside the lesson, and at the end feel that they have accomplished something that others can appreciate and that they themselves can be proud of. These ideas will be picked up and revisited in the upcoming chapters because they link to principles that define children's active participation in research.

Premise 2: Children Have Valuable Insights to Share about Important Matters, and We Need to Listen to Them

Over the decades of working with children, I have been constructing and reconstructing a personal conception of childhood, and, as a result, I have come to see children as resourceful and competent – often more competent than we would first imagine – and full of potential and promise. I have experienced again and again that when children are approached respectfully, trusted to make their own choices and given space to think for themselves, they can act responsibly and will often surprise adults with their contributions. Malaguzzi, the well-known founder of the Reggio Emilia schools, which will be discussed in later chapters, once said: 'All children, whatever their culture, whatever their lives, are rich, better equipped, more talented, stronger and more intelligent than we can suppose' (Cagliari et al., 2016, p. 397). Malaguzzi's own work was with young children in pre-schools, but such conceptions can and must surely be applied to children of all ages. Such views and beliefs about children have resonated with me since the beginning of my career, and over the years these beliefs have grown into a stronger conviction. The need to listen to children and take their views seriously will be one of the cornerstones of the upcoming arguments about child-focussed research.

For sure, I am not on my own with these beliefs about children. However, in applied linguistics, and particularly in child L2 education, such beliefs and conceptions are not routinely talked about. In fact, the literature in applied linguistics to date has not explicitly addressed adult conceptions of childhood and the status of children as language learners. We also have not 'problematized the role of English in children's lives' (López-Gopar, 2016, p. 7) and have not asked serious questions about why and how children might or might not want to learn second or foreign languages. Very few studies have attempted to find out about children's English language learning experiences other than by asking narrow questions framed by adult perspectives. I would like to argue that we also need to ask open-ended questions to explore children's views and perspectives about L2 learning and invite them to work with us in a more holistic way. Currently, we know very little about children's concerns and priorities, and in order to understand children's perspectives better, we need to develop a genuine space for dialogue and to listen and act on what we hear. Engaging with children in genuine dialogue will be the foundation of their potential active engagement in research.

Premise 3: It Is of Benefit to Cross-Fertilise Research from Different Discipline Areas with a Focus on Children

One reason why children's views and perspectives have not been given much attention in applied linguistics is because the field has been largely driven by the desire to push the boundaries of scientific knowledge about L2 language learning processes in childhood rather than by a desire to ask questions about how the participants themselves might see, benefit from and experience language learning and related research. Recently, scholars such as Crookes (2005), Ortega (2005), Ushioda (2021), and Yates (2005) have all begun to draw our attention to the importance of interrogating our practices in terms of the values of our research, that is, why we do the work that we do, who the true beneficiaries of our research are, and who we might be serving with our research. In a quest to serve the children, as primary beneficiaries of child second language education research, I have turned to work in other disciplines for inspiration. Such an attempt to bring together ideas from a wide variety of traditions and ways of working is challenging but also refreshing. Of course, it is not possible in this volume to give justice to the rich literatures in these discipline areas, and I do not claim to do that. Instead, the upcoming chapters will attempt to introduce some illustrative work to give a flavour of the type of child-focussed research that has been undertaken outside our field. My hope is that researchers interested in engaging children in applied linguistics research will take up the challenge of continuing this exploration, working on building bridges to connect us to scholars interested in children in other fields of study so that we can benefit and enrich each other's work.

Premise 4: Processes of Teaching, Learning and Researching Are All Connected

The main focus and interest in this volume is on promoting active roles for children in research that takes place in school contexts, emerging from but not necessarily limited to second language (mostly English as an L2) classrooms. In fact, the intention is to explore all kinds of possibilities for researching *with* children, in both short-term and longitudinal projects undertaken by teachers, academic facilitators or by teams of adults and children. The starting point will be to raise awareness about the possibility of inviting children as active participants and to generate ideas about how to involve them in various active roles in second language classroom research. The initial focus will be on possible ways of exploring the L2 classroom, but as will be illustrated in later chapters, projects can grow well beyond those. When children experience researching in active roles alongside adult facilitators, such experience will inevitably have an impact on how they come to think about their everyday teaching/learning experiences. It does not make sense to trust, respect and listen to a child intently only while they participate in a research project but not in everyday teaching. Looking at it from the other side, if children enjoy high degrees of autonomy in less hierarchical institutions, they are likely to be more prepared for active roles in research as well.

Child-centred approaches to learning and teaching emphasise that learners become active enquirers and feel motivated because they are genuinely interested in the selected topic or learning material and sustain enthusiasm for their project in the long term. Having had the privilege of working with children who played active roles in research, I have witnessed the zeal, enthusiasm and deep engagement on the children's part when they were working alongside adults as co-researchers and as novice researchers taking their first steps in child-led research projects (Pinter, 2019; Pinter et al., 2016). These children were keen to work independently on topics that were of interest to them; they were excited to take responsibility and make decisions for themselves; and they showed a huge appetite to take on more and more work and make a difference with their work. These potential advantages of involving children in more active roles in research can naturally cross over to teaching and learning processes.

Premise 5: A New Framework Is Needed to Supplement Current, More Traditional Approaches

There are four possible ways of involving children in research, which are research 'on' and 'about' children as well as research 'with' and

Table 1.1 Types of research involving children, adapted from Kellett (2010a) and Mayne and Howitt (2015)

Research on children	Research about children
Children's perspectives are interpreted by adults alone	Children's perspectives are interpreted by adults alone
Typically observations or tests	Interest in unique trajectories of children
	Typically small-scale, longitudinal case studies and other qualitative studies
Research with children	**Research by children**
('weaker' and 'stronger' forms)	Empowering children to undertake their own research
Respect for children's capacities	
Focus on listening to children	Implementing their own agenda
Partnership and collaboration	Holistic engagement from selecting questions to dissemination
Information sharing, dialogue	
Co-constructing knowledge	Adult guiding and supporting children to conduct their own research

'by' children (Kellett, 2010a; Mayne & Howitt, 2015; see Table 1.1). I will argue that in addition to the more passive roles of 'on' and 'about', we need the more active roles of 'with' and 'by'. This volume will adopt this categorisation throughout the upcoming chapters to describe and analyse what children actually do in different research studies. The categories from research 'on' children to research 'by' children also represent a continuum, and attempting to categorise studies will help to highlight how and when children can move towards more active roles.

Extending the framework with active roles does not intend to replace traditional research or suggest that passive roles are somehow inferior but to add new possibilities to the repertoire of those researchers who are interested in exploring alternatives.

These four separate categories, which also sit on a continuum, will be used as reference points in the upcoming chapters, and returning to these categories will help us to navigate the analysis of different studies.

1.3 The Title of the Volume

The title of this volume is *Engaging Children in Applied Linguistics Research*.

When inviting children to participate in research in active roles, they are being recognised as 'experts', that is, experts of their own lives and experiences. Handing over to them some responsibility in the research process represents a continuum from minimal participation to full participation. This elevation of children to the role of experts – in contrast to traditional research – brings potential political and activist overtones and an explicit questioning of traditional views on hierarchy, power and knowledge creation in research.

Promoting children's active roles in research is also associated with certain educational philosophies and pedagogical practices embedded in learner-centredness, experimentation, inquiry-based approaches, and democratic and inclusive ways of working. However, beyond all that, for many childhood scholars, researching with children or enabling children to become researchers in their own right is bound up with an explicit ethical stance that thrives on a deep commitment that children must be respected as individuals in their own right and as rights-bearing citizens (Convention on the Rights of the Child, 1989). What this means for some is that conducting our research must serve and benefit the very participants we work with.

Active roles refer to the kinds of research engagement where children's views are taken seriously and their insights are respected. This may mean including children as consultants, helpers or partners in adult-initiated or jointly initiated research, and or it can refer to the possibility of inviting children to undertake their own research. In effect, this volume is dedicated to critically examining what types of participation in applied linguistics may be possible (from weaker to stronger forms of active engagement) and to developing arguments for broadening the currently limited framework for research.

Working with children who take up active roles in research is closely associated with a sociological approach to studying children and childhood, often referred to as the 'New Childhood Studies' (James & Prout, 1990). In the last thirty or more years, the sociological view of childhood has had a tremendous influence on a range of disciplines interested in children, such as law, education, health care, social care and climate change education. This volume's overall aim is to make a plea for research with children as active participants in our field, applied linguistics, where this influence has been largely missing to date. By promoting an alternative way of working with children, this volume aims to open up new, creative possibilities for researchers interested in understanding children's life worlds and their second and foreign language learning experiences, motivations and priorities. Working with children in this way in applied linguistics can also unlock opportunities that can take us beyond the classroom walls, exploring important topics and issues of local and global interest and thus connecting language learning to real-life needs and interests.

1.4 Why Is This Book Needed Now?

In the twenty-first century, as part of the global trend of introducing English into primary and pre-primary education, more and more children are learning English in formal school contexts. Almost exactly a decade ago, Ellis and Knagg (2013) estimated the number of young English learners globally to be somewhere around half a billion. This is a staggering statistic, and numbers since 2013 have increased further. Children are learning English in a variety of contexts worldwide, including state schools, private schools, pre-schools and kindergartens of all kinds in both developed and developing countries.

Most children are learning English because it is now compulsory in their schools or because their parents have chosen it for them. Believing that learning English will lead to enhanced life opportunities, parents in some contexts spend huge amounts of money on their children's English language education (Brown & Lauder, 2012; Butler, 2017a). By contrast, English is also taught to children in large under-resourced classrooms in marginalised communities, sometimes in very difficult circumstances, including war-torn areas, refugee camps and other conflict zones. These children's experiences with L2 English and other languages must be vastly different, and yet we know very little about their day-to-day experiences or their perspectives. What sense do children make of the role of English in their lives? What types of learning materials and activities do they find meaningful and purposeful, what it is they enjoy or do not enjoy, and why?

With growing numbers of children learning English worldwide, more and more research is targeting children as second/foreign language learners, as evidenced by publications of the last decade (e.g. Bland, 2016; Butler, 2015; Copland & Garton, 2014; Enever, 2011; Enever & Lindgren, 2017; García Mayo, 2017; Garton & Copland, 2019; Mourão & Lourenço, 2015; Murphy, 2014; Murphy & Evangelou, 2016; Nikolov, 2016; Pinter, 2011; Rich, 2014).

The vast majority of research is 'on' and 'about' children rather than 'with' or 'by' children, meaning that children play entirely passive roles in the research, with the consequence that their language learning experiences are exclusively described through an adult lens. Given that children are passive participants, at times they may even be unaware that research is going on, and their contributions are restricted to following adult instructions to respond to tasks, just like they do every day when interacting with their teachers in their ordinary lessons. Research 'with' and 'by' children, as expected, stands in sharp contrast to this perspective as such options imply a more active, aware and motivated engagement on the part of the child participant and a different perspective, awareness and intention on the part of the adult. This contrast between passive and more active roles taken up by children will be unpacked and critically examined in the upcoming chapters.

The current status quo is, of course, completely understandable, and there are many reasons why applied linguistics research involving children has not embraced more active roles for children. One reason is that teaching, learning and researching work in applied linguistics is mostly undertaken in a second language. Exploring children's views in depth and encouraging them to participate in research actively may not be possible via the second or foreign language, but instead children may need to 'fall back on' the use of their strongest or dominant language, their L1, or their multilingual repertoire.

Child L2 education as a field is the mirror image of the adult field. As Oliver and Azkarai (2017) suggest, second language acquisition (SLA) as a field is entirely adult-oriented and follows an adult agenda. Initially, the focus on young learners was prompted by the widespread observation that children in immigrant families, as opposed to their parents and grandparents, typically acquire a second language with ease and with better overall outcomes. Inspired by Lenneberg's (1967) theory, a sub-field of adult SLA began to develop, focussing on the impact of age in L2 acquisition. But studies focussing on children tend to employ methods, tools, questions and analytical frameworks inherited from adult SLA studies. To date, much of the work undertaken in the broad field of child second language education is largely derivative of the adult literature, addressing questions mirrored by that literature and using the same or similar approaches and methods (e.g. Philp et al., 2008).

In this volume I argue that we need to broaden the scope of research by incorporating studies that target the unique views and understandings of children about language learning processes, not just as data sources but also as active contributors to research.

Butler (2022) similarly comments that in current child SLA 'we may need more fundamentally unique approaches to child L2 studies, not simple modifications and adjustments of adult-based models' (p. 198). She proposes that 'research with children requires rethinking established research methods and practices in L2 development' (p. 199), and she advocates so-called child-centred views or approaches to research.

This volume embraces one possible interpretation of child-centredness in applied linguistics by suggesting that focussing on children's perspectives and engaging them actively in research are promising avenues to understand many different aspects of child second language learning as well as child second language learners as whole persons.

We need to consider the following key questions:

- Who should speak for children in applied linguistics and SLA research? Should it be only adults, or is there room for children's perspectives and views as well?
- Is it only adults who can be considered experts, or can children be acknowledged as experts of their own language learning experiences inasmuch as they may have relevant insights to share about what it is like to learn and use their L2 in different contexts?
- If children are seen as experts, is it the adults' duty to consider their expertise in addition to their own?
- If children are experts, can they contribute to research in applied linguistics more actively, assuming different roles, not just passive ones as data sources?
- Who and what is child second language education research for? Who gets to do research in this field? What gets researched focussing on what populations, with what questions and approaches in mind?
- Does the research we do respond to children's needs, priorities, wellbeing and challenges? Is the research relevant? Is it relevant to the children?
- What kind of new research 'with' and 'by' children is feasible? What kinds of participation of children in research might be feasible? With what benefits and challenges?

The central narrative that will run through this volume underscores the argument that child second/foreign language education as a field could benefit from embracing children's perspectives more systematically by opening up possibilities for researchers to explore their learners' views and experiences in different active roles, since attention so far has largely focussed on studies where children were invisible in passive object roles or had limited roles to play as data sources.

Including children's perspectives in research is a commitment advocated by a sociological approach to the study of childhood and children, one that has explicitly positioned children as 'active subjects' rather than just 'passive objects' of adult control and influence. Embracing this shift in perspective by conceptualising children as active, capable subjects whose opinions matter and who are able to speak for themselves is aligned with the principles articulated by researchers working within the (New) Childhood Studies or (New) Sociology of Childhood approach (James & Prout, 1990; Kehily, 2009), which are associated with studying children with a focus on their 'rights', 'agency' and the kinds of 'participation' that may be possible to achieve in different contexts.

Such a shift towards a focus on children as social actors and a need to uncover their perspectives has been underlined by a number of justifications. First, giving learners a voice in educational policy-making or research is an epistemological necessity in that the reality experienced by children cannot be fully appreciated by adults. Since children inhabit so-called subcultures that are not visible or accessible to adults (Kellett, 2010a), the meanings that they attach to their experiences are not the same as adults' meanings (Lloyd-Smith & Tarr, 2000). From a political/ethical perspective, the publication and the international ratification of the United Nations Convention on the Rights of the Child (1989) provided further impetus for reconsidering the status of children as 'rights-bearing' citizens whose contributions need to be elicited, listened to and taken seriously in all areas of their lives. From a policy perspective, services, materials and resources for children can be improved when their input is considered. Equally, teaching and learning processes in formal education can be substantially improved when learner contributions are taken seriously both in research and everyday teaching.

Taking children's perspectives seriously and listening to and acting on their voices in applied linguistics will lead to a better understanding of children's life worlds, their ecologies, their needs, interests and ever-changing priorities and identities within language learning and beyond. Adult researchers, teachers, teacher educators and policy-makers would benefit from better understanding how children conceptualise language learning and the role of English (and/or other languages) in their lives, what they enjoy and do not enjoy or find difficult, and what they may be interested in exploring in collaborative research projects with adults or on their own.

1.5 The Use of Key Terms

To avoid ambiguity, it is essential to explain and justify the intended meaning of some key terms used in the volume.

'Applied linguistics' is used as an umbrella term to refer to the broad field, which itself suffers from a lack of consensus regarding its exact definition. In this volume my core concern is with second and foreign language education in childhood, with a focus on instructed learning contexts in classrooms and schools rather than community or heritage language learning, although those contexts may also be able to draw some implications from the content. While it is the case that the majority of the examples in this volume will come from English as an L2 contexts, the discussion and the principles throughout the book relating to the theoretical, philosophical, methodological and ethical issues could also be made relevant to researching other language learning scenarios. I will use the term 'child second language education' to refer to the narrower field, which I see as nested inside applied linguistics. Again, mostly this will imply English as a second or foreign language as it is by far the most widely taught second and foreign language in schools worldwide. Nonetheless, occasionally, other L2s will also be mentioned.

'Children' rather than 'young learners' is selected for the title, and this is a conscious choice following the core literature that inspired this book, which is the New Sociology of Childhood. Following the definitions used in international legislation, such as by the Convention on the Rights of the Child (1989) and UNICEF (2002), the term children will be extended and thus include all minors under eighteen years of age. The age ranges covered in the book thus will include children in pre-schools, primary schools and secondary schools, all the way up to the age of eighteen years of age. Young learners, which is a term used in applied linguistics, tends to describe learners between the ages of five and twelve, an age bracket that roughly covers the primary school years in most contexts but one that chooses to cut off sharply any work either side involving older or younger children. This broad definition, in contrast, helps to emphasise continuity and fluidity in development rather than rigidity and the specific characteristics associated with a specific age range. I am aware that this broad definition of children and childhood is perhaps somewhat awkward and even counterintuitive, but it is more in line with the argument that agency and voice as well as participation are not characteristics of a specific age but of experience and careful training. My selected definition is also more appreciative of the fact that children who share the same chronological age often vary enormously in terms of their abilities, skills and interests, so rigid age brackets may not be as useful as we imagine. Finally, a broad definition allows for the inclusion of a larger variety of studies illustrating how increasingly more sophisticated approaches can be promoted in research with children.

In addition to the labels 'child' or 'children', the terms 'young people' or 'youth' for older children will also be used (Heath et al., 2009), typically referring to those aged fourteen to fifteen or above. According to Skelton (2008) 'young people' is used as a label by these older children to describe themselves, placing themselves somewhere between the binary categories of children and adults. The definition of childhood and children will be further unpacked and discussed in upcoming chapters.

'Research' in this volume covers a multiplicity of different meanings and types of research, from academic research to all kinds of practitioner research, teacher research as well as, and perhaps most importantly, children's research. The various types and interpretations will be elaborated on in the different chapters of the book, including the suggestion that all research may sit on a continuum from high-prestige research in academic journals (research with a capital 'R') undertaken by academics, mostly to generate new theories, all the way to practically oriented research (research with a lower-case 'r') aiming to investigate a practical issue or problem of interest to make a change or take action.

The 'R–r continuum' represents different types of research from more formal to less formal but also represents a potential growth trajectory from less to more sophisticated levels of knowledge, skills and growing expertise in research. Both adults and children sit somewhere on this continuum. New researchers, whether adults or children, start with a rudimentary understanding of research and a limited set of skills and knowledge, but with training and experience over a longer period of time, they can, if they wish to and have the opportunity, develop and move towards more sophisticated levels and types of research engagement.

1.6 The Map of the Book

The book is structured as laid out in Table 1.2. This chapter (Chapter 1) has set the scene, introduced my personal motivation to write this book and outlined where the gap is in the child second language literature and why it would be desirable to complement the currently largely adult-focussed research by incorporating children's views and perspectives, in particular by encouraging more active roles for children in research. I have outlined some basic premises that this book is based on and defined the key terms used.

Chapter 2 provides a brief historical overview of childhood and children, illustrating how the concept of childhood has developed over time into our contemporary understanding. The discussion focusses on

Table 1.2 Structure of the book

Framing chapter	Introduction of relevant concepts and principles from interdisciplinary literature	Exploration of relevance for applied linguistics	Framing chapter
Chapter 1	Chapters 2–4	Chapters 5–7	Chapter 8

how adults, including applied linguists working with children, need to reflect on the implications of their belief systems and specifically their conceptions of children and childhood when it comes to their work with children, whether it is research or otherwise. The chapter then elaborates on the most notable conception of childhood, which is the natural child, based on developmental psychology and representing a biological, universal view of childhood. The critical views that attacked developmental psychology and its conception of children as universal 'becomings' led to the emergence of Childhood Studies more than thirty years ago. This multidisciplinary, bottom-up approach takes a very different view of children. Rather than passive becomings, children are seen as social constructions, active agents and unique 'beings' worthy of interest in themselves, not just as developing adults. The Convention on the Rights of the Child (1989) and its proposal that children are rights-bearing citizens whose voices must be heard will be introduced next, and the discussion will address how the proposed rights can be realised in practice by schools, communities and individual adult researchers in their ongoing work with children. The main contributions of Childhood Studies over the last three and half decades will be summarised to draw attention to some current issues and concerns. Finally, this chapter outlines the main components of the extended framework, which includes possibilities of conducting studies not just 'on' and 'about' but also 'with' and 'by' children.

Chapter 3 explores and critically evaluates the main tenets of Childhood Studies via addressing the key concepts of voice, agency, participation and children's rights. The discussion will start with exploring the challenges of working with child voice, highlighting that voices can never be authentic but instead they are messy and multi-layered, heavily influenced by social, cultural and institutional discourses. Like voice, agency must also be understood within intergenerational relationships. A large part of this chapter discusses the differences between the various definitions and descriptions of participation 'frameworks' (such as Fielding, 2001; Hart, 1992; Lundy, 2007; Shier, 2001) with a view to drawing out actual roles children can take in research studies (such as consultants, partners or researchers in child-led research projects). Similarities and differences between research 'with' children and research 'by' children will be discussed. Three types of studies are identified: (1) those that use participatory tools to elicit children's views and attempt to create more natural and meaningful conditions for children to be able to take some control of the process (although these are still passive roles); (2) studies where children are active participants and work collaboratively with adults as partners, taking over some aspects of the research process, and finally (3), studies where children become enabled to undertake their own research, which is labelled as child-led research. Addressing opportunities and limitations drawn out of current debates in empirical research will highlight the most important implications and opportunities for child second language research.

Chapter 4 explores how schools and other institutions can embrace a focus on participatory research with children or child-led research, should they wish to do that. First of all, the concept of child-centredness or learner-centredness is explored. Child-centred research is linked to child-centred education and early childhood education, which has a long history emphasising children's agency and freedom to choose, their autonomy, creativity and the importance of dialogue and democratic or horizontal relationships between adults and children. Child-centred approaches to research, such as those inspired by the work of Freire (1970, 1973), have been linked to being participatory in an emancipatory sense. Child-centredness is also rooted in the key articles of the Convention on the Rights of the Child (1989) emphasising children's voice and rights. Such an approach promotes active roles for children (e.g. research 'with' and 'by' children), although the Convention on the Rights of the Child messages are not as consistent and unambiguous as we might like. Child-centredness is also congruous with more democratic working patterns and autonomous ways of learning (Little et al., 2017), with autonomy-promoting schools driven by the core principles of Self-Determination Theory (Deci & Ryan, 2012) and alternative inquiry-based pedagogies (Hatch, 2014; Partnership for 21st Century Skills, 2009). Schools and institutions that embrace a child-centred approach to teaching and learning and take student voice, students' rights and a democratic way of working seriously will be able to accommodate child-led research or research with children more easily and more meaningfully. At the end of Chapter 4 the alternative framework to research with children promoted in this volume will be revisited to tease out the main opportunities and challenges associated with the framework, including issues not just related to the adult researcher and their belief systems, knowledge, experience and intentions but also those that arise from actual institutional structures and the philosophies of education they embody.

Chapter 5 discusses features of research involving children in applied linguistics. Drawn from comprehensive overviews of the field, the main areas of research interest are highlighted. Then, based on a strategically selected 'slice' of the literature, that is, a survey of child L2 studies in five key applied linguistics journals over a period of a decade (2011–2021), a close analysis of children's status and roles in research is undertaken. Observations are made about the type of studies (methodological solutions, tools and approaches) dominating the field and about what is missing. Examples of studies in child second language education where children take up different types of passive roles are discussed and analysed. A handful of examples identified in the sample, where the status and the roles of the children have been shifted away from entirely passive roles, will also be discussed. These examples are closely examined to identify the extent of active involvement which does not move beyond a 'weak' form of research 'with' children. The continuum of possibilities, research on-about-with-by children (Kellett, 2010a), is revisited here for further reflection. While the literature sample (with 324 studies) can only be a limited source for this analysis, it is believed to be representative of the existing research in terms of children's status and the roles they play.

Chapter 6 addresses the gap identified in the earlier chapters and asks the following question: Based on the previous chapters and the overview of the field, what kind of research is needed now in applied linguistics? Seventeen studies will be used to showcase children's roles, illustrating varying degrees of active participation. Studies are included in the three main categories identified in Chapter 3. Building on examples taken from other disciplines, such as climate change education, health care, geography or social work, tools and approaches are introduced with a commentary about how these ideas might be incorporated or further built on when addressing research in child second language classrooms and beyond. This chapter offers ideas and raises awareness among researchers about the variety of opportunities for incorporating the new extended framework when working with children in applied linguistics.

Chapter 7 addresses the most important global and local (macro and micro) ethical dilemmas and challenges when working with children, in particular when working with children in active roles. It outlines generic ethical issues relevant to research with under-eighteens and also addresses ethical issues in research when moving from research 'on' and 'about' children to research 'with' and 'by' children. In addition to addressing the origins and main dilemmas of child-focussed ethics, the chapter critically evaluates a selection of existing international ethics guidelines for research involving child participants, potentially relevant for applied linguistics, drawing out challenges, opportunities and tensions. This chapter revisits the key messages of the Convention on the Rights of the Child, this time as a point of reference for ethical practice in research. The chapter also addresses the process of securing child consent or assent and discusses good practice regarding securing permissions from other stakeholders.

Ethical issues, specifically when working with multilingual children and families, will be covered as well as how ethical guidelines have to be sensitive to cultural, social and contextual circumstances, making reference to challenging issues in different contexts, including contexts in the Global South.

Chapter 8, the final chapter, summarises the main arguments developed in the book and reiterates the case for promoting the extended framework of working with children in applied linguistics. The chapter discusses the main opportunities and challenges going forward and emphasises that future research with children needs to stay relevant and address children's future needs and realities. Incorporating the extended framework into applied linguistics research would mean rebalancing the current trend in research and serving the communities of children more directly. Future studies where researchers embrace more active roles for children will spark inspired debate and discussion and will have the potential to move the field forward.

1.7 Conclusion

While the main purpose of this book is to promote an alternative approach (research 'with' children and 'by' children), it is nonetheless important to make it clear that this approach is seen as complementary, representing an additional 'angle' rather than aiming to replace traditional research 'on' children. A central thesis of this volume is that all kinds of research are needed but that research 'with' and 'by' children is still largely lacking in our field. Opening up these new potential possibilities does not intend to negate or diminish the research knowledge that has emerged and will continue to emerge from the traditional methods. The volume will bring together the core principles and benefits of working with children as active participants in research in any context, from mainstream and 'elite' schools to average and difficult contexts, including contexts where children and teachers lack resources or may face hardship or difficulties of all kinds. The key message of the volume is that no matter what the local circumstances may be, wherever we find ourselves as adult researchers, engaging children in research in active roles is always an option, and it carries the promise or even the very real possibility of improving the lives of all those involved.

2 From Traditional to Contemporary Conceptions of Childhood

2.1 Introduction

In order to develop the new framework, which includes research 'with' and 'by' children, this chapter begins to set out the background to the emergence of the New Childhood Studies movement, with its conceptualisation of children as active and capable social agents. Given that this conceptualisation of children and childhood is largely missing in applied linguistics, such a shift in perspective will be significant and will lead to opening up new opportunities for children, teachers and researchers.

First of all, this chapter offers a brief overview of how childhood has been conceptualised throughout history to provide a background to how the most widespread twentieth-century conception of the 'natural, universal child' emerged and got entrenched as the only way of looking at children. It was this conception, associated with developmental psychology, that was criticised by a sociological approach, eventually leading to the concept of the social child.

2.2 Who Is a Child?

Being a child is understood in a binary relationship with an adult and is considered a universal phenomenon. Despite the fact that 'children' and 'adults' are commonly used labels whose use seems largely unproblematic in everyday discourse, defining exactly who a child is as opposed to an adult turns out to be a surprisingly challenging task. Drawing a precise line between children and adults will in fact be impossible, especially in a way that works across different domains, such as education, law, biology, politics or economics. For example, young people in many countries cannot consent to participating in research until they are 18 years of age without their parents' or guardians' involvement, and yet they can vote, drive, drink alcohol or get married by the time they are 16 or 17.

A clear distinction between adult and child language learners is similarly difficult to draw in the language education literature, even though much discussion and research have targeted the significance of age itself in SLA. Studies focussed on the age factor have centred around questions such as what is the best age during childhood to start a second or foreign language, and whether there is a critical period (e.g. Pfenninger & Singleton, 2017) for second/foreign language learning. If there is indeed a critical period for learning a foreign language, then what exact age brackets for onset and offset apply? These questions have generated complex literatures and lively debates but not clear-cut answers. In fact, even though everyone in SLA agrees that age does influence the process of language learning, it is difficult to tease out exactly how due to the complex interplay of many associated factors, such as the quantity and quality of input, levels of motivation and opportunities for practice and receiving feedback in a non-threatening environment. So, in a move away from precise age brackets, most scholars are in agreement that it is not age per se but the actual circumstances in the learning context that help children enjoy some advantages as language learners. In addition to the lack of definite answers in the Critical Period Hypothesis literature, there is also an ongoing debate about how to define young L2 learners as opposed to balanced bilingual learners who grow up with two languages from birth. Research in this area is buoyant, and although there are disagreements, the consensus is that L2 child learners are those who start a second/foreign language once their L1 grammatical system has been firmly established. Questions also arise about the top end of the age range. At what point is a L2 child learner no longer labelled as a child learner but instead turns into a (young) adult learner? Impossible to say exactly.

A precise definition with exact age brackets of who a child language learner is therefore eludes us, so the best we can do is apply somewhat arbitrary age brackets for pragmatic reasons. For example, conference organisers, publishers and research communities within applied linguists who are interested in the study of children as second/foreign language learners work with arbitrary age brackets, such as 5–12 years of age, and refer to older children as teenagers or adolescents. Different special interest groups and book series decide on their own definitions and age brackets, but these do not necessarily align with each other even within the same body of research literature.

As adults, we cannot know what it is like to be a child. At some level, of course, childhood is a familiar experience to us all. We all remember some of our early experiences vividly, and as we tell stories about ourselves, we constantly revisit and reinterpret our early memories, creating our unique childhood story. Many adults have children of their own, have close relatives or friends who have children, or work with children and thus claim some expertise in 'knowing' children. And yet, the paradox is that to know what it is like to be a child in current times is knowledge and first-hand experience that is firmly denied to all of us. The perspectives of children, today or at any time, are unique to them and are uniquely shaped by a specific time and place in both historical and cultural terms, sharing some but certainly not all features with previous generations of children.

Ultimately, such unique perspectives can only be gained from the children themselves. This underscores the need to gain insights from children about their lived experiences – in the case of this volume, putting the emphasis on children's second/foreign language learning experiences. Such insights and accounts of experiences need to be given more weight in applied linguistics. Graue and Walsh (1998) suggest that researching children and asking them about their views helps us to challenge our own dominant adult views. The authors urge us to find out and understand better what children think 'and to keep finding it out, because if we do not find it out, someone will make it up' (Graue & Walsh, 1998, p. xvi). For adults the temptation is to assume that they know everything best and thus must set all the rules and make all the decisions for children, often without finding things out first. As will be argued in this volume, the fact is we know very little about second language learning experiences from children's own point of view.

What (we think) we know about children is rooted in our images and conceptions of childhood, which are also the products of historical, political and cultural influences as well as our own unique individual experiences as adults, parents, teachers and researchers. For example, what a teacher or researcher working with children believes and understands about children and childhood is determined by their personal and professional experiences mediated by contextual, political, cultural and historical circumstances and prevailing discourses about childhood. Such belief systems may be rendered unexplored, unless explicit and systematic reflection is encouraged by one's training and professional development. Hence it is essential for every teacher and researcher working with children to reflect on their answers to these key questions:

- What is my image/conception of the child?
- What is my image/conception of the teacher/researcher (myself)?

Answers to these questions will begin to feed into decision making and increased reflexivity in any research project.

2.3 A Brief Historical Overview of Studying Children

Before examining the belief systems behind the proposed conception of this volume (i.e. the *active, agentive child*), it is useful here to pause and explore some historically significant conceptualisations. As Gittins (2009, p. 37) comments, images and conceptions of childhood have been changing across the ages, and 'how that status is conceived by adults also varies and changes: sometimes it has been defined by physical and/or sexual maturity, sometimes by legal status, sometimes by chronological age alone'.

The earliest accounts of children can be traced back to the Middle Ages. Aries (1986) speculates that adults in ancient times perhaps were not so concerned about children or their development and wellbeing. It was only around the sixteenth century when children began to appear much more frequently in historical records of all kinds (e.g. paintings), reflecting profound cultural changes relating to the growth of interest in family life and domestic issues. Within the family unit, influenced by religious beliefs and teachings, parents began to devote attention to children by trying to educate them about good behaviour and morality through a very strict upbringing. This was influenced by the idea that children were evil and born with original sin and, consequently, needed education, control and discipline to achieve enlightenment. By the seventeenth century Locke challenged this conception by suggesting that children were neither good nor bad but simply the product of their environment, referring to them as blank slates (tabulae rasa). Then the view of childhood changed completely in the eighteenth century following the ideas promoted by Rousseau. Children became associated with the opposite of sin and evil, and it was suggested that adult society was the source of all sin and that children were in fact naturally good and innocent. In this way becoming an adult meant losing one's childhood innocence.

By the nineteenth century, romantic constructions of childhood became the norm in wealthy middle-class families, with the idea that childhood is a special time to be protected and devoted to play and learning. At the same time, working-class childhoods were very different, with large-scale industrialisation and child labour becoming the norm for poor families. Towards the very end of the nineteenth century, mass schooling was introduced with the main purpose of teaching the poor, helping to keep crime rates down and providing moral education to the masses, referred to as savages (Walkerdine, 2009). Historically, the introduction of mass schooling coincided with the rise of Darwinism and the idea that children could be studied in terms of an evolutionary process on their journey of development from being savages to becoming civilised rational adults. 'Childhood in this way became a developmental process in which adaptation to the environment was understood as a natural stage-wise progression towards a rational and civilized adulthood, which was to be the basis for liberal government' (Walkerdine, 2009, p. 115).

Interestingly, mass schooling was put in place as the mirror image of factories in the growth of industrialisation. Children were divided into classes according to their age and instruction was put in place, with the bell ringing for breaks just like in factories. This basic image of schools is still prevailing in our times, even though much criticism has been raised about these practices that many see as outdated. Schools throughout the twentieth century became important places for research. Children were seen as the future of nation states, and large-scale research on health, nutrition and education were put in place with the aim of protecting and nourishing childhood and better understanding the process of growing up. Based on such large-scale research, education authorities in different countries made decisions about what to teach, how and for how long. In order to gain insights into the learning mechanisms in childhood, school-based research focussed on what was considered typical and normal in terms of cognitive abilities for various age groups. This was based on the underlying assumption that childhood and development were controllable, following a clear chronological stage-like process, and with the right approach to teaching, competent, rational adult citizens would be created.

2.4 Developmental Psychology

By the 1920s childhood research became firmly established, and a new field was born: developmental psychology. The idea of development is historically significant in the age of Darwinism with its paradigm organised around the metaphor of growth and, accordingly, orderly stages of development. In developmental psychology data are collected from large numbers of children to encourage comparisons, standardisation and normalisation. The average abilities of children of a certain age performing on the same task can result in identifying what is 'normal', and this becomes the basis for setting curricula and instructional materials for various age groups.

The core idea in the developmental psychology paradigm is that children are only partially rational, becoming more and more rational with age until they become fully functioning adults. Consequently, childhood is always understood as an incomplete state of 'becoming' and is seen as preparation for adulthood, which is in turn associated with the finished/complete state of 'being'. It is the process that describes what happens on the journey from childhood to adulthood that constitutes the focus of research interest, rather than the particularities of any one individual child. Piaget's work is a good example of an attempt to describe the journey from childhood to adulthood. His well-known universal stage development theory addresses in detail how children acquire the rules of formal logic and the Kantian categories of space, time and causality through four universal stages. These stages always follow in the same order, and no stage can be skipped. Piaget's theory, though immensely influential and impactful, has been widely criticised as reductionist because the tasks were stripped of cultural and contextual influences, leaving the young child confused about the adult's intentions and the true meaning of the tasks. Yet despite this criticism, Piaget's pivotal influence cannot be underestimated today, even though the parallel alternative influence of social constructivism promoted by Vygotsky and his followers have also gained just as much ground.

The establishment of developmental psychology as a new discipline at the beginning of the twentieth century has been the source of much evidence relating to what we know about children and childhood today, with its methods and approaches having been mirrored across various disciplines and fields of study devoted to children, including applied linguistics. As discussed above, the predominant approach to research with children in developmental psychology consists of observation and experimental methods since these are believed to yield 'objective evidence'. Typically, asking children's views and trusting their accounts are approaches that do not sit well in this paradigm because of the assumption that children lack the ability to reflect on their experiences, are easily distracted and do not have the cognitive or linguistic skills to talk about their lives, and that what they say may not be coherent and trustworthy. As a consequence, children's voices have traditionally been muted in research (Hardman, 1973).

Developmental psychology as a way of conceptualising children and childhood, with its hugely important body of knowledge amassed over many decades, is a 'particularly powerful story of childhood because it plausibly accounts for the fixed biological nature of development, making it difficult for us to view childhood any differently' (Wyness, 2019, p. 17). Indeed, conceptions of childhood originating in developmental psychology are accepted as universal, and the way families, schools and the whole of society view and treat children is fully consistent with this conception.

2.5 The Emergence of the New Sociology of Childhood

Criticism of the traditional paradigm and developmental psychology started building up in the second half of the twentieth century. By the

1970s research approaches began to diversify, with attention moving away from experiments while the significance of context in research began to be addressed and Vygotsky's influence also increased. Margaret Donaldson (1986) and her colleagues' work, which reappraised some of Piaget's claims about younger children and their limited ability to solve problems and reflect on their experiences, cast doubt on about the stage-like development theory. For example, questions were raised about the context of these experiments and the actual language use of the experimenters as well as the types of scenarios presented to the children. When the same Piagetian experiments were subsequently rerun with tasks presented in a more familiar context and with adults using more natural language, young children's performance improved, indicating that the original judgements of children lacking logical thought at a young age were too harsh. Parallel to this, in sociology more individual accounts of socialisation, such as Mead's (1934) work were produced, and a gradual realisation slowly began to grow that children should be listened to and respected as individuals and competent meaning makers in their own right.

The most important movement that explicitly suggested an alternative to the traditional paradigm was called New Childhood Studies, which began to gain ground in the late 1980s and early 1990s. This sociological approach to childhood, in stark contrast to developmental psychology, promoted a new perspective that some refer to as an entirely new paradigm. The main tenet of this new approach is that children are 'competent social actors' who are worthy of study in their own right rather than just as future adults in the making. New Childhood Studies is fiercely critical of all approaches objectifying children and contends that children should be studied not just as 'becomings' (i.e. situated somewhere en route to adulthood) but as social 'beings' (Qvortrup, 1994) in their own right. Some scholars also argue that this new approach is more ethical in the sense that it is more contextual and bottom-up, rather than top-down (i.e., it intentionally looks up to children rather than looking down on them). Such a bottom-up approach is more respectful and allows for a more open-ended, exploratory stance in the quest to understand children.

The sociological approach to studying children embraces a conception of childhood that sees children as responsible, competent, resourceful, and active in shaping their own lives. Accordingly, adult observations and accounts of children's experiences can only ever give us a partial understanding of children, and it is now widely accepted across various disciplines that children can and should contribute their views and that these views are worthwhile (Fraser et al., 2014). There is also mounting empirical evidence to suggest that children can be trusted to provide reliable accounts of their experiences and can assist adults in a variety of different roles. In fact, children's accounts of their own experiences are essential, and adults cannot understand their life worlds without consulting them (Rinaldi, 2005). In current sociological approaches to studying children, the emphasis is on understanding children's views and experiences from their own point of view, adhering to the principle that those are worthy of study in their own right and can usefully complement adult insights. As we will see in the upcoming chapters, even though children's ability to share their perspectives is now widely accepted in theory, the challenge is how such perspectives can be elicited and acted on by adults.

James et al. (1998) argue that, despite the widely accepted need to listen to children, traditional conceptions of childhood continue to influence if not dominate our thinking by being deeply embedded in our everyday attitudes to children. These traditional conceptions (see Table 2.1) make up what James et al. (1998, p. 9) refer to as 'conventional wisdom' shaping our shared consciousness about childhood. The lasting effect is observable cumulatively and clearly traceable in practices, attitudes and even policy decisions today. Many of these conceptions are reminiscent of historical approaches and even theories of childhood proposed centuries ago. For example, institutional practices that promote tight control originate from the first conception (the evil child), assuming that without such control institutions such as schools would become chaotic and anarchical places.

Armed with a new sociological conception of childhood, two eminent scholars, James and Prout (1990), in a milestone publication identified the key features of this new 'paradigm' by making the following claims (pp. 8–9):

(1) Childhood is a social construction: it is nether universal nor natural but a specific structural and cultural component of many societies.
(2) Childhood is one variable of social analysis, and it is intertwined with class, gender and ethnicity; childhood is a variable rather than a universal phenomenon.
(3) Children's social relationships and cultures are worthy of study in their own right (not through an adult lens).
(4) Children are active in the constructions of their own social lives and those around them and the societies they live in.
(5) Ethnography is a useful methodology; it allows children a more direct voice and participation.
(6) To proclaim a new paradigm is to engage in reconstructing childhood.

Table 2.1 Traditional conceptions of childhood (adapted from James et al., 1998)

1. *The evil child.* The suggestion that children are born as harbouring potentially dark forces goes back to the Old Testament. If evil is the primary element of childhood, it follows that children must be shaped and restrained by control and discipline. Parents and adults in general will have to exercise absolute power and authority and demand complete subordination of children. Such a conception leads to harshness and brutality in childrearing practices and a strict control over children.
2. *The innocent child.* A directly opposing view to the above suggests that children are pure in heart. Originally proposed by Rousseau, this view states that children have natural goodness and clarity of vision. Childhood is worth our attention for its own sake. Children's inherent goodness and innocence is to be nurtured, and it is the adults' responsibility to promote high standards of care. Many consider this conception as the foundation of contemporary child-centred education.
3. *The immanent child.* This conception of childhood suggests that children are imbued with vitality and immanence. Locke's contention is that children are neither good nor bad but in fact they are clean slates (tabulae rasa) to be filled with knowledge, which will be acquired through experience.
4. *The naturally developing child.* At the heart of this conception lies the 'growth' metaphor, suggesting that growth and development are natural and universal processes of childhood. Indeed, the main focus of developmental psychology as a field is to study the natural stages of development which describe how children become fully fledged adults. Children are viewed as 'becomings' rather than 'beings', and they are routinely described in terms of what they still lack as compared to adults. Reminiscent of this conception of childhood, much current education is based on establishing average performances while children are compared with their peers; they face constant testing and evaluation against a gold standard.

In this way, childhood is seen not just as a universal phenomenon but instead as a social construction unfolding in unique contexts. If childhood is a social construction, then it is just another social variable and, as such, dynamically interacts with other categories, such as gender, class, ethnicity and educational affordances. Childhood in societies is defined following largely arbitrary culturally and socially set conventions (James & Prout, 1990), but the key social mechanism that helps to constitute children's position in society is law. It is through law, rather than simply due to the ageing process, that children in fact achieve adulthood. The categorical stage of adulthood is therefore also arbitrarily fixed by social practices of custom and law. Lacking full personhood is what makes children different from adults, and this leads to institutional separation. Children are rigidly controlled by restricting where they can be present. As Wyness comments (2019, p. 171) one of the 'most powerful norms of Western childhood is that children be in the right place at the right time'.

To document this process of social construction, James and Prout (2004) suggest that ethnographic approaches might be particularly suitable in research when working with children. These methods lend themselves naturally to inviting children to have a 'direct voice' and more active 'participation'. Mayall (2002) proposes that the new paradigm intends to study children in a more contextualised way, by looking 'up' to them, treating them as actors and knowers, rather than looking down at them. This is a radically different approach from the conventional/traditional approaches, which treated children as subordinates from a symbolically higher adult vantage point. Respecting the child's voice, however, 'strikes at the heart of conventional authority relationships between children and the adults who regulate their lives' (Woodhead, 2005, p. 92) both at school and outside school. Quite how this tension can be navigated will be revisited in the upcoming chapters.

In essence, a socially constructed childhood emphasises the unique trajectory of each and every child and directs researchers' attention to the multitudes of childhoods around us rather than the universal, typical child. Modern Western childhood is highly structured and is centred around the home, the school, the classroom and the playground, as well as increasingly around online environments such as gaming, using tablet devices and smartphones, and interacting with peers virtually. However, other childhoods (e.g. those in parts of the Global South) can be remarkably different, with children having to earn money to make ends meet or look after younger siblings to support their wider families in addition to or even instead of school (López-Gopar, 2016). Many children's lives around the world are in stark contrast to the normalised images of Western childhood, including children living on the street, in inner-city slums, in conflict zones or on the move to seek new homes as unaccompanied child refugees. Such a variety of childhood experiences has certainly not been fully reflected in second language education research, where the focus has been largely confined to more readily accessible contexts in the West. This harks back to Chapter 1 and the question about who our research is for and what it should be about (Ortega, 2005). In our field, with the increasing number of children learning L2 English in various contexts, attention also needs to be directed to the diversity of children's experiences. English language learning opportunities for children range from contexts where well-trained teachers work with small groups of learners using modern technology and materials to those where teachers have no formal teaching qualifications, no access to suitable materials, and where classrooms may be as large as catering for 100–200 students. The experiences, interests and needs of children across these contexts will be remarkably different, and therefore more bottom-up insights from all these contexts are urgently needed if we want to better understand child second language learning processes.

2.6 The Social Child: A 'Rights-Bearing' Citizen

The emergence of the New Childhood Studies coincided and has been bolstered by international political developments, in particular by the 1989 publication of the Convention on the Rights of the Child, which is considered one of the most important international documents relating to children. The Convention will be discussed in the upcoming chapters, so here I am just introducing it briefly, outlining its purpose, content and overall impact.

The Convention is an extension of Universal Human Rights Document, with fifty-four articles devoted to children's rights. It is an important advocacy tool that promotes children's welfare as a matter of justice rather than charity (Veerman, 1992, p. 184), and it is also the first document that considers children as subjects in their own right rather than simply objects of adult intervention. Accordingly, children have the right to self-determination (Article 1), to non-discrimination (Article 2), to decisions that follow their best interest (Article 3), to life, survival and development (Article 6), to freedom to participate (Article 12) and to see, receive and communicate information relevant to their lives (Articles 13 & 17).

There are three kinds of rights declared in the Convention, often referred to as the three Ps. These include provision, protection and participation rights. The content overall is comprehensive, containing general rights, linguistic rights, rights to protective measures, rights concerning civil status, rights to preserve identity, to be reunited with family and rights to health, basic services and social security. The Convention also addresses the rights of children in special circumstances, such as refugee children and indigenous groups, and it covers regulations on adoption and the prohibition of the recruitment of child soldiers.

Wyness comments that it is a crucial document in 'establishing a social ontology for children' (2019, p. 207), with Article 4 stating that children should be seen as equals alongside adults.

The Convention on the Rights of the Child has been ratified by most countries in the world, and many states have incorporated it into national law. The first declaration dates back to 1924 and the second to 1959, but it was only in the 1970s that work on the current document finally started (Freeman, 2011), and it took over ten years to agree its content. There were several areas of contention, most notably around the concept of freedom of thought and religion, but also debates were devoted to the basic definition of the child, the right of the unborn child, traditional cultural practices and children's duties to parents which were seen as socially and culturally acceptable in some contexts but not in others (Freeman, 2011).

It is mainly the rights around 'participation' that have been taken up, explored and interpreted by those interested in the New Sociology of Childhood, and it is the concept of participation that is central to the active children's roles proposed in applied linguistics research. By all accounts, Article 12 is the most widely quoted section, emphasising children's rights to voice their opinions about important matters in their lives. It [requires states to] 'assure to the child, who is capable of forming his or her own views, the rights to express those views freely, on all matters affecting the child, the views of the child being given due consideration in accordance with the age and maturity of the child' (Convention on the Rights of the Child, 1989).

Whenever children are enabled to become active partners or collaborators in research (i.e. where research 'with' children or 'by' children rather than 'on' children is mentioned), it is this article of the Convention that is often referred to, citing children's right to have their voices heard and highlighting the legal imperative that children's views about *all aspects* of their lives need to be taken seriously. Exactly how this imperative plays out in different types of research involving children in more or less active roles will vary, but the core principle is associated with the adult's obligation to consider how a rights-based approach can be implemented in practical terms in their own local circumstances.

The Convention articles are open to interpretation, and different readers and researchers have taken different views on the key messages. Some argue that children's participation in *research* is not in fact mentioned in the document explicitly, and for many it is not considered to be an important matter at all, especially compared to other needs or rights. Others point to the dual emphasis in the document on children's voices as well as their parents' and other adults' voices (see more about this in Chapter 7). As Hammersley (2015, p. 572) argues, the imperative to seek children's perspectives about important matters is framed with the caveat that adults need to first make judgements about children's competences 'in accordance with the age and maturity of the child'. Conflicting interpretations of the document have led to continuing debates and discussions about the document and its articles.

While the Convention is an important international document, its actual implementation is certainly patchy. A continuing difficulty is that different societies have different understandings of childhood, parent–child relationships, education, the role of punishment or child labour (Freeman, 2011). A common criticism of the Convention is that suffers from a Western bias and does not take the reality of childhoods in the Global South into account. Ironically, there is no evidence that any children or groups of children were consulted in the construction of the document, and as such, therefore, it is an adult-initiated document entirely, although steps have been taken since to involve children in the work that is associated with its implementation internationally.

For those countries signed up to the document, there is a monitoring mechanism in place whereby ministries of education or those national institutions responsible for children are required to submit reports every five years to the UN to demonstrate compliance and to report on progress with issues related to the Convention. However, there is no mechanism of enforcement, and in reality little progress has been made in promoting children's rights internationally. For many, the Convention remains a political token and a moral document only. Nonetheless, the imperative to listen to children and respect their rights is now enshrined in law in most countries, and all adults accordingly need to work towards finding opportunities to respect the Convention principles in their practice with children. Even though the document is open to different interpretations, its basic message that children have rights is well accepted. Therefore, in applied linguistics, as in other disciplines, adults working with children need to engage with the document and its articles and need to reflect on their personal interpretations of these rights and how they are to be acted on and implemented in everyday practice.

Taking children's views seriously following the Convention is also directly linked to children's overall wellbeing and social justice concerns. Kumpulainen and Ouakrim-Soivio (2019, p. 184) argue that listening to children, 'their meanings, experiences, opinions, and perspectives in relation to their life worlds, creates avenues for educators to learn about children, and hence to support their holistic learning and wellbeing'. In the context of second/foreign language education, participation refers to the right of children to fair participation in decisions about their educational and linguistic rights. Including children's voices in educational discourses can also promote educational equity and fair opportunities (Kumpulainen et al., 2014). Kellett (2010a) claims that high levels of child involvement in research lead to the potential for transformation and for empowering and emancipating marginalised groups.

Quennerstedt and Moody (2020) argue that for educational stakeholders (researchers or teachers) it is important to understand the messages of the Convention regarding children's rights to education. Three different types of rights are important: rights *to* education, rights *in* education and rights *through* education. Rights to education at a basic level refers to accessing good-quality education, while rights in education deals with how rights are respected in educational institutions, and finally, rights through education refers to how children's attitudes and knowledge can be affected by rights-infused environments. Quennerstedt and Moody (2020) recommend that the following questions must be asked in every school:

- Do our schools secure children's participation rights?
- How is Article 12 implemented in our schools?
- Is children's decision making given due weight?
- How do children understand their own participation rights?
- Are participation rights central to learning/teaching?
- How are children affected by environments that respect their rights?

The authors suggest that, overall, opportunities for children in schools to exercise their rights are still rare and that children have little scope to influence educational institutions. Teachers' knowledge, as well as the actual enactment of children's rights, is weak, and there is a general scepticism about teaching children as rights holders.

> We have not to any large extent studied how a child, learning about her/his rights and the values underpinning them gradually becomes a bearer of rights, capable of claiming them for her or himself and defending them for others. We have not given close scrutiny to the educational context and the pedagogical processes that can support children to develop into capable and responsible rights holders, who understand the complexity of human rights and the violations of them.
>
> (Quennerstedt & Moody, 2020, p. 201)

In UK schools, for example, a desire to develop participation rights and give children a voice has led to the establishment of school councils. Children represent their peers and hold office in preparation for adult life as citizens. A major criticism of school councils, however, is that even though the adults present the school council as participatory, in reality it is often only symbolic, with low levels of consultation. Wyness (2018) argues that consultation revolves around specific events only and that engagement wanes in between these. Being a member of the school council is also considered a privileged position, only available to a selected few, thus implying that not all children's participation is equally important. In addition, the views of children selected to be included tend to come from those who are highly articulate. This opens the question of whether current methods of participation for children and young people in the school environment favours an elite, conformist section of school society and in this respect are merely tokenistic. Kellett (2014) concurs that, paradoxically, in school councils children are being invited to speak up in a context where virtually nothing is under their control.

2.7 Childhood Studies from the 1990s to Current Times and Children as Future Makers

At the beginning of this chapter I discussed the gradual emergence of Childhood Studies and elaborated on how it developed its scholarship in an attempt to oppose the previous paradigm (i.e. developmental psychology and a traditional view of children as passive 'becomings'). Although these ideas were introduced as progressive, more in tune with contemporary conceptions of childhood, it is important to note that Childhood Studies as a movement has been around for a long time; it has naturally evolved since its beginnings and has encountered its own challenges.

Over the last thirty or more years, Childhood Studies has moved away from earlier sentimental views of children to more balanced views, acknowledging that children's active participation is not a panacea and that their active contributions must always be carefully contextualised.

James and Prout's (1990) original criticism of the traditional approaches and developmental psychology was harsh for a good reason: they wanted to break away from what was the only way to view children and make a convincing case for a new paradigm. Looking back, many would argue that their criticism of developmental psychology was perhaps too strong and that when they completely dismissed traditional approaches, they went too far (Spyrou, 2018). They rejected claims about the naturalness and universal aspect of childhoods and went as far as to say that experimental methods were inadequate to do justice to children's rich lives and experiences. At the same time Qvortrup's (1994) work drew attention to the fact that children were considered as 'becomings' even though they were a permanent feature of all societies.

The early work by James and Prout, Qvortrup and their colleagues inspired a great deal of work exploring children's views, opinions and life worlds in different discipline areas, with innovative methodologies illustrating how children acted as social agents. However, despite more work accumulating in various disciplines illustrating what children were saying and believing, there was also a gradual realisation that the movement was producing more of the same thing. James and Prout began to acknowledge that the divide between the natural and the social child was perhaps too sharp, calling for more balanced approaches. Critical voices also addressed the rather romantic ideals upheld by scholars in some of the early work, and a view was widely acknowledged that more critical approaches were needed that intersected discipline areas and connected work to ongoing philosophical debates and dialogue in the literature outside the study of children and childhood (Carnevale, 2020; Facca et al., 2020).

Conceptions of children and childhood are changing fast, and they continue to be shaped dynamically by contemporary events. It is a widely held view that modern children grow up too fast. The premature loss of innocence in childhood, the early sexualisation and commercialisation of childhoods, and children's (excessive) use of modern technology are often cited as negative aspects of growing up today. Children's lives are more highly controlled than ever by levels of surveillance never known in history before. Increasing control and surveillance are required to protect children, but these measures are starkly at odds with the image of the active, responsible and capable child.

Current modern childhoods have also been described in a positive way, as remarkably proactive, visible and forceful. Appadurai (2013) talks about 'children as future makers' who embody a dynamic, fresh kind of agency that is capable of driving new initiatives. For example, children recently attracted a great deal of attention as a result of the international progressive resistance movement around topics such as the climate crises. Holmberg and Alvinius (2020, p. 88) mention the emergence of 'children's progressive resistance' in the context of the global influence of Greta Thunberg. Greta herself started her awareness-raising campaign about environmental issues by sitting outside the Swedish parliament building during school hours in 2018 and 2019, subsequently becoming an internationally recognised climate activist who has since addressed UN Climate Change conferences and recorded TED talks and was nominated for the Nobel Peace Prize in 2019. Her activities have inspired children and young people all over the world to attend school strikes, with the most comprehensive global strike having taken place in March 2019, involving 1.6 million people in 2,000 locations.

Up until now children's political interest has always been considered negligible, but the recent international proactive movement indicates that children's knowledge and levels of awareness may be transforming rapidly. Greta has set an example of a loud and bold child voice, openly challenging world leaders, politicians and large companies, blaming the whole system of capitalism and demanding concrete steps for change immediately. There is very little research on children's resistance to global issues to date, but thanks to the opportunities offered by rapid social media, this new form of global activity has started to grow and will likely continue to do so. The positive, forceful, proactive child image is fully in line with the proposed active participation of children in research and adds a fresh hue to the active agentive conception of children and childhood.

2.8 Towards a New Framework in Working with Children in Applied Linguistics

Having reviewed the background to the emergence of Childhood Studies and its main mission and focus, alongside the principles advocated by the Convention, it is time to consider what this will mean for the extended research framework when it comes to child participants in applied linguistics (see Figure 2.1). Here the key components of the new framework will be outlined, to be further elaborated on at the end of Chapter 4 after examining different participation types and contextual affordances in the interdisciplinary literature (Chapters 3–4).

The research any adult can undertake can be categorised as research 'on', 'about', 'with' or 'by' children (Figure 2.2; see Chapter 1; Kellett, 2010a; Mayne & Howitt, 2015).

Based on the adult researchers' intentions, beliefs, values and conceptions of childhood and children, whether they embrace the rights-based approach to working with children (as enshrined in the Convention) or whether they have a choice about the type of research questions they are exploring and the kind of epistemology and corresponding methods they are comfortable with, they can place themselves somewhere on this continuum between research 'on' and 'by' children.

Research 'on' and 'about' children, although separate categories, both represent studies where children's responses and contributions are interpreted from the adults' point of view alone and the child participants have no input into the shape and focus of the research project. Typically, studies 'on' children rely on adult observations, experiments or interventions of different kinds where tests or tasks

2.8 A New Framework in Working with Children

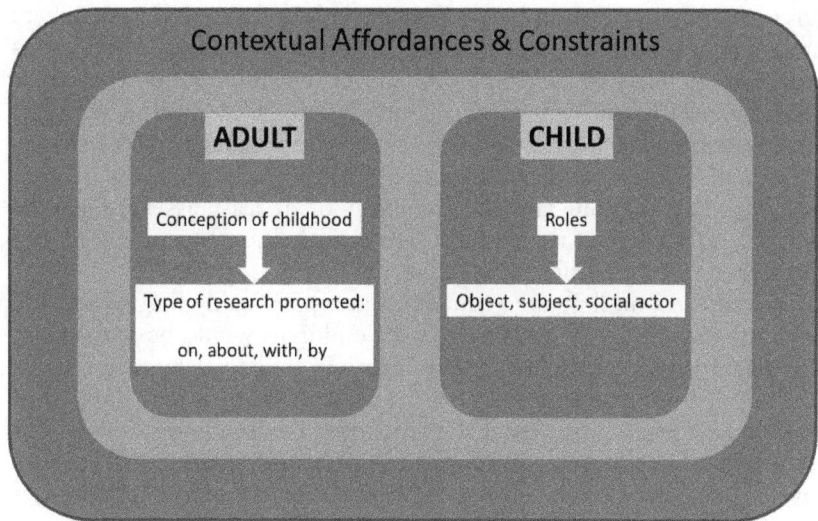

Figure 2.1 Key elements in the extended framework of research involving children in second language education

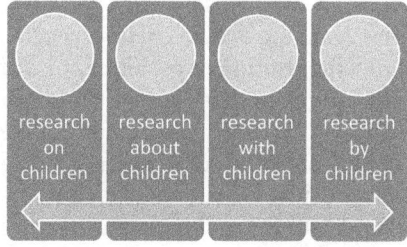

Figure 2.2 Types of Research: 'On', 'about', 'with' and 'by' (on a continuum)

are administered and children's responses are elicited to be counted or measured and often compared to some kind of a benchmark. This approach is broadly consistent with the passive object status of children. As passive objects, children are routinely assumed not to be able to understand or to be interested in the purpose of research and to lack the ability to offer any useful insights. Parents/guardians will decide about and consent to their children's participation, and the children themselves are often not consulted at all or not fully consulted.

Research 'about' children is still conducted completely through the adult lens, but these studies are often smaller in scale and qualitative in nature, allowing for a more explicit interest on the part of the adult researcher to explore the unique trajectories of individual children.

In their attempt to understand children's behaviours, researchers might elicit multiple types of data in a longitudinal design. While this approach is likely to yield rich data about the children involved, their participation is still defined and controlled by adults following adult judgements about their ability based on assumed competence. Although in these studies children are more likely to be aware that research is going on, and their consent or at least assent might be sought, all aspects of the research are nonetheless conceptualised and presented from an adult perspective.

In child second language education, a typical study that would fall into the first category (i.e. research on children) would be one where, for example, a vocabulary test is administered to a large group of children before and after a treatment of introducing a new method of vocabulary teaching to see if the treatment has been effective. In this type of study children are assumed not to be interested in the purpose of the research. The second type of study, research 'about' children, is likely to be a more qualitative study and might, for example, explore a specific group of children's language development by observing/ recording their talk, analysing their writing over time and getting the children to reflect on what new language they think they have learnt. Research 'about' children might use a variety of tools to gain deeper understanding of the learning trajectories of each child and would attempt to understand the unique experiences of different children in terms of their second language development, but with regard to how such a study is planned, conceptualised, undertaken, analysed and made sense of, it is still entirely adult dominated and the children's input is still non-existent, just like in the previous category.

Both studies 'on' and 'about' children treat them as passive participants, that is, data sources only.

Naturally, these two types of studies make up the vast majority of the second language education literature with child participants (see more in Chapter 5). Studies with children's more active involvement have been rare, with the consequence that children's roles and status in research in applied linguistics simply has not been explicitly problematised (Pinter, 2014). The traditional framework with its exclusive focus on research 'on' and 'about' children is a natural consequence of the lack of attention devoted to children as language learners in SLA and the kinds of priorities that have been pursued to date.

The new elements in the framework point to participatory opportunities from less to more participation and are labelled as undertaking research 'with' children or even 'by' children (i.e. children themselves initiating and completing their own research projects). While these new roles present great opportunities for both the children and the adult facilitators involved, the complexities surrounding these roles in terms of constraints of various kinds are numerous, and these will be further explored with the help of illustrative studies from a range of discipline areas in Chapters 3 and 4.

In the category of research 'with' children, a whole range of active child roles are possible (from weaker to stronger types of participation), and these are often labelled differently in different studies. Weaker roles allow for minimal involvement, whereas stronger roles are more reminiscent of partnerships. Co-researcher roles are qualitatively different from the roles that fully fledged child researchers play. Kellett (2010a, p. 50) explains that the difference between co-researchers and researchers is in the 'size of contribution, ownership and responsibility'. Using the metaphor of a sandwich, she suggests that co-researchers tend to make up the filling only while child researchers represent the whole sandwich, including the bread as well (i.e. having responsibility for all stages of the research, from beginning to end, albeit under adult guidance).

Alderson (2008) highlights three different ways in which children can become familiar with research. The first, most basic step is via exposure to research at school. This is the practising stage, when children are undertaking a project as a pedagogic activity. The second possibility is that children become interested and involved in a research project that is led by adults and are offered the opportunity to take on various co-researcher roles. In this scenario children help to plan questions, analyse data and report evidence, and over time their involvement may increase. Finally, some may decide to undertake their own research initiated by themselves into an issue of interest to them. This suggests that teaching research skills at school and encouraging children to undertake research at school is the most meaningful preparation for projects that the children might one day want to initiate outside school, for example in their community. School-based research may start from a pedagogically focussed set of activities initiated by the adult, yet over time, in some cases, it may have the potential to develop into the type of activity that Kim (2016) labels as more 'authentic' and more in line with the core principle of participation as citizens in society at large. Children's understanding of what research is, what it is for and what it can achieve will have the potential to thrive if they can be involved in projects at school and have frequent opportunities to take more and more responsibility while the adult facilitation is carefully phased out.

Becoming a researcher takes time and training (Kellett, 2010a), and it is certainly not something that would be feasible and of interest to all children everywhere. But in some contexts, some children may take an interest in this role as a result of working in co-researcher roles first. At the beginning children may be able to and interested in contributing to adult-initiated research in a consulting role, such as by giving advice on a data collection tool designed by the adult. At a later stage, they may contribute more substantially by, for example, providing input into the research questions, collecting data from their peers or collaborating with the adult teacher or researcher on the data analysis. At the most advanced end of the scale, some children in some contexts may become interested and inspired to undertake their own investigations. Chapters 3, 4 and 6 will elaborate on the opportunities and challenges in such studies.

Research 'with' and 'by' children involves varying degrees of involvement and commitment by the children, but all these projects have the potential to promote democratic, more horizontal relationships between children and adults. While the adults' roles change from studies categorised as 'with' and 'by', there is always a focus on listening to children, information sharing and ongoing dialogue. Researching with children and ultimately helping them to undertake their own research relies on inherent respect for children's capacities and is consistent with an active subject role or social actor status rather than a passive status (as in the traditional framework).

As Mayne and Howitt (2015, p. 37) comment, 'research that upholds the rights-based ideals of the Convention does not just happen by chance, but requires strategic choices at both planning and implementation stages of a research project'.

From the adults' point of view the research can be 'on', 'about', 'with' and 'by' children, but in terms of the children's own roles, they can be categorised as objects, subjects, social actors and active participants (Table 2.2).

Across different disciplines, evidence has been accumulating that some children in some circumstances (although not all) are able and keen to undertake research and that the process of researching can be beneficial to both children and the adults who work with or alongside them. Kellett (2010a, p. 105) comments that 'children observe with different eyes, ask different questions – they sometimes ask questions that adults do not even think of – have different concerns and immediate access to a peer culture where adults are outsiders. The research agendas children prioritise, the research questions they frame and the way in which they collect data are also quintessentially different from adults.'

Table 2.2 *Child roles in research (framework adapted from Mayne & Howitt, 2015 and Christensen & Prout, 2002, p. 480)*

Object	• Children are unknowing objects
	• Paternalistic methods are used
	• Underlying assumption: children are not capable of understanding the purpose of research
	• Children lack the ability to consent and to have any input
Subject	• Recognising subjectivity
	• Children's level of involvement is defined in accordance with adult judgements regarding ability (age-based criteria)
	• Everything is still conceptualised and presented from an adult perspective
Social actor	• Direct link with New Childhood Studies
	• Recognising children as a equals
	• Co-construction of knowledge between adults and children
	• Participatory, flexible approaches
Children as active participants	• Link to the ethical imperative in Convention on the Rights of the Child Article 12
	• Social actors contribute to all or some stages of the research process
	• Fully aware and committed to the research

2.9 Children as Social Actors in Second Language Education Research

In applied linguistics, what is our image of the child language learner, and what roles can they take in research? What is the purpose and the goal of our research, and who are the beneficiaries? Depending on the answers to these questions, different adult researchers will approach their work differently, but it is important that such questions are raised for reflection in our field, and every teacher as well as every researcher working with children must consider their responses. Bucknall (2014, p. 82) reminds us that the opportunity for children to learn about research and the possibility of becoming more active participants in research alongside adults is 'in the gift of' the adult researcher or teacher (i.e. children are not in a position to come forward, inform the adult and claim their rights to participation).

The Convention and its rights-based approach to working with children, even if difficult to implement and open to debate, cannot be ignored in applied linguistics. A commitment to listening to children, taking their views and opinions seriously, and inviting them to participate actively in research is relevant and important in language learning as well as other disciplines. It is therefore important for all teachers, teacher trainers and researchers to raise questions and reflect on:

- How do I see the children's role and status in my own teaching and research?
- What is the purpose of my research, and who benefits?
- How can I understand more about the children's experiences of language learning from their point of view?
- How can I listen better to the children's views and opinions in my teaching and research?
- How can I involve them in more active roles in my research?

The Content and Focus of Research

Children can be encouraged to take an active role researching their own and their peers' language learning processes and experiences. For example, questions like the following might emerge.

Broader Topics

- Who am I or who are we, and why are we leaning English?
- What use can we make of English in our lives?
- What books do we read in English in this class, and why?

Narrower Topics

- What English language (online) games do we play in this class?
- What do we learn from playing these games?
- How do we in my class learn new vocabulary?
- How much time do children in my class spend practising English outside the class?
- How do children in grades 3 and 6 use their English outside the classroom?
- What kind of help do children get at home with English homework?
- What kinds of English language apps are used by children in my class?
- Which English games and activities do children like in my class?

Once some insights have been gathered about these or other topics, it is important to follow up the results and the findings. If some activities have been found to be less enjoyable and less effective, for example, according to the children's views or their research, it is essential that changes are made to teaching and learning practices. Without such follow-up, the research undertaken can become hollow and ultimately meaningless.

Children may also become interested in researching *in the L2* but with a focus on topics/issues of great interest in the class, the school, the local community or beyond. The ultimate aim of such research will be to make a change or make a difference. If appropriate, English (the L2) can be used, or a variety of languages might be used in bilingual or multilingual communities. In bilingual schools or in content and language integrated learning (CLIL) contexts, the use of L2 may be particularly meaningful as a vehicle for undertaking, presenting and disseminating the research, but multilingual and translanguaging approaches may also be appropriate.

It may be the case that a traditional project is planned by the adult (i.e. a study on or about children), but opportunities will still naturally arise to take the children's input and feedback on board, with the consequence that an original research plan may be adapted or extended. Embracing insights and input from the children has the potential to enhance the study overall.

2.10 Conclusion

This chapter has introduced the concept of the social child and explained how and why such a focus emerged in the literature. Taking children's views and perspectives seriously in research is associated with new ways of working with them. Listening to and acting on their voices in applied linguistics will lead to a better understanding of children's life worlds, their needs, interests and ever-changing priorities with regard to language learning and beyond. Understanding their perspectives will lay the foundation for effective partnerships in research with children. In order to develop the tools and approaches to work in this way, the next two chapters will explore the interdisciplinary literature to review key concepts, such as voice, agency and participation (Chapter 3), and educational philosophies and structures that promote child-centredness, children's voice and rights-based approaches (Chapter 4).

3 Voice, Agency and Participation

3.1 Introduction

Having explored reasons behind the emergence of Childhood Studies, the aim of this chapter is to go deeper by focussing on the key concepts of voice, agency and participation, which are considered the main pillars of this alternative approach to studying childhood (Spyrou, 2018). Understanding how voice and agency are conceptualised and how participation is defined, enabled and enacted in different ways in different contexts will begin to illustrate what is realistically achievable with children as active contributors to research.

This chapter will first address the evolution of the key concepts from their first appearance as somewhat naïve and celebratory ideas to more critical interpretations. Then, participatory tools and methods will be reviewed to indicate a move away from research 'on' children towards research 'about' and 'with' children. In order to access children's 'voices', participatory, creative, visual or arts-based tools may be used. These tools can give children some control over how they contribute, although they stop short of assigning active roles (research 'about' children and weaker versions of research 'with' children). Finally, active roles in research 'with' and 'by' children will be explored with examples that illustrate typical engagement as co-researchers alongside their adult counterparts or researchers exploring topics by themselves.

3.2 The Key Concepts

Due to the existing social order (i.e. the fact that adults routinely exercise complete control and authority over children both at home and in schools), it has become a commonplace to talk about the need to hand over control or give children a voice in the traditionally adult-dominated arena of research. The concept of the 'social actor' as promoted by James and Prout (1990) underscores children's ability to exercise their agency as opposed to simply being restricted by adult structures. It is also understood that in order to exercise their rights as laid out in the Convention on the Rights of the Child (1989), children need opportunities for meaningful participation in all areas of their lives. While at a superficial level all these concepts (voice, agency and participation) can be considered commodities to be handed over to children, scholars have cautioned against these sentimental ideas and have suggested that more critical approaches are needed when defining and operationalising them.

3.2.1 Voice

Before the 1990s research had been entirely adult-dominated, and children and their voices and views had not been sought at all, not in second language education research nor elsewhere. Following the initial recommendations made by early Childhood Studies scholars in the 1990s, a great deal of work began to be devoted in different disciplines to 'listening to children's voices', in search of the authenticity of such voices. This early approach suggested that if only adults were willing to listen, children were ready to come forward and have a great deal to say. This image of the willing, 'knowledgeable, self-reflexive child-actor' (Spyrou, 2018, p. 85) is characteristic of these early studies.

More critical approaches pointed to the fact that there is no such thing as a child's authentic voice. Beyond it being an idealised, symbolic concept, the child's one true voice' would be difficult to pin down as no two children's views and voices could be entirely the same, and just like adults, children speak with different voices (Thomson, 2008). At school, for example, children speak with 'schooled voices' because of their exposure to certain types of pedagogic regimes and discourses and the prevailing hierarchical structures that constrain their voice. 'Being able to say what you think, in the ways that you want, is highly dependent on what you are asked by whom, about what, and what is expected of you' (Thomson, 2008, p. 6). At school, most of what children say is in response to teachers' questions and instructions both in and outside lessons. A child will tell a different story in different settings and offer alternative responses and views about any one issue to different people, these being the product of the particular interaction and the time and place in context. When working with an adult researcher, other than the physical context, the adults' class, gender, ethnicity and age will all contribute to what is eventually being told or indeed withheld by the child. When children do speak up, they may voice views and opinions that they feel will satisfy adult expectations, fitting with their understanding of what will please the adult in question. 'These issues around voice(s) are writ large in research with children and young people, who may be particularly reluctant to say anything which they judge may displease the interviewer or may feel that they need to speak with a particular kind of voice since that is not what is expected of them' (Thomson, 2008, p. 6).

When we listen to children's voices, we need to therefore situate these voices in interactional, institutional and local cultural discourse contexts. This situatedness will help adults understand children's complex and multi-layered meanings (Pinter & Zandian, 2015; Spyrou, 2011, 2016). In fact, deeper layers of understanding can represent complex, contradictory views, and uncovering these requires sustained engagement. Komulainen (2007) warns that children's words are often reminiscent of adult discourses, such as teacher voices or parent discourses. Researchers thus need to become familiar with the influences on children's voices but also become more aware of the discourses that inform their own analyses and interpretations (Aro, 2012; Spyrou, 2011). Reflexive research accepts that children's voices are potentially messy, multi-layered and dynamic and need to be analysed and interpreted within their micro-contexts. At the same time, of course, adult researchers can never quite overcome their own biases, and these need to be factored into analysis and interpretation as well.

When it comes to how children's voices are understood, analysed and represented, Spyrou observes that children's voices tend to be interpreted verbatim (i.e. whatever children may say is accepted and celebrated without any questioning). In a more critical attempt, he recommends that we need to go further and ask ourselves: What do children's words actually mean? How are they to be interpreted? 'In the absence of an in-depth investigation of children's own semantic categories, adult researchers may simply reify children's voices by transposing on them their own adult, interpretive frameworks' (Spyrou, 2018, p. 104).

This suggests that beyond simply quoting what children say or comment about an issue, the adult's task is to look deeper for interpretation. This can be achieved by developing relationships, working together for relatively longer periods of time and making sure judgements and interpretations are based on children's 'thick voices' (Carnevale, 2020, p. 3), that is, multiple layers of data analysis undertaken iteratively in a way that acknowledges that the voices are relationally embedded. 'Theorizing voice includes acknowledging voice as always already relational, that voice has no authentic or fixed point of origin, which means that voice should be treated and

3.2 The Key Concepts

accounted for, as it is in critical qualitative research practices, as a complex construction where meanings are always situated and open to multiple interpretations' (Facca et al., 2020, p. 10).

While voice is emphasised, we must also attend to silence. Silences are just as important as voice as they can convey a range of meanings from resistance to shyness, hesitation, lack of interest or boredom, just to name a few. Silence may be a non-response, denial, a long pause, a sigh, deflection or a reframing of an original question. The child–adult encounter is particularly interesting regarding silence because it has a layer of complexity due to the social power distance and the likely effect of being silenced by authority. This can be particularly acute in certain cultural and institutional contexts where children are not used to being asked their opinions (see, for example, Kuchah & Milligan, 2021). In such situations an initial silence can be interpreted as a sign of being surprised and confused because of the adults' unexpected interest. When children give one-word answers, show a general lack of enthusiasm or interest through fidgeting or being distracted, adult researchers need to take notice and interpret these as important signals that the children may not want to continue the conversation (Andrews, 2021). Young children may get distracted more easily and may wish to slip in and out of the research process by taking breaks and re-joining a group, for example. The important thing to remember is that silence is never neutral (Lewis, 2010) or empty, and it must be an integral part of the analysis even though it is a challenge to 'hear' it Mazzei (2003). Spyrou (2016, p. 12) also reminds us that silence may trigger questions about ethics too. He describes a 'wavering back and forth' type of silence or reluctance where children may be wondering what to disclose and what to hold back. The phrase 'I don't know' is also often used to close down a line of questioning, not to have to talk about something they don't want to. 'Encouraging children to talk about aspects of their lives that they resist talking about carries ethical implications' (Spyrou, 2016, p. 19).

Bucknall (2014) discusses how 'giving' children a voice is associated with the intention to reduce the power gap in the normal social order. Much discussion in the literature has been devoted to how adult interlocutors may present themselves as more child-like and child-friendly – again, to ease children into the research. Mandell (1988, p. 435), for example, suggested that when working with children, adult researchers should take a so-called least adult role, that is, adults should pretend to be and act like children so that they blend in and no longer appear to have control or power. However, this radical solution is problematic, as children will always be aware of the adult presence, so, instead, it is recommended that adults may present themselves as simply lacking knowledge and experience in a topic area that the children happen to have expertise in (Mayall, 2002). Such a hybrid identity, which explicitly presents the adult as less 'powerful' because they are lacking knowledge that the children have, has the potential to balance out the initial hierarchical status quo and can create a more balanced basis for genuine dialogue. Hybrid roles (such as the adult researcher in the role of a graduate student) will have to be explained to the children carefully, giving them the opportunity to ask questions, make comments and verbalise their doubts and surprises (e.g. Kuchah & Pinter, 2012).

When children's voices are captured in creative ways and they are being carefully listened to, power imbalances between children and adults may be altered slightly (Graham et al., 2016), especially if the relationship is carefully negotiated over time, but of course ultimately no single method, creative or otherwise on its own, can guarantee that power between children and adults is equally distributed. Rather, power is always dynamic and constantly negotiated in any context where adults and/or children work together. Based on a Foucaultian understanding of power, Gallagher (2008, p. 147) reminds us that power is exercised between people through a diverse array of actions and that researchers are always caught in a complex web of power relations: 'Participatory techniques may provide interesting ways to intervene in games of power, but they do not provide a way to transcend such games.'

There are also important existing power relationships between children in any group, with some of them being shy or reluctant to talk to adults and even peers while others come across dominant, communicative and forthcoming. In any one situation, power is dynamically negotiated, and how exactly it plays out depends on the complex relationships between adults and children, as well as between different children in a peer group. Kellett (2010a) argues that children's class, age, linguistic skills, physical ability and popularity will impact on the power dynamics between groups of children and adult researchers.

In some cases, children using their power may also exploit, contest, resist and refuse participatory techniques or any other activity in a research project (Gallagher, 2008). Such instances call for a careful handling of key ethical guidelines to do with informed consent and possible withdrawal from the study, and it is the adult's responsibility to notice the need to evoke these steps (see Chapter 7).

3.2.2 Agency

Like voice, agency is also a politically significant concept: the 'child agent' was emphasised in the seminal publication by James and Prout (1990) alongside the parallel concept of voice. If children are not 'becomings' but instead 'beings' in their own right, their agency needs to be investigated and paid close attention to.

The analysis of child agency originates from Giddens' theory (1984), which defines the agent as an autonomous individual who exercises power and thus can make a difference to their own lives. Recognising that children are in this sense not actually fully autonomous individuals as they are unable to make a difference through their actions in the world, Mayall (2002) suggests that children are social actors rather than agents. Even though a focus on agency has been enlightening, the original emphasis in early publications was somewhat overstated, ignoring the fact that children's lives are always highly structured and controlled by adult systems. Just like with voice and its associated power, the romanticised understanding of agency has been criticised. A more careful and balanced approach to studying agency focusses on when, how, with whom and under what circumstances children choose to or are invited to exercise their agency rather than just taking it for granted that they possess agency.

Agency, like voice, must be understood within the prevailing constraints embedded in intergenerational relationships that limit children's worlds. Leonard (2016) proposes the term 'generagency' and suggests that we must focus on the relational processes in intergenerational relationships when we attempt to understand how children's agency is enacted in the context of the limitations of their structural realities.

Some would argue that children's agency (as well as voice) is always ultimately adult controlled since in these intergenerational relationships they are only appreciated by adults when their views and actions conform with adult normative conceptions of what is desirable.

3.2.3 Degrees of Participation

In Childhood Studies it is argued that both voice and agency are part and parcel of participation, with participation being a broader concept, usually described as a process that may manifest various degrees of active involvement in research. The purpose of participation may be to uphold children's rights, improve their services, enhance democracy, promote child protection, enhance children's skills and knowledge or empower or enhance children's self-esteem, all of which have been associated with benefits (Thomas, 2007). Wyness (2015) cautions that participation is understood with a Western frame of the participating child and does not comfortably apply to all contexts, such as, for example, the argument that children have the right to participate in the labour market. The Western ideal of participation is increasingly coming under criticism as not necessarily authentic and fully applicable to all contexts.

By using their voice and agency, children can seek participation, but one of the major obstacles to children's participation is that they themselves cannot initiate it. Opportunities for children to participate actively in research or in other spheres of their lives (such as schools, for example) must always be initiated by interested adults. Participation at schools, which is where children spend most of their time, is very patchy, often minimal and rarely meaningful, despite research that strongly backs up its advantages. Thomson and Gunter (2009, p. 412) comment that even when schools offer some form of participation, children are least likely to be asked their opinions about important matters such as classroom processes and the curriculum, and instead their participation remains tokenistic and about less serious questions (see more about this in Chapter 4).

Various scholars have described and characterised degrees and stages of participation by creating frameworks to illustrate the possibilities from more tokenistic to genuine/full participation. In 1992 Hart published one of the best-known models, which has inspired many other frameworks and much empirical work in the literature. This framework uses the metaphor of a ladder to illustrate eight steps taken towards increasingly more genuine types of participation (Figure 3.1).

At the bottom of Hart's ladder is non-participation or tokenistic participation. At the next level children are assigned some roles and consulted about adult decisions but still contribute only minimally. This is followed by increasing levels of participation, including stages where the children share gradually more decisions with adults, and finally, it reaches the top rung where children initiate a research project and adults assist them in the background. It is not implied that all studies with children need to aim as high as possible on this ladder, but instead the ladder raises adults' awareness about the various possibilities that might be applicable in a certain context. As Wilkinson and Wilkinson (2018, p. 20) note, 'the ladder of participation should not be used as a measuring stick of quality', adding that 'it is not necessary that children always operate on the highest rungs of the ladder'. Treseder (1997) suggests that there is no obvious or right way to progress across the rungs either.

Many other scholars have offered alternative participation frameworks, such as Fielding (2001), Lansdown (2005) and Shier (2001). Fielding's model consists of four levels where the learner is seen as simply a data source (level 1), then active respondent (level 2), then co-researcher (level 3) and finally a researcher (level 4). Lansdown's (2005) model differentiates between consultation, participatory processes and self-initiation. In consultation mode children respond to a preconceived adult agenda and lack any real possibility to control the

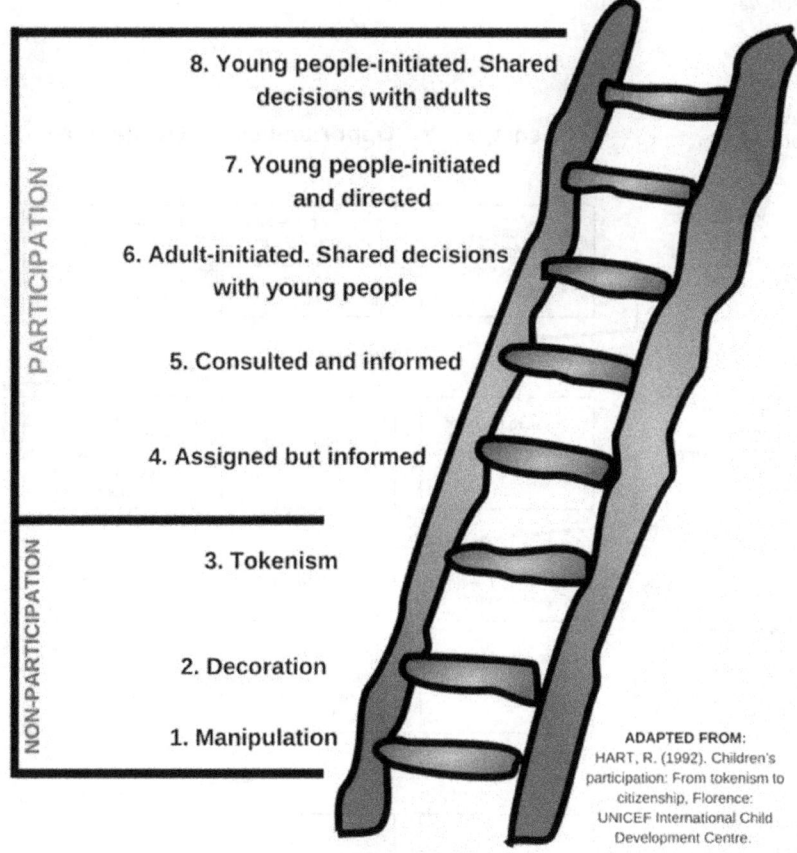

Figure 3.1 Hart's ladder of participation

process or the outcomes of the work, whereas in participatory processes the relationship is more equal. Finally, in self-initiation the learner engagement is fully autonomous.

One of the most detailed models, inspired by Hart, has been developed by Shier (2001). This model is particularly attractive because it adds contextual elements to illustrate how participation can be supported systematically within institutions. The model elaborates on the affordances and opportunities in the given context in order to give adult researchers and practitioners clear guidelines as to what to do if they wish to encourage children to take on more active roles. This Pathways to Participation model (Figure 3.2) includes five steps, which are:

50 Voice, Agency and Participation

Pathways to Participation
Harry Shier 2001

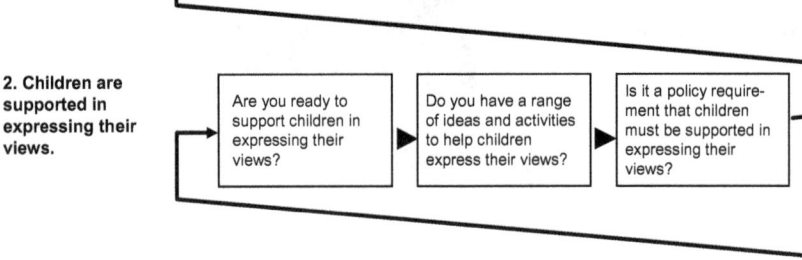

From: Shier, H. (2001). Pathways to Participation: Openings, Opportunities and Obligations. *Children and Society*, 15: 107-117.

Figure 3.2 Pathways to participation

3.2 The Key Concepts

(1) Children are listened to.
(2) Children are supported in expressing their views.
(3) Children's views are taken into account.
(4) Children are involved in decision-making processes.
(5) Children share power and responsibility for decision making.

Shier points out that there is no obligation to reach the last stage of his framework (i.e. stage 5) according to the Convention on the Rights of the Child (1989), but instead organisations and schools can decide what level is appropriate or desirable. The emphasis in this framework is on the dialogic sharing process with adults, and children's independent decision making (i.e. active roles where they undertake their own research) therefore is not included here.

Each step or level has openings, opportunities and obligations. Openings stand for personal commitment and statement of intent, whereas opportunities require resources to be available and procedures to be in place to enable the individual or the organisation to act. Finally, obligations stand for an agreed policy that has been embedded, meaning that all adults in the organisation should be expected to operate at this level. Stating these obligations explicitly guarantees that the given level is built into the system and is being adhered to by everyone.

Shier (2001) suggests that children's involvement in decision making can improve the quality of provision, increase children's sense of ownership, self-esteem and responsibility and facilitate the groundwork for citizenship and democratic participation. Importantly, if children do not want to take responsibility, they do not have to and should not be forced. This is, however, rarely a problem because in reality adults are more likely to deny children this responsibility than force too much of it on them.

Finally, Lundy's model (2007) is worth mentioning because of its popularity and its emphasis on the importance of creating a context that gives plenty of space and time to eliciting children's voices. This framework promotes four elements: space, voice, audience and influence, suggesting that, first of all, appropriate physical spaces need to be made available where children feel ready to voice their opinions. Lundy further highlights the importance of a sympathetic audience who can hear the voices, meaning adults in the position to take on these messages and act on them to make changes.

The model provides key questions to consider within each segment of the circle: space, voice, audience and influence (Figure 3.3).

52   *Voice, Agency and Participation*

Figure 3.3 Lundy's model of participation: Guiding questions

Although, in general, deeper levels of participation are promoted by all frameworks, interestingly, Lundy (2018) defends minimal participation and even tokenism.

She suggests that it is better than no involvement at all:

[T]okenism is sometimes a start. Not listening to children's views on matters that affect them is always wrong – a breach of their human rights. Not seeking their input on the basis that it would be tokenistic is therefore also wrong. Seeking children's views and doing so in a tokenistic fashion is also wrong but arguably not as wrong as not starting at all. As always in participation, there is no one right way to do it. However, moving forward, it is admitted that it will often be better to begin a process of collective participation that could be tokenistic and then put in some checks and balances that foster a conducive environment for meaningful engagement with children's views.

(Lundy, 2018, pp. 351–352)

3.3 Using Participatory Methods and Tools

Participatory methods and tools have proliferated more recently (e.g. Carter & Coyne, 2018; Groundwater-Smith et al., 2015; Groundwater-Smith & Mocklet, 2016) with a great deal of variety across studies regarding exact definitions and implementations.

Accessing children's voices, giving children agency and encouraging their participation have together produced a large, rich interdisciplinary literature. A major concern in this literature has been the conviction that children require alternative creative methods to elicit their views because traditional elicitation methods, such as ordinary interviews, are inadequate as they are rigid and reliant on adult ways of communicating. In these situations children find it hard to express themselves verbally, following a 'question and answer' format reminiscent of school discourse, with the expectation that adults know best and there is a right answer. As Hart (1992, p. 14) suggested, 'unfortunately, most social science research with children is still of the distant, adult-controlled type: questionnaires and structured interviews which barely scrape the surface of what children are able to tell'.

While traditional research has marginalised children (Alderson, 1995; James et al., 1998; Morrow & Richards, 1996) participatory techniques arguably offer an emancipatory alternative. Encouraging children to voice their views and inviting them to respond in ways that may be more suitable, natural and meaningful do not necessarily lead to active participation.

Some of these tools and methods are inspired by the work of Freire (1970, 1973), who called them Participatory Rural Appraisal tools. Freire's approach to research was characterised by respect for diversity and complexity, a commitment to enhance local capabilities and an ongoing active dialogue between researchers and researched. Participatory tools are embedded into ongoing dialogue rather than used in isolation. Even though the adult proposes the tools themselves, children have some control over their responses as compared to simple question and answer interviews. In some cases it is also possible for the child to adjust the tools or co-create these with the adult. Creative or participatory methods are not easy to administer, though, and considerable training and experience might be needed on the part of the adult. Using open-ended participatory tools that override verbal exchanges can be challenging to implement (e.g. Blaisdell et al., 2019) because adults can get impatient and give in to the temptation to retreat to the security of verbal voice and question and answer routines, especially if the more open-ended methods do not immediately work.

In the rest of this section some popular participatory tools and methods will be reviewed, drawing on examples from the interdisciplinary literature. Even though the use of these tools and approaches is directly applicable to applied linguistics, in this chapter the discussion will focus on the characteristics of these tools, while actual language education-related examples will be discussed in detail later, in Chapter 6.

Popular participatory tools and methods include various types of role plays, drama, drawings, photos, videos and film making, scrapbooks, collages and other arts-based approaches. As Greene and Hill (2005) suggest, the choice of method will influence what kind of data we get from children, and children of different ages in different formal or less formal contexts may enjoy and be comfortable with very different methods. Adults may need to spend some time deciding what type of participatory tools might be most suitable in a given context. If possible, it is good practice to involve children in the decisions about choosing the tools. Even though power differentials between adults and children can never be denied, these participatory/creative approaches can facilitate the process of breaking down power barriers to some extent in the sense that they may be more in line with children's preferred ways of expressing themselves.

In contrast to traditional verbal methods, creative and art-based methods can also elicit and invoke emotional and aesthetic responses. Dreissnack and Furukawa (2012), for example, discuss the advantages of art-based approaches with children in health care research and claim that these methods are particularly useful when adults are trying to elicit emotional or sensitive stories from children by putting them at ease. Drawings can serve as catalysts for conversations, and puppets, masks and dolls help children to remove themselves from their own situations and talk about their experiences more generally.

There has been a growing interest across discipline areas in the use of visual methods with children, to the extent that some scholars talk about the 'visual turn'. Visual prompts will work with all children, but they may be particularly suitable for children who are less vocal, do not speak the language of the interviewer well or who have some form of a learning difficulty. In these cases visual/alternative methods can be argued to be more 'ethical choices' than traditional methods because they make participation more inclusive. Thomas and O'Kane (1998) and O'Kane (2008) advocate a diverse use and the mixing of such methods to elicit rich data. It must be kept in mind, though, that using visual or arts-based methods will not solve issues around the complexities of representation. Drawings, photos or collages cannot be equated with the 'authentic' depictions of children's voices either, and a careful and critical approach to analysis will still need to be adopted. Working with visual artefacts is common in Childhood Studies and, while we do not have to be artists to make use of these tools in our research, Thomson (2008, p. 15) suggests that 'it certainly helps if we can see the visual as something beyond technique, and as a social practice which has traditions, genres, debates, grammars, and hierarchies of distinction'.

The current spike in interest in the visual is linked to the development of affordable cameras, mobile devices, and the general proliferation of image-based systems of communication. The photo image is not a simple window on the world (Thomson, 2008). Images are the result of human construction, and they are never neutral. They are typically put through processes of selection, processing and editing. Images are also embedded in specific micro and macro-cultures and may be read in multiple ways by various audiences, and thus interpretations can also vary. 'There are a myriad of such decisions and choices that are made by the image producer and these decisions are themselves in part determined by virtue of who the person or team is, where they are, and what they think is important, their intentions, values, and their historical position and membership' (Thomson, 2008, p. 10).

Accordingly, when images are produced by children in research, efforts are to be made to elicit a commentary from the image maker or photo taker.

The easiest and most often used visuals in research are drawings: adult researchers ask children to draw something relevant to the topic of the investigation. For example, children can draw themselves, their teachers, scenes from their lessons, their school, their family or even more abstract or distant ideas such as their hopes and fears or imaged future identities as language learners. These drawings can be used as prompts and a starting point for dialogue. Drawings give children some control or choice over the content and can be inclusive, although not all children like drawing, and older children especially might decline an invitation to draw anything at all. On the plus side, drawing is a relaxing activity, and while engaged with it, children have time to think about what they want to say. Drawings can be changed or added to and thus certainly offer children some flexibility regarding their responses (Punch, 2002).

Given that ever younger children now carry smartphones and routinely use mobile devices, drawings are becoming less popular, with photos taking over. Photos are quick, easy and cheap to take, and children are just as good at this as adults. Both digital photos and disposable cameras have been used extensively with children in social science research (e.g. Clark, 2010; Cook & Hess, 2007; Einarsdottir, 2014). Photos taken by children often surprise adults in that children see different things in their environment; they focus on things at a different eye level and notice things that adults might not pay attention to at all. Although simple and easy, there are still practical challenges with photos, such as making sure that children are not instructed by other adults, siblings or parents about what to take a picture of and that they can save and access the photos they have taken.

Whether children are taking photos in groups or individually, the number of photos taken can vary a great deal in different studies. Generally speaking, more photos will give more insights, and indeed the most common approach is to invite children take several photos and then get them to select a particularly important one from the batch to start the dialogue with the adult. For example, in a study by Burke (2008), children were given disposable cameras and invited to compile a visual diary documenting their play activities at school. The children could take as many pictures as they wanted. Once the pictures were developed, conversations were arranged between each child and the adult researcher. The adult started the conversation by laying out randomly all the photos taken by a child before the child was asked to choose one significant photo to talk about. This was followed by the adult choosing a different photo and asking the child to comment on it. Taking turns with selecting photos at least gives some space to children's choices and priorities in terms of negotiating the content of the dialogue and giving them a sense that they can initiate some topics for discussion.

Photos create focal points around which negotiation of meaning happens, and they have the power to evoke meaning while being moved across time, space and context (Lipponen et al., 2016). Taking an image or photo is an individual act but also an act that can materialise collective experiences and pass them through time. When these photos are used in interaction between the children and the researcher, the interaction is mediated through these cultural artefacts; in other words, photos help children to communicate things that otherwise would be difficult to convey. At the same time, photos also offer a shared reference. It is possible for the parties to see what each other see, and they also serve as memory support. The artefact is always relative to the social situation it is used in. Sharing an experience using photos will affect what part of the story or experience gets emphasised. This construction and reconstruction of experience is shaped by the present situation as well as imagined future situations (i.e. for whom and for what purpose the photo is taken). An artefact also always implies possible uses other than the intended one, and thus discussing photos with a researcher can lead to opening up new interpretations and alternative meanings and new topics for discussion.

Collages and zines are also based on drawings and photos, but they can both carry more complex messages and capture experience more holistically. They involve cutting and pasting pictures from magazines or brochures and combining these with the person's own drawings, writing or photos (see Figure 3.4). Zines 'constitute an empowering tool for self-expression and an alternative knowledge production and sharing' (Valli, 2021, p. 6) as they are often politically and emotionally charged and promote change. As inclusive artistic tools, by going beyond any verbal communication, both collages and zines are particularly suitable for exploring children's or young people's experiences, especially in eliciting summative reflections and recommendations for change (Prasad, 2013, 2020, 2021; Vacchelli, 2018).

Film making can be used to record interviews, reflections or observations. One attractive approach of using video to record reflections is to tap into culturally familiar forms of recording, such as the *Big Brother*-style diary room used by Noyes (2008). In this setup a video recorder is placed in a room where children can enter and record their reflections when they are ready to contribute by switching the machine on and off themselves. In this study by Noyes (2008) 9–10-year-old children's thoughts and feelings about learning maths were recorded following the conventions in the *Big Brother* TV show. The diary room with a video camera was available one day of the week for several months, and the children were encouraged to visit this room to make their own video entries regularly, documenting their own thoughts, feelings, and experiences in relation to learning maths. The use of video diaries allowed the adult researcher to hand over some of the responsibility for data collection to the children, and this successfully moved away from the conventional question and answer format, giving children the opportunity to reveal and withhold whatever they felt appropriate given the context and the topic at hand. Recording feelings and experiences this way also helped with the reflection

Figure 3.4 Identity collage created by a multilingual child (Sophie's collage, from Prasad, 2020, p. 919)

process as children had time and space to think about what they wished to share with the adult researcher.

In addition to using it for recording purposes, film or video can also be a creative narrative technique with its own communicative power and affective qualities (Parry, 2015). When used as an artistic expression to facilitate children's insights and opinions, films are about meaning making and aesthetic effect. Media production can facilitate group collaboration and enable pedagogies of shared negotiation and research. When using film with children, one has to accept 'the mess, uncertainty and ambiguity of research' rather than follow a neat research plan (Parry, 2015, p. 89), but it allows otherwise hidden messages come to the surface, such as feelings and emotions that might be harder to communicate in other ways.

The challenge of eliciting the views and insights of younger children is even more acute than that of older children. Participatory approaches and methods, therefore, are very popular, in particular with early years' researchers and practitioners working with pre-school children.

With young children who cannot read or write yet, Hohti and Karlsson (2014, p. 550) recommend the use of an emergent and flexible approach they call 'story-crafting'. This is an open-ended opportunity to tell the researcher any story. The approach is contingent on the discourses and the social, material and physical resources available and takes time and patience, but it serves as an open-ended space to capture young children's voices in a spontaneous way. The adult invites the child to tell a story that is written down and read back to the child for checking. The child is invited to add additional details and corrections to the version that is read back to them. Interpreting children's stories will require reflexivity by taking 'an uncomfortable distance' (Hohti & Karlsson, 2014, p. 559) from our assumptions, meaning that the stories we may hear are not what we expected.

A widely implemented, exciting initiative with pre-school children is associated with the mosaic approach and the original inspiring work of Clark and Moss (2011, 2005) involving pre-school children in active roles. This approach to research is based on the amalgamation of traditional observation with multiple creative, visual tools. Although many variations are possible, the original mosaic approach consists of three main stages:

- Stage 1 is devoted to gathering data from all participants, including children and adults.
- Stage 2 is about piecing together information for discussion and reflection.
- Stage 3 is for interpreting the data and feeding it into decision making.

Clark (2001, p. 334) explains that

[The] mosaic approach is a multi-method framework, which combines the traditional methodology of observation and interviewing with the introduction of participatory tools including the use of cameras, tours and mapping. Other tools such as drawing and role play can also be added. Each tool forms one piece of the mosaic. In stage 2 these pieces are brought together with parents' and practitioners' comments to form the basis of dialogue, reflection and interpretation. The mosaic, which is made, is a form of documentation co-constructed by the children and adults.

The resulting mosaic is rich with layers of data, but of course the whole process of creating it is just as important as the product itself, since all three stages are characterised by productive dialogue, which is recorded for further reflection. The perspectives of young children are actively sought, but these are also supplemented by adult views. Rather than juxtaposing these views, the mosaic aims to bring them together 'in the construction of dialogues in which there is mutual respect, active participation and the negotiation of co-construction of meaning' (Pascal & Bertram 2009, p. 254). Such joint dialogue building opens up new spaces for listening, exploration and co-constructing new knowledge with children.

The challenge for adults is how to tune into the world of children, who are considered skilful communicators with important things to share (Nutbrown, 1996). Many of the mosaic tools and techniques, such as photo elicitation or map making, could be used on their own, but the real appeal of the mosaic approach is the careful combination of several tools and the way they draw together all these different sources of data. Once the mosaic is created, reflection and interpretation take place, and further dialogue is encouraged between groups of children, practitioners and researchers, children and researchers, and between parents, children and researchers. The mosaic that fully documents the contributions is referred to as visible listening as it attempts to document children's views in a visual form (Rinaldi, 2001). The mosaic, as a central focus on display, can be revisited, extended and reflected on for as long as there is willingness and interest to sustain the process.

The philosophy of listening to young children encapsulated in the mosaic approach is an approach that has influenced many researchers and educators working with young children. Due to its flexibility and adaptability, it has inspired a wealth of research (e.g. Dahlberg & Moss, 2005; Greenfield, 2011; Rogers & Boyd, 2020; Zhang, 2015).

3.4 Types of Participation: Research 'with' and 'by' Children

The participatory tools discussed above help elicit children's views, opinions and experiences, and some of these tools help to move away from studies 'on' and 'about' children to studies that can be labelled as studies 'with' children, but children's roles do not automatically change from passive to active participants just because participatory tools are used.

Using participatory techniques signals that adult researchers have given careful thought to how they can help children express their views in a way that is more natural, easier, more meaningful or even enjoyable, but these are still passive roles, labelled as research 'about' children or a so-called weaker form of research with children.

In this section, attention is turned to examples of studies where children are positioned in explicitly active roles, as co-researchers/partners or as fully fledged researchers in their own right.

When it comes to research 'with' children, weaker or stronger forms of engagement and participation are possible, and many suggest that it is all a matter of degree. Various definitions of child co-research or partnership with adults can be detected in the literature (Spriggs & Gillam, 2019). The terminology used is inconsistent, with some studies referring to children as active participants, advisers, consultants or researchers, while others do not use such labels and yet the children clearly play active roles. Depending on the specific role in any given study, children will be more or less active, more or less committed and more or less involved in the research. The focus of the project may be one that the adult researcher has selected, and as such it may be less important or relevant to the children, or the topic can be of joint interest to the adults and the children. Co-researchers collaborate with the adult in at least one or more stages of the research; they might be involved in determining the research questions, collecting data or interpreting and analysing results. Franks (2011, p. 18) talks about 'pockets of participation', which means that the children may choose to be involved in some stages but leave the rest to the adults, depending on their interests and experience. The more the children are involved, the more balanced the partnership may be.

Scholars writing about children's active participation in research frequently refer to the various participation frameworks (such as Hart, Shier, Fielding or Lundy) and identify a particular stage, step or rung on the ladder to describe the type of engagement they are promoting. Others simply use a term such as 'co-researcher' and then define it in unique terms to fit with their contexts. Thomas (2017, p. 161) suggests that the most common labels are 'children as research assistants', 'children as research partners' and 'children as research leaders'.

Let us now take a look at an example of research 'with' children, where the children actively shape the research project and work alongside the adults in active roles, and another example where children undertake their own research.

Example 1 Research with children (Johnson, 2008)

In this study, children are labelled as co-researchers. The study introduces participatory tools, but the children are trained to become co-researchers and help collect and analyse the data with the adult. The children's contributions clearly impact the outcomes of the study as well as the changes that are made to the school afterwards.

Johnson (2008), a new headteacher of a primary school in Australia, invited children to help her understand what places in and around the school needed improvement. She asked the children where and how they enjoyed spending time in school and what suggestions they had for improving the school. The ultimate goal was to initiate change and make a positive difference to the school environment in a way that took the children's perspectives into account. Since there were some deaf children and some non-English speaking children in the school, Johnson was keen to use tools that were suitable for everyone and allowed all to participate, so some participatory tools (such as photos and artwork) were incorporated. The design of the study did not just invite the children to take photos and produce artwork to express their views and opinions about school places, but the children were also trained as visual researchers as part of the process. After the initial discussions with the children, the adult researcher invited the children to discuss a draft research plan. Specific skills, in particular the use of visual representations in research based on Kress and van Leeuwen's (1990) analytic framework, were taught to the children. The children were helped to notice both the denotative as well as the symbolic, connotative meanings of visuals. Ethnographic research workshops were run where the children were introduced to information contained in visuals, encouraging them to carefully scrutinise these visuals and challenging them to recognise that a photograph is a representation created by the photographer and that the meaning of the photo is always co-constructed by the maker and the viewer.

First, the children looked at the photos Johnson took on her first day at the school, and they discussed the intentions behind the photos together. They were challenged to look 'beyond the material characteristics' of the photos. She asked them questions such as: What can you see? So, what does this really mean? What does it tell us about what is valued? Is this a concern? For whom? Now what is our response? Next, visuals in carefully selected picture books were also examined to see how these books used the visuals to communicate with the reader.

After the training, the children were asked to create artwork and take photos around the school to locate the best parts of the school and those in need of improvement. All children could create as many pieces of artwork as they wanted, using whatever methods and materials they chose. Some children took several days to complete their artwork. Photos of places in need of improvement were taken by small groups who shared a disposable camera. This meant that the children were encouraged to discuss their choices together. Finally, at the last stage, children selected their photographs for discussion and analysed and interpreted the visuals to determine what action was needed to make changes to various places in their school. The adult researcher and the children discussed the findings together, and the children's input was ultimately translated into priorities in the next school budget and into making changes to the school environment.

Example 2 Research by children (Bucknall, 2012 and a summary of children's research taken from Kellett, 2005)

One of the most well-documented initiatives of children as researchers (CAR) has been associated with projects run by the Open University Child Research Centre with 9–11-year-olds. In the CAR projects, academic staff run training sessions for interested schools. In some schools whole classes are involved, while in others only small groups or a handful of individuals. Some schools incorporate the research activity into the curriculum, while others (most) run it as an add-on or as a research club.

Academic researchers work in schools for weeks or months to run research training for the children and facilitate their projects to undertake their own research. Evidence is plentiful from both adults and children that undertaking research is associated with many benefits, such as acquiring new skills and confidence, practising and developing transferable skills and higher order thinking skills as well as ICT skills, and pride in achieving something useful and tangible (Bucknall, 2012).

The facilitators' job is to make sure the children develop an authentic interest and curiosity in the topic they choose; otherwise, they may lose interest and struggle to persevere with the project, so cultivating children's passion and interest in the topic is the foundation of the process. Children's research questions do not emerge from the literature but from their experiences and the activities, although some children do read about what other people have found out by consulting websites, school policy documents, newspapers, magazines or other young researchers' work. The involvement of external researchers leads to qualitatively different relationships between children and adults as compared to teacher–learner relationships. Children comment that they feel different and that they appreciate being taken more seriously. Children also say that the kind of research they carry out in CAR is very different from the research they might do at school, such as looking things up on the Internet. Children are invited to work in pairs or groups supporting each other. 'It was striking that where children were able to decide for themselves to work in pairs or in groups, they were able, despite some disagreements, to draw on each other's strengths to carry out research with very little direct adult involvement' (Bucknall 2012, p. 15).

The selection of child researchers is a challenging process since, often, more children want to volunteer than it is possible to include. Consent is also a challenging process, and discussions about ethics and consent need to start in advance of the project. 'Class teachers, for example, act as "gatekeepers" for potential research participants in their classes, and it can cause some difficulty and confusion if a young researcher asks to talk to a class but the teacher knows nothing about the research initiative' (Bucknall, 2012, p. 45).

Writing up the findings can take many forms, such as reports, research posters, audio/video recording or PowerPoint presentations. Dissemination is essential. Often this happens through local neighbourhood groups, local newspapers, teacher conferences, school partnership meetings, school managers'/governors' meetings or teacher training events.

The following report (Table 3.1) is an example of a project that was initiated as a result of the children's genuine interest in the possibility of playing mixed-gender football tournaments at school. The comprehensive research training provided to the children made it possible for them to mix different research methods, including a student questionnaire, observations of actual play and interviews with the captains of the mixed-gender teams. The two child researchers read widely about the topic in newspapers, allowing them to put their research questions in context. The results are well summarised and justified with empirical data, and the young researchers interpret and evaluate their findings too. This is an abridged version of original text with some details taken out, but readers are invited to consult the full version complete with tables and figures (https://dx.doi.org/10.4135/9781446212288). The text gives a flavour of the type of research project this pair of children were able undertake, and it describes the steps they took. Further detail is available in the original about the detailed decisions they made when designing the various research tools, such as the types of questions asked.

Table 3.1 An actual CAR project (adapted from Kellett, 2005)

Girls Want to Play too! Investigating the Views of 9–11-Year-Old Pupils about Mixed-Gender Football

Introduction

We wanted to base our research project on men's and women's football because it is a subject that we are both particularly interested in. Direct comparisons between women's and men's football show huge differences between the two. Men's football is one of the richest and most publicised sports in the world. It has been speculated that David Beckham of Real Madrid earns an average wage of £120,000 a week, whereas Mia Hamm, one of the best female footballers in the world, earns approximately £714 a week, which equals roughly £40,000 a year (*Match Magazine*, October 2003, Edition 442). We calculated that David Beckham is earning three times as much in a week as Mia Hamm does in a year.

Research (observations and a close look at newspapers) showed that:

Not everyone thinks women and men should not play together. We think that mixed-gender football is very popular and wanted to find out what other people our age thought about it. We both started off doing different projects, but we thought that it would make the projects more interesting to have male and female views. It also helps that both of us play for local football teams and at school.

Research Question

What are the views of girls and boys on mixed-gender football?

Methodology

We decided to use a multi-methods approach to answering our research question. We thought this would allow us to answer the question in the most thorough way possible.

1. Questionnaire to the whole class
2. Experiment/observations of mixed-gender and single-gender games
3. Players' questionnaires
4. Captains' interviews

Findings

We started our analysis by looking at the questionnaire that we gave to the whole class. We found that 82% of all children would like a mixed-gender league, with 57% of the 82% strongly agreed to there being a mixed-gender football league. Seventy-seven per cent of children agreed that mixed male and female teams are better than all-male or all-female teams, whilst 23% of children disagreed. We found that 30% thought that female or mixed teams were not as good as male-only teams, but 70% thought they were as good. Similarly, 70% disagreed that female-only teams were better than male or mixed-gender teams. These results show us that the general opinion of the class towards mixed football is positive. It is clear that a majority of children think mixed-gender is better than single-gender football.

The statement that produced the strongest opinions was to do with a mixed men's and women's Premier League. We can't say why this statement produced the

(*continued*)

Table 3.1 (cont.)

strongest opinions, but it could be because the premier league is on TV and in the papers so much. We asked the people who thought that mixed-gender teams were not as good as single-gender teams why they thought this, and they thought it might be because they had been brought up with only single-gender leagues.

Seventy-three per cent of people agreed that mixed football is better for spectators to watch; 65% thought it would improve players' behaviour on the pitch, whilst 78% thought it would improve spectators' behaviour. Seventy-three per cent thought that there is fair play in women's football, whilst 69% thought there is fair play in men's football. These results again show that people's opinion of mixed-gender football is positive. The majority of children believe that mixed-gender football would be better to watch and would improve the behaviour of players and spectators. There was no difference in the opinions on fair play, with the majority of people believing that there is fair play in both men's and women's football.

The results show the majority of people expressing positive opinions towards mixed-gender football: 68% thought that football would be more enjoyable if males and females played together, whilst 77% thought that mixed-gender football would encourage people to be more social. Seventy-seven per cent of people also thought that there is fairer play in mixed football, with 50% of these strongly agreeing.

Observations

We were quite surprised at what we found in the observations that we made. The boys involved the girls a lot more than we anticipated, though they did pass it more to their gender. Three of the observations we made about the boys were to do with them changing the way they played when they played with the girls. Boys were less rough with the girls then they were with their own sex. Boys were more relaxed playing with their own gender, and they passed the football about more when they were playing on the single-sex team. These observations indicate that the boys are treating the mixed-gender football differently to playing solely with boys.

The observations of the girls showed that they joined in more in the mixed-gender football; they were also more dedicated to the match, whereas some boys were messing about in the mixed-gender game. This again indicates that the boys weren't taking the game seriously, whereas the girls were.

Overall, the girls and boys worked as a team. The mixed-gender football was not as physical. Also, the boys helped the girls get into the games. However, we thought that the boys felt that they were playing against a lower-class team in the boys vs girls single-gender game. Both teams were equally willing to tackle and argue with the referee. The mixed-gender games were a lot more exciting, and everyone seemed to enjoy them more.

Players Questionnaire

When asked about the differences they noticed in mixed games, both boys and girls gave answers that indicated the games changed (e.g. more social, not as rough, played differently together, more fun). Three of the girls compared to one boy

(continued)

Table 3.1 (cont.)

mentioned differences between the girls' and boys' ability (e.g. girls good, boys not; girls played better). One boy thought that the boys and girls worked together, whereas no girl agreed with this. Both boys and girls agreed that the games were not as rough. All of the girls thought that they played better, whereas no boy agreed with this. One boy thought that there were no differences in the mixed-gender game. These answers indicate again that there were some differences between the mixed-gender and single-sex games in the way that they were played.

This is supported by the finding that 71% of the boys and 75% of the girls said they played differently in the joint games compared to how they would normally play when they were just with their own gender.

When asked about whether they would like to play mixed football again, only 11% of boys and girls showed little interest in playing in a mixed team game again.

The majority of both boys and girls did not think that the referee was easier on either the girls or the boys.

These results from the players' questionnaire show again that there were some differences in the way that the mixed-gender games were played. However, these differences don't seem to affect the enjoyment or motivation to play in a mixed game again.

Captains' Interviews

All captains enjoyed the matches and would play again, even though not everyone thought that the teams were fair. Nobody thought that the referee was strict. Three of the four captains thought that their teams played well; the other thought that they could have played better. These answers support the finding that the mixed-gender games were as enjoyable as the single-sex games and that the captains would want to play in them again.

Discussion

We are pleased with our results, and we think that this was because we enjoyed this subject. From the analysis we think we have found three main findings. Firstly, the general opinion towards mixed-gender football of both boys and girls is positive. We thought that it was absolutely brilliant that 82% of our class would like a mixed-gender football league. Other significant results that indicated the positive opinions of children to mixed-gender football are 77% of children agreeing that mixed male and female teams are better than all-male or all-female, while 73% thought mixed football was better to watch.

The second main finding we found was that the boys and girls seemed to treat the mixed-gender games differently. This is supported by our observations of the football matches in the experiment and the answers given to some of the questions on the players' questionnaire. For example, 71% of the boys and 75% of the girls said they played differently in the mixed-gender games.

We don't know why this is but think it could be because the boys feel that the girls are not as physically strong. More research on this would need to be done before we could definitely say why the boys and girls changed the way they played.

(continued)

Table 3.1 (cont.)

The third main finding was that the mixed-gender games were enjoyable to play in. This finding came out in the observations, players' questionnaires and captains' interviews. For example, 88% of both boys and girls gave an answer between 8 and 10 to indicate whether they would like to play in a mixed-gender game again.

Conclusions

We have both enjoyed writing this report as it is a subject that we are very interested in. We think that female football would have the same universal publicity if it had been taken into consideration earlier. We both love and play football for a local team, but we are both angry at F.I.F.A (Federal International Football Association) as they have refused to accept mixed-gender football as a proper type of football. We are also angry at the English association, who even though they are trying to increase the amount of mixed-gender football leagues are not doing enough to promote it.

Therefore, we decided to base our project on these subjects. Our project has turned out very well, and the results we received were very interesting. They showed us that girls would love to play football with boys, but they are just not able to because of the poor understanding of the original basis of football. Boys are able to find somewhere to play very easily, while girls find it a lot harder. We feel this is decreasing the real talent and potential of females.

We think that the physical differences aren't as big as people make out. In men's football there is a whole range of physical differences, and we think some women would be as strong as some of the men. Further research on the exact differences is needed. If there are some women who are as strong as men playing in the Premiership, shouldn't they be allowed to play? We hope that our project will help to highlight these issues to the football community.

There have always been males commanding football who only let males into their teams; they think that females are not as physically strong and as good. However, most male and female players have equal ability. We do not understand why the Football Association refuses to change the norm.

We hope that in the future projects like this one will help change the minds of the leading minds in football.

3.5 The Relationship between Co-Researching (with) and Child-Led Research (by)

What is the relationship between research 'with' children and research 'by' children? For some scholars there is a link between these two activities (i.e. co-researching and child-led research). For example, adults, having inspired children to take active co-researcher roles in one project, may encourage children to go on to new projects with more substantial roles or even to lead their own research. If this

3.5 Co-Researching (with) and Child-Led Research (by)   69

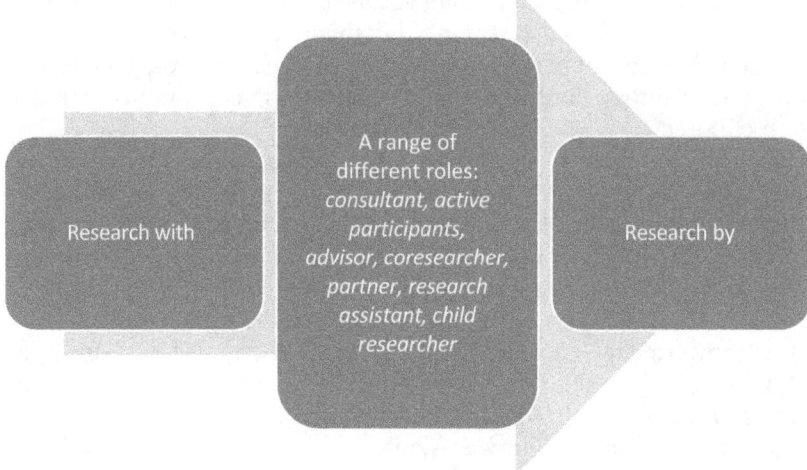

Figure 3.5 The continuum between research 'with' and research 'by' children

process can be facilitated by putting a training programme in place and supporting children in increasingly more active roles, gradual progression from co-researching to wanting to undertake their own research might be a possibility (Figure 3.5).

Kellett acknowledges that it is very unlikely that very young children can undertake research on their own, but she also suggests that 'supporting very young children (aged 3–6 years) to engage in research is about introducing them to *some* of the processes and developing *some* of their embryonic research skills rather than getting them to undertake a whole empirical study' (2010a, p. 109, author's emphasis). This view fits well with the idea that rudimentary research skills can develop into more sophisticated research skills as a result of training, practice and experience accumulated over time.

The alternative way to look at research 'with' and 'by' children is that they are very different activities. While research with children has many shades, research by children is more clearly defined, and child-led research is more likely to be explicitly labelled as such, as Kellett (2010a) observes. In child-led research children will take responsibility for all parts of the research, and thus such research (Alderson, 2001; Davis, 2009; Kellett et al., 2004) is very different from the partnerships in which children are enabled to take control of the whole process and then left to take full responsibility for the project from start to finish.

During the research process itself the roles of adults and children are different in research 'with' and research 'by' children. The proportions of responsibility change, although adults are ultimately accountable in both cases. In child-led research adults watch more from a distance, consciously and deliberately letting go of their control, whereas in joint research they take an active partner role in continuous dialogue with children.

Overall, the merits of research where children have acted as co-researchers have been documented widely. Co-researching with children promotes inclusivity, and knowledge created by children gives us adults a more holistic view of whatever they are researching. Children gain confidence (e.g. Alderson, 2001; Lundy et al., 2011; Lundy & McEvoy, 2012), enhanced critical thinking (Kellett, 2006) and a sense of empowerment (e.g. Alderson, 2001; Kellett, 2005; Lundy & McEvoy, 2012; Schäfer & Yarwood, 2008). Children have also demonstrated considerable competence in planning research (Kellett et al., 2004), data collection (Gray & Winter, 2011; Jones, 2004) and interpretation (e.g. Coad & Evans, 2008; Lundy et al., 2011). Nonetheless, critical views maintain that there are difficult ethical issues to navigate in such projects. Spriggs and Gillam (2019) raise concerns about possible drawbacks. Some of the concerns include children's right to participate at the expense of others and practical difficulties faced by the child, such as taking advantage of the children's existing relationships and networks, or the children might be under pressure to comply with unspoken adult expectations, or they may be exposed to distressing information. It is important that the training the children receive covers these potential challenges, not just technical questions about research.

In the case of research 'by' children, or child-led research, there is a move away from adult research questions to a focus on what matters to the children. The relationship between adults and children still matters just as much, but after the training where children acquire necessary research skills, the adult needs to stay in the background. Child-led research thrives especially when schools support it and consider it an integral beneficial activity rather than a luxury extra activity. Child-led research is rare, and decisions to undertake research are never within the children's control. It can only happen in contexts where there is a trained adult to pursue this possibility, one who is willing to navigate the challenges and obstacles in the way (Bucknall, 2012). Kellett et al. (2004) suggest that if more adults were willing and available to engage children in research, more child-led research could be made a reality: 'many more children... could be encouraged to become active researchers, if the level of support was differentiated accordingly, and if the research methods were developed specifically tailored to their interests and skills' (p. 341).

3.5 Co-Researching (with) and Child-Led Research (by)

Originally, child-led research was promoted as the insider perspective which is supposed to produce superior knowledge about childhood because of the children's expertise and unique insights about their own lives. This rather enthusiastic claim has been revised to accept that children do not produce superior knowledge compared to adults but will simply have qualitatively different insights and produce different knowledge. Children's research is not the same as adult academic research, so it should not be compared or juxtaposed to adult academic scholarship and should not be assessed against the same criteria. Thomas (2017, p. 174) suggests that 'research by children is not one thing but rather a hybrid phenomenon, situated somewhere between academic research, community-based action research and education for children'. Child-led research will require training which follows adult methods but breaks them down and teaches them gradually and carefully, first focussing on the most rudimentary concepts needed, then slowly building on those as the children's interest increases. With sustained involvement, more and more sophisticated training content can be delivered.

Most studies that discuss research 'with' children will be written up by the adults and published in academic journals. Child-led research is unlikely to find its way into academic journals, and indeed children would be unlikely to read it. Thomas (2021, pp. 12–13) suggests that

> most child-led research results are likely to be consumed by the children themselves, by their peers in school or other settings, and perhaps by policy makers and service providers to whom demands for change are addressed. Research by academics in which children take an active role is another matter. Much of this, where it occurs, will continue to be aimed at an academic readership and judged by academic standards, and the way in which children's participation is handled will of course continue to be subject to critical review.

Nonetheless, academic articles have been published with additional sections in them that have been written by children and child researchers, and some scholars have recommended considering possible co-authoring with children (Bradbury-Jones & Taylor, 2015; Kellett, 2010b; Kellett et al., 2004; Kinash & Hofman, 2008; Larkins & Young Researchers, 2014). Co-authoring can happen in different ways. Kellett (2010b) and Kellett et al. (2004) incorporated the children's full research presentations into the academic publication and used the space to critically analyse the process the children went through. Kinash and Hoffman's (2008) paper is an example where a child researcher and the adult partner worked together to reflect on their collaboration, and the final paper is a genuinely collaborative piece. In Larkins and Young Researchers (2014), the adult has worked together with a group of young researchers who were reflecting on their research experience and defining together what the most essential ingredients of child-led research might be.

Since children's research often targets their peer groups, they can often have success in getting responses from other children more readily than adults. Their work and findings contribute to the body of knowledge about children's experiences, and the dissemination and ownership of the research is an important vehicle for making their voice heard. The whole experience can be an empowering process, giving increased confidence and self-esteem.

O'Donnell (2017) echoes this and adds that children also gain a greater sense of pride and satisfaction, learn to communicate more effectively and work cooperatively with others, learn to become a reflective and critical thinker and enjoy feeling respected, listened to and taken seriously by adults.

Some scholars are more enthusiastic about incorporating child-led research into school than others. Thomas says that (2021, p. 7) 'there is no reason in principle why participation in research could not in some form be offered to all children', and he lists three justifications for this (pp. 11–12):

- Children have rights in relation to research, including the right to be offered an opportunity to take a direct part in the research if that is appropriate.
- Agency and competence are empirical issues. Depending on their own capacities and on the constraints and affordances in their immediate and wider environment, different children will be more or less interested or ready to get involved in research in active roles.
- Research can mean different things. '[A]ll research seeks to generate knowledge: the question then becomes what kind of knowledge, for what purpose and to whom it is important? We do research in order to find out something we do not already know, or to test something that we think we know but cannot be sure' (p. 12).

Thomson and Gunter (2007, p. 331) argue that student-led research can be an important way in which participation becomes meaningful because it addresses issues of importance to students, allows marginalised perspectives to come centre stage and uses students' subjectivities and experiences to develop approaches, tools, representations and validities.

For adolescents, Sandoval and Messiou (2022) suggest the so-called youth participatory action research as the most popular form of

3.5 Co-Researching (with) and Child-Led Research (by)

research with active involvement. This provides young people with opportunities to study social problems affecting their lives and then determine actions to make changes. The content of the training sessions also varies: some train technical skills only while others also train relational skills (like how to be a good listener). Training may take place at universities, or at schools with the possibility of embedding research into class time. Like younger children, student researchers usually collect data from peers rather than adults, and findings are presented to their school and to senior management or even at conferences or local radio or exhibition venues.

Just like with agency, voice and participation, the literature discussing child-led research has evolved from early over-enthusiastic promotion of it at all costs to a more balanced and critical view that acknowledges its special status compared to academic research and discusses both its benefits and its challenges and problems. As Thomas (2021, p. 10) remarks: 'We can acknowledge that some of the claims made for child-led research may have been over-enthusiastic or naïve, or on occasion somewhat dogmatic in asserting that it should be the only path for researchers to take.' Critical and more sceptical views point to the seemingly unresolvable tension between child-led research and rigid school cultures, and the impossibility of incorporating it meaningfully into schools (Barratt Hacking & Barratt, 2009; Lomax, 2012; Robinson & Taylor, 2013).

Robinson and Taylor (2013), for example, caution that giving children voice even in the most advanced form, by forming student as researcher (SAR) groups with the intention of empowering these children, does not necessarily negate larger forces and power dynamics that are structurally inherent in the existing school systems and in the context at large.

Having implemented two such projects (one in primary and one in secondary), they conclude that even in schools which were open and enthusiastic to embrace child-led research *on the surface*, there were concerns raised regarding the impact and the meaningfulness of the projects. While the academic researcher was invited to work with the children, the authors felt that the presence of the outsider researcher may in fact have disempowered both staff and students. The expert with the perceived legitimacy of elite modes of knowledge production was seen as the authority. Power relationships were also evident within student groups, with some more confident and talkative members silencing others. Choosing just a handful of students meant that many were inevitably excluded. 'A detailed analysis of the complex micro-processes at play in the running of these projects reveals how, despite the best intentions, the projects continued to replicate the dominant power relations present in other school practices' (Robinson & Taylor, 2013, p. 33). It was understood that adults should not interfere with the child-led projects, but the mere presence of these adults still meant that certain topics were off-limits. All this constitutes hidden dominant power.

Lomax (2012) also echoes these concerns and refers to highly institutionalised practices into which some try to insert child-led research. Child-led research is supposed to be inclusive, but in fact some of these projects are driven by adult agendas, time frames and priorities. Children are constantly curtailed by the constructions of childhood deployed by adults around them. In Lomax's study (2012) children's voices were mediated by hierarchies of 'cool' as they were observed to deliberately or inadvertently diminish the participation of some of their peers, which meant that some children were sidelined. The creative methods used did not necessarily sidestep verbal skills. 'Rather, children's verbal skills are a crucial means by which children and young people are able to negotiate their place within the peer-led research group and with the adults and children they encounter, photograph and interview' (Lomax, 2012, pp. 114–115).

3.6 Conclusion

In this chapter I have looked at the key tenets of Childhood Studies and examined how voice, agency and participation are converted into methodological solutions in studies involving children. Both benefits and challenges of studies with varying levels of active participation have been discussed.

It is clear that children's contributions in active roles in research will be unique in every context, and as Spyrou (2018, p. 174) suggests, both children and adults *can* contribute to knowledge production, but when children participate, we need to 'recognise the role of both children and adults in the process and acknowledge that the knowledge produced is the outcome of interaction and exchange, collaboration and negotiation'. This will be the case in any study, whether it is research 'with' children or 'by' children.

In light of the enthusiastic endorsement of children's active involvement in research and at the same time the criticism of the impossibility of making this happen in schools, institutional structures and underlying philosophical principles will be examined in the next chapter.

4 Child-Centredness and Democratic School Structures

4.1 Introduction

In Chapter 3 the key concepts of voice, agency and participation were examined to highlight how these lend themselves to specific methodological interpretations and solutions, and how they play out in research 'with' and 'by' children. Various examples of participatory tools were described, and two typical examples of research with and by children were included. The purpose of this chapter is to shine light on actual contexts as well as educational philosophies that underlie and support institutional structures. The question is: What kinds of contextual and institutional structures allow, support or even encourage research 'with' and 'by' children?

Research 'with' children can take various forms, from short, surface-level participation to longer projects where research training for children is provided, but only the most impactful projects have the potential or the explicit aspiration to shift traditional hierarchical structures within schools towards more balanced and democratic structures. However, unless these structural changes are enabled and supported from the very top, obstacles and restrictions are likely to stand in the way of incorporating high levels of learner participation consistently. Of course, active child participation in research can also happen outside schools, or at least outside regular school hours, such as in after-school clubs and other less formal venues in the community.

This chapter will explore educational philosophies as well as enabling institutional structures that have the potential to tolerate, support or encourage child participation. Bringing educational philosophies and institutional structures into alignment with child participation will mean that children's active involvement in research does not have to be an isolated event.

The chapter will start by exploring the concept of child-centredness and learner-centredness and will suggest that enabling institutional structures can be characterised by a range of key principles that emphasise meaningful learning opportunities based on learners' interests and needs, an approach that cuts across traditional subject areas and allows for exploration, inquiry and autonomous decision making. Learner-centredness is also associated with active participation and the opportunity to take some control over what is being learnt in partnership with teachers in more dialogic, collaborative and democratic relationships.

4.2 Child-Centredness

Active child participation in research is only possible when children work in trusting partnerships with adults. Children will likely be genuinely engaged in activities only when they have a stake and interest in them and have chosen these interests themselves.

Ownership of the research process comes with high levels of motivation, enthusiasm and genuine, deep engagement. Children immersed in the process will exhibit high levels of control or autonomy over what they do, such as what information they want to look up, what questions they need to ask and what methods they need to use. Studies have documented the benefits experienced by children when they have the opportunity of engaging in research as active participants (see Chapter 3), including acquiring new skills, engaging in authentic and deep learning, developing self-esteem and confidence, and taking ownership and pride in their work and accomplishments. Researching means finding things out and making a change or difference based on some empirical evidence gathered, but at its core every research project is also a learning opportunity.

However, participating actively in research is a very different type of learning experience from the everyday learning experiences typically observed in most schools. So, the following question arises: What can be learnt from these research experiences to improve everyday learning or to make these two processes more compatible with each other? Can the gap between everyday activities and research with children's active participation be narrowed? How can children's participation become a normal part of school life? What types of schools are ideally placed to welcome such research?

Whether any research 'by' children or 'with' children is seen as incompatible with the rest of school life will also depend on the length, intensity and structure of the project. For example, an afternoon club with the involvement of a small group of children is not likely to be incompatible with traditional schooling practices. Incompatibility, when it arises, will be a source of frustration for all involved, especially in the case of longer projects with lasting consequences (e.g. Mathew & Pinter, 2021).

At their core, both effective teaching/learning processes and research processes with children's active involvement can be traced back to the so-called learner-centred approaches. Schweisfurth defines learner-centred education as 'a pedagogical approach which gives learners, and demands from them, a relatively high level of active control over the content and process of learning. What is learnt, and how, are therefore shaped by learners' needs, capacities and interests' (2013, p. 20).

Learner-centredness is a pedagogical approach that can be characterised by a set of features sitting on a continuum signalling a movement away from teacher-centredness. The more a particular pedagogical approach embraces features on the right-hand side of the contrasts listed below, the more it can be related to learner-centredness. These features include:

- Chalk and talk, transmission *versus* inquiry, group-based learning
- Authoritarian teacher *versus* democratic teacher
- Extrinsic learner motivation *versus* intrinsic learner motivation
- Knowledge as fixed *versus* knowledge as fluid
- Curriculum content fixed *versus* curriculum content negotiated
- Teacher as a controller *versus* teacher as a facilitator

Learner-centredness is not new. In fact, it has a long history with scholarship reaching back centuries, promoting the basic ideas of a learner's active participation in his or her own learning and the central role of the relationship with the adult. Socrates (470–399 BC) stressed the importance of meaningful dialogues and good relationships between teachers and students. Rousseau (1712–1778) suggested that children's education must follow their natural interests and that their education should focus on positive values and personal freedom. Guiding children towards what is right should happen using gentle encouragement rather than coercion or punishment. Froebel (1782–1852) emphasised creativity and free play in learning and maintained that children expressed themselves through free imaginative play, and he is, in fact, credited with first using the term 'child-centred'. Perhaps the most influential historic figure is Dewey (1859–1952), who embraced child-centred education fully by promoting experiential learning and teacher–learner partnerships. He believed that every child engaged differently and that it was important to acknowledge the uniqueness of all learners. Further, he suggested that schools were communities and that education and democracy were intrinsically linked. He cultivated the teaching of thinking skills and believed that it was important for learners to draw from their own experiences. He appreciated that learners' perspectives were worthwhile and important to elicit and listen to. One other figure that deserves a mention here is Montessori (1870–1952) because of her widespread influence on alternative pre-school education and her direct association with the Reggio Emilia movement. Montessori was interested in children with special needs and promoted the importance of teaching social skills and empathy. The environment where children's learning was to take place had to be a welcoming and stimulating place where learning through all the senses could be accommodated. She suggested that in this kind of environment children could enjoy and take responsibility for their own learning. These ideas all strongly align with the principles of child-centredness and child participation.

A contemporary interpretation of child-centredness proposed by Moss (2019) promotes an image of the capable child, who is a co-constructor of their knowledge, identity and culture (p. 51), is born equipped to learn and is active and competent and thus worth listening to. Much of Moss's work and this contemporary image of the child is inspired by Reggio Emilia, an iconic network of schools for early childhood education in Italy that is famous for an emphasis on child-centredness, meaning creativity, experimentation and participatory pedagogy. Following Dewey, educators in Reggio Emilia believe that democracy is key in schooling: 'This is democracy understood as an approach to living and relating, an ethos and a culture, that can and should pervade all aspects of everyday, living not least in the school' (Moss, 2014, p. 122).

Reggio Emilia scholars conceptualise the child as rich, competent and one who speaks with 'a hundred languages'. Such a conception of childhood dictates an approach to teaching that is founded on co-construction and collaborative meaning making. Relationships between children and adults are characterised by interconnections and interdependency, and the teaching and learning processes are open-ended, unpredictable and full of amazement and wonder. This means that rather than putting the emphasis on learning static facts, education is about trying out different ideas and new things and exploring what is not yet known. Knowledge is likened to a tangle of spaghetti or a rhizome (Deleuze & Guattari, 2004), where in contrast to linear step-by-step development, we conceptualise the process of learning as shooting off in all directions. A rhizome has no fixed beginning or end point; it is something that always changes; it is never complete or perfect but instead is always a form of compromise. As Moss (2019, p. 118) contends, 'a rhizome with its endless possibilities for making new connections, provoking new lines of flight going in new directions moves us away from closed and binary thinking, where we can always find new possibilities, new directions to take'. Such uncertainty is the motor of learning, and the parallel processes of teaching/learning and researching are cycles of joint experimentation, documentation, reflection and analysis involving both adults and children.

Moss (2019) associated this view of child-centredness with a 'resistance movement', with scholars drawn together to contest dominant discourses in education and take inspiration from timeless principles such as autonomy, creativity and open-ended enquiry.

The evidence is strong in terms of underlying research that child-centred approaches should be used in all schools (Schweisfurth, 2013, p. 144). People of all ages, including children, learn best when learning activities align with basic principles set out in the cognitive literature, such as engagement, motivation, appropriate levels of challenge and dialogue. Learner-centred education can help with preparing learners for democratic and economic citizenship by constantly modelling desired behaviours. These approaches are also dynamic and flexible and thus seen as suited to our modern and diverse world, where rapid change results in having to cope with uncertainty and ever-new demands and priorities. In view of this, traditional approaches and curricula are being re-considered, and new approaches are promoted with key skills such as creativity, critical thinking and problem solving, all rooted in a learner-centred approach. Nonetheless, in some cultures and contexts, ideas about learner-centredness and child-centredness are met with outright opposition because child-rearing practices and the roles of parents and teaches are conceptualised very differently, and this goes beyond the traditional distinction between Western and Global South contexts.

How do learner-centred principles relate to research 'with' children and 'by' children? A teacher who takes children's views seriously when it comes to research and decides to involve them in active roles must surely think about the consequences and the impact of this kind of research on everyday teaching/learning situations as well. Trusting that learners can take responsibility for their learning is a core principle of both learning/teaching and researching with children. In contexts where children experience sustained engagement with research that invites them to be active participants, questions about everyday learning processes will arise, such as how children can be trusted to undertake their own research yet be subjected to rote learning, transmission approaches and tools, methods and tasks that are in conflict with learner-centredness as a core principle. The opposite is also true. Children and learners who are invited by their teachers to take active roles in their everyday teaching/learning (e.g. Porto, 2016; Villacañas de Castro et al., 2021) will surely be more ready and willing to take on potential active roles in research projects that are meaningful to them, should the adult introduce this idea.

4.3 Learner-Centredness in Applied Linguistics

The literature in applied linguistics has long embraced the principles of learner-centredness, although with almost exclusive attention to adults. In the early days the promotion of communicative language teaching (CLT), both in its strong and weak forms, was based on the need to put the learner and his or her needs squarely in the middle of the teaching process, contributing to a growing understanding about language learners' needs and unique interests. With a strong desire to meet learners' real-life communicative needs, CLT promoted, for example, task-based approaches to attempt to increase learners' opportunities to engage in authentic communication with various interlocutors, making the learning experience as personally useful and meaningful as possible.

The so-called project approach to teaching and learning is particularly strongly associated with a learner-centredness in second language education (Arnold et al., 2019). Project work revolves around CLT approaches with a focus on meaning-based, contextualised and personalised approaches. Interpretations of what a project might look like will vary a great deal, but most projects require some independent research, and it takes more than a single lesson to complete a project, meaning that substantial amounts of work outside the class might be required. Even though ultimately the teacher controls the planning, projects are driven forward by the students' ideas and input.

The use of L2 projects for both adults and children has been noteworthy, with international textbooks often promoting units that culminate in project work that allows the learners to personalise, extend and consolidate their knowledge as well as encouraging additional learning and researching. Projects are designed to explore real-world issues and involve some practical problem solving. Projects must be challenging, requiring sustained engagement where the authentic learner voice is invited. Many educational reforms recommend projects. The big issue is whether to use L1 or L2 during project work. Beckett and Slater (2005), Holm (2011) and Mukhurjee (2015) report many benefits of projects but note broader curricular and institutional restrictions. Nonetheless, in a classroom where project work is common practice, research *with* children and *by* children may be more attractive and feasible to introduce.

Another interpretation of learner-centredness in second language education is linked to learner agency (Ahearn, 2001; Benson, 2007; Gao, 2013; Mercer, 2012) and learner autonomy, focussing on the core idea that learners are individuals who will succeed when they are able to take charge of their language learning (Legenhausen, 2001; Little, 2011; Little et al., 2017; Miliander & Trebbi, 2008). Most work in the autonomy literature in second or foreign language education goes back to the original conceptualisations of the autonomous language learner as defined by Holec (1981). However, Little (2022) also credits Dam's (1995) classrooms in Danish schools with young adolescents (aged 10–15) as inspirational in conceptualising autonomous language learning. Learners in Dam's classrooms were able to and ready to set their own learning task, make their own materials, monitor their own progress and evaluate their own outcomes. As autonomous learners they seemed to be enjoying their language learning and were confident and highly proficient users of the target language (English).

In Dam's (1995) classroom the teacher and the learners negotiated a 'process syllabus', but within that the learners enjoyed a great deal of freedom to make decisions about their own learning tasks, and they created or selected their own authentic materials. The content of these tasks always centred around the identity of the students and their interests.

The learners plan, implement and evaluate their learning in their groups and then report back to the class about their progress. The teacher's role is described as orchestrating the lessons, promoting reflection, encouraging self- and peer assessment, and attending to any questions that arise.

By prioritising the use of the target language (both speaking and writing) and focussing on what the learners are interested in, the learners become autonomous operators in the L2: 'When the focus of formal learning is a foreign language, we should want our learners to be able to exercise their autonomy in that language, and they will be able to do that only if their learning is grounded in agentive target language use.' (Little, 2022, p. 70)

When learners enjoy the learning process and have control over it, they will be able to sustain their motivation to work hard. When children work in groups alongside the adult as co-researchers or work on their own projects as researchers, they, too, need to be autonomous in planning, implementing and evaluating a research project in order to work on topics that are important to them.

4.4 Self-Determination Theory

One of the most oft-cited psychological theories that supports learner-centred principles is Deci and Ryan's Self-Determination Theory (2012). This theory proposes that all humans, including children, have basic psychological needs for autonomy, competence and relatedness. While people are naturally prone to psychological growth, integration, mastery learning and connection with others, these processes are not automatic, and therefore it is important to provide supporting conditions for them in any given learning context, including schools.

As discussed above by Little (2022), autonomy refers to the learners' sense that they have some control over what they do rather than being forced or compelled to do something. Autonomy does not mean working in isolation; it can be highly social. Autonomy-supportive teaching helps to foster learner engagement via involving choice and allowing for diverse and flexible ways of working. 'Key autonomy-supportive behaviours include building in an element of choice where possible, involving learners in decision-making processes, permitting a diversity of working styles and learning outcomes, encouraging open communication with learners, and respecting and motivating learners as individuals' (Reeve 2006, p. 651).

Even more important than choice is relevance. Learners need to see the clear relevance of what they are doing to real life. Shernoff (2013) points out that many traditional teaching activities have no actual purpose, making it hard for the learners to appreciate any relevance other than the educational value of the exercise itself.

Ryan and Deci (2020) suggest that teachers who support students' autonomy attempt to understand and acknowledge students' perspectives and are responsive to these perspectives. They provide opportunities for students to take ownership and initiative regarding schoolwork, provide meaningful choices and engage students' interests. Autonomy support entails an interest in the learner's needs, barriers and resources, whether these are cultural, cognitive or emotional.

For example, teachers can support their learners by cultivating their sense of competence and a growth mindset. A sense of competence is related to what Bandura (1997) calls expectancy beliefs about whether one can complete a specific task or not (Mercer, 2019). It is related to an overall judgement of one's abilities and self-concept in a particular domain. Mindsets (Dweck, 2006), that is, beliefs that learners hold about the degree to which they feel that their abilities are developed through conscious effort and hard work (a growth mindset) or whether they believe that these are fixed, unchangeable characteristics (a fixed mindset) play a big role in a learner's sense of competence.

A learner with a growth mindset will not give up on completing the task at hand but will persevere, trying alternative strategies.

Relatedness is the need to belong, such as a sense of belonging to the classroom or a group, but it also connects to the relationship with the teacher as well as the family. A sense of relatedness will increase with higher levels of participation and where children can see evidence that their views are respected and consistently sought. These positive, supportive and non-hierarchical relationships are reminiscent of co-researchers' and child researchers' relationships with facilitating adults. When taking active roles in research, in particular in child-led research, it is of paramount importance that children sustain an interest in their selected topic and stay engaged in the process. What are the main ingredient of high levels of engagement? And in what kinds of classrooms can engagement thrive?

4.5 Engagement and Positive Emotional States

Skinner et al. (2009, p. 225) define engagement as 'energized, directed and sustained actions towards a goal'. Engagement is multifaceted and comprises three component dimensions: behavioural (action), affective (feeling) and cognitive (thinking), always situated in a social context. Mercer (2019) suggests that it is possible to be engaged in one dimension, such as the behavioural dimension, but not in the other two, so the best type of engagement requires all three dimensions working together.

Connecting tasks with real-world purposes can lead to ownership (Newmann et al., 2007). There is a need to provide academic tasks that are relevant to the students' concerns and tasks in which students have some freedom to choose, with opportunities to work in cooperative groups over longer periods of time. It is paramount that students have the opportunity to follow their interests. Teacher and student engagement can create a virtuous circle which consists of cycles of hard work, joy and learning, as well as increasing feelings of connectedness, competence in teaching and learning, and autonomy.

Skinner and Pitzer (2012, p. 35) discuss the importance of active participation and engagement in those tasks that are 'project based, relevant, progressive, and integrated across subject matter, or in other words, intrinsically motivating, inherently interesting, and fun'.

Parallels with children's active involvement in research are, again, quite clear. Child-led research is often characterised by bursts of engagement that are similar to 'flow', when a person's body and mind are stretched to the limits to accomplish something worthwhile (Csikszentmihalyi, 1990, 2003). Such complete concentration and engagement lead to the learner being fully immersed in the task and becoming oblivious to the passing of time. Once fully engaged and motivated, learners are also charged with positive emotions. A related concept of 'mastery motivation' (Barrett & Morgan, 2018) refers to individuals' persistent thriving to complete a task in the face of moderate challenge by keeping at it rather than giving up. What learners do as a result of often playfully engaging with the task can lead to mastery, which then functions as a reward and source of motivation.

It is often observed that for children to learn effectively and engage with the task at hand, they need to feel secure and happy. In fact, Noddings (2003, p. 246) suggests that '[t]he atmosphere in the classroom should reflect the universal desire for happiness. There should be a minimum of pain (and none deliberately inflicted), many opportunities for pleasure, and overt recognition of the connection between the development of desirable dispositions and happiness'.

Noddings (2003, p. 241) sees education 'as a mode of living and learning together' with a careful and sensitive balance between inferred needs versus expressed needs. Coercion must be avoided, and trust is all important. Teachers and students need to stay together for a longish period of time in order to develop and cultivate trust and get to know each other.

She suggests that the best schools are like best homes:

The best homes provide continuity of caring relations, attend to and continuously evaluate both inferred and expressed needs, protect from harm without deliberately inflicting pain, communicate so as to develop common and individual interests, work together cooperatively, promote joy in genuine learning, guide moral and spiritual development (including the development of an uneasy conscience), contribute to the appreciation of arts and other great cultural achievements, encourage love of place and protection of the natural word, and educate for both self-understanding and group understanding.

(Noddings, 2003, p. 260)

The best homes and the best schools are happy places. Happiness is both the means and the end. Happy children will seize their educational opportunities with delight.

4.6 Twenty-First Century Demands and Twenty-First Century Skills: Future-Proofing Education

Learner-centredness is also a key theme in the so-called twenty-first century learning frameworks (e.g. Partnership for 21st Century Skills, 2009). One pressing reason for leaners or children to become more

Table 4.1 A framework of twenty-first century skills (adapted from Binkley et al., 2012)

This framework defines ten skills grouped into four categories:
- *Ways of Thinking*

Creativity and innovation
Critical thinking, problem solving, decision making
Learning to learn, metacognition
- *Ways of Working*

Communication
Collaboration (teamwork)
- *Tools for Working*

Information literacy (includes research on sources, evidence, biases, etc.)
ICT literacy
- *Living in the World*

Citizenship – local and global
Life and career
Personal and social responsibility – including cultural awareness and competence

---

active in their own learning and for educational institutions to re-think traditional approaches to teaching and learning is that the future is definitely uncertain. Whatever we are teaching today is likely to become out of date faster than ever, and we simply cannot predict the actual future needs of current generations of children. Responding to these uncertainties and the likely demands on future citizens who will be solving new types of problems in new kinds of jobs, many educators around the world have been united in arguing that twenty-first century realities require new approaches to educating children and young people so that they are better prepared for a variety of unexpected challenges. These new educational developments have collectively been referred to as 'twenty-first century skills'.

Many frameworks have been generated in the literature, and Table 4.1 summarises the most commonly cited skills (Binkley et al., 2012). This particular framework brings together ten key skills in four categories, which are 'ways of thinking', 'ways of working', 'tools for working' and 'living in the world'.

Among other things, twenty-first century approaches to education encompass independent action, critical thinking and creativity, and the cultivation of effective communication skills with both peers and adults. Rich learning tasks include multi-disciplinary group projects which require deep learning, researching information, collaborating with others, problem solving, creative thinking and presenting findings to each other. Self-direction and autonomy are core. Dynamic learning opportunities arise with the affordance of new technologies, such as, for example learning with online applications or games. Children's perceived learning gains when engaging with online games on tablets, smartphones or computers has also been linked directly to twenty-first century skills, such as collaboration, problem solving, communication, self-regulation and controlling negative emotions (e.g. Kahila et al., 2021).

When children work as co-researchers or researchers, they will need to tap into similar skills. In fact, undertaking research will naturally incorporate and activate the use of some of these skills. For example, young researchers need to exercise critical thinking and solve problems; they need to reflect on their thinking processes and interpretations of their findings; and they need to be able to communicate effectively with both adult facilitators and peers, collaborate with peers on group projects, use ICT tools and choose topics of local or global interest. Thus, schools that embrace the implementation of twenty-first century skills may be conducive to introducing active learner participation and research 'with' and 'by' children.

4.7 From Traditional to Democratic School Structures

Regarding the implications of the Self-Determination Theory, a considerable amount of empirical research internationally has been devoted to implementing this theory into actual school policy decisions. Research in Israeli primary schools, for example, clearly illustrates that after introducing an autonomy-supportive programme, it was possible to make changes to the culture of the whole school (Assor et al., 2002).

Schools as autonomy-supporting places create an atmosphere where students' choices are taken into account and where students are supported as they formulate their inner compass – their values, goals and interests – and classroom conditions that allow them to experience autonomy. Such schools would be designed in ways that 'nurtured and satisfied students' need for autonomy' and would 'offer frequent opportunities for students to experience autonomy during their learning activities' (Reeve & Assor, 2011, p. 120).

Assor et al. (2002) also suggest that fostering choice is not enough because some pupils may not yet have clear goals and therefore cannot make good choices. If they do not see any connection between their interests and schoolwork, some additional help will be needed to make connections and find the relevance of school work in relation to the rest of their lives.

[B]eing able to choose one's schoolwork may not be important to students because none of the choices seem related to their personal goals or interest, or because they do not have clear goals or interest.

(p. 273)

To foster the relevance of schoolwork for children, teachers need to take an emphatic-active role in relation to their students. This role requires the teacher first to understand students' goals, interests and needs, and then to link school tasks to those goals, interests and needs.

(p. 265)

This suggests that children who might not be interested in anything at all can become interested in various topics following relevance-fostering exercises where teachers or other adults help them to discover new interests. Effective 'relevance fostering' can also mean that certain activities (despite their initial extrinsic source) can be internalised and eventually experienced as autonomous. In research *with* children and *by* children, facilitating adults may have similar roles in introducing learners to ideas and topics that can become interesting to children and be the focus of their future inquiry. This may be particularly important with first-time researchers and those who are not quite sure about whether they would like to participate in research in active roles.

Autonomy-promoting schools need to adapt both SVE and FIV strategies. SVE stands for 'support of value/goal exploration'. This refers to discussions and activities that enable learners to examine their developing goals and values in a personally meaningful way. FIV stands for fostering inner directed valuing processes, meaning that teachers need to help students make serious decisions while encouraging the examination of one's values and goals when faced with difficult decisions. Teachers can also encourage the consideration of alternatives and relevant information before making decisions (Kanat-Maymon & Assor, 2010). Table 4.2 summarises strategies used in middle schools, but the overall approach can be adapted to younger or older learners as well.

Autonomy-supporting schools nurture learners' inner motivational resources to communicate how any learning activity represents an opportunity to make progress towards an intrinsic goal rather than obey a directive, fulfil a request or earn credits. In such schools adults rely on non-controlling language by providing explanatory rationales without exerting pressures. Instead of using commands and directives, teachers display patience to allow time for self-paced learning and personal development. Students are listened to and given time to work in their own ways. In autonomy-promoting schools, therefore, research 'with' or 'by' children may find synergies with already existing practices.

Table 4.2 Six attributes of autonomy-promoting schools (adapted from Reeve & Assor, 2011)

Characteristics of autonomy-promoting schools	Relevance for researching 'with' and 'by' children
(1) Each teacher is responsible for a small group of students with whom he or she has *regularly scheduled dialogues*. Teachers as growth-promoting allies: the teacher develops *close relationships*. This helps the students feel that the teacher is really interested in their growth and basic needs. The meetings have to be regular; teachers understand their students better and find *greater fulfilment and satisfaction* in their profession; emphatic, respectful and *trusting relationship*s form the foundation for fostering inner valuing processes and interest explorations in students.	In research 'with' and 'by' children, the adult–child relationship and regular dialogue are equally important. Teachers' in-depth knowledge of the students is an excellent basis on which to build a possible collaborative research project. Teachers being familiar with students' interests can be helpful in identifying topics that might be worth exploring in research.
(2) Students have *considerable influence* and *responsibility* (democratic participation): an organisational structure where *students are partners,* (e.g. in discipline laws, budget allocation, selecting learning content, knowledge objectives and assessment procedures). This gives students the evidence that their *competence is deeply respected*.	Learner participation in research needs to be serious and meaningful. If learners have influence, this gives them the message that their opinions and views matter, which leads to an expectation that their research projects, findings and suggestions for change will also be listened to and taken seriously.
(3) Fostering the development of *individual interests:* considerable time is devoted to students exploring various domains of potential interest to develop enduring intrinsic interests.	Fostering interests: What to research or investigate, either individually or in groups? This may be particularly useful and important for child-led research, exploring topics such as local and global issues of importance.
(4) Supporting exploration of and open reflection on important social and moral identity-defining values and issues (SVE): regular activities where students discuss their views on *important social and moral issues* in	In collaborative research where adults and children work together, a space needs to be created for honest dialogue where views and opinions, sensitive issues and problems can be openly discussed.

(continued)

Table 4.2 (cont.)

Characteristics of autonomy-promoting schools	Relevance for researching 'with' and 'by' children
an atmosphere that is *tolerant and accepting of different views*. Teachers encourage inner directed valuing processes (FIV): it is OK to take time, to stay with ambiguity before making a commitment or to avoid making a decision because of social pressure. This becomes even more important with secondary level students.	
(5) Pro-social activities that are satisfying and choiceful: pro-social and altruistic values (helping the needy, caring for others); specific activities and structure that allow students to discover the satisfaction that can be derived from *pro-social action* and involvement; pro-social and moral values are an important component of a healthy identity, the 'unshakeable core of one's inner compass' (p. 124); *choice is important*, choosing from different activities.	In child-led research the focus of the research is often a topic/issue that the children care about (such as climate change, community services, school improvement, serving the local community).
(6) *Reduce the amount of information students are tested on and the frequency of comparative achievement tests*: tests increase tension, and preparation for them takes away time from other important activities (such as pro-social activities or teacher–student dialogue). In the information age there is not much point in transmitting great amounts of information; better to put *focus on effective knowledge search and organisation skills and logical and critical thinking*.	If testing is reduced, more time can be devoted to learning through enquiry and undertaking research. More meaningful learning is directed towards what is personally relevant.

4.8 Learner-Centred Education and International Baccalaureate Schools

Arguably at the elite end of the scale, International Baccalaureate (IB) schools (https://www.ibo.org/programmes/primary-years-programme) promote explicit learner-centred approaches to teaching and learning. Primary IB programmes claim to follow a 'whole child approach', with a transdisciplinary curriculum where student-led inquiry is the foundation of all learning processes. The IB learner in the primary context is an inquirer, a thinker, and a communicator who is knowledgeable, principled, open-minded and caring. The IB primary curriculum is based on child-led inquiries culminating in the Grade 5 project and an exhibition of children's work to be showcased, celebrated and discussed with various audiences. Five elements are important in these outcomes: knowledge, concepts, skills, attitudes and action. In order to prepare for the exhibition, children undertake some 'research' with the help of an adult teacher/mentor in a topic area that is personally important to them but also significant and meaningful to the local community. These projects reflect knowledge of key concepts, skills but also attitudes, as well as a plan for action. Although the projects are not explicitly referred to as research, the principle that children choose topics of interest that are of importance to themselves, their peers and the local community links closely with the idea of children undertaking their own research following research training, which is provided as a form of mentoring in IB primary schools.

The IB project demands sustained high levels of engagement and motivation, and the exhibition that allows authentic audiences to engage with the children's work makes it deeply meaningful and purposeful. Gathering and analysing data for the project is reminiscent of the processes observed in studies where research 'with' and 'by' children is discussed. Finally, presenting your findings in an attractive manner to captive audiences is not much different from the dissemination of findings in child-led research. While the term child-led research is not used in the IB context, and the children clearly do not receive explicit research training, working with a teacher/mentor while preparing a project that is a major undertaking resembles steps in child-led research.

4.9 Active Self-Directed Learning in Maker Spaces

Just like schools promoting twenty-first century approaches to curricula or IB schools with a focus on inquiry-based learning, maker spaces are relatively new, alternative learning communities that promote learner-centred approaches to education. Maker spaces, as will be discussed here and in Chapter 6, are particularly conducive to conducting research 'with' and 'by' children.

Originally conceptualised as a hands-on approach to teaching STEM subjects, maker or player spaces allow for a wide range of creative learning opportunities, including learning about research. They can be created in both formal and informal settings, can be temporary or permanent and can be set up in museums, libraries, after-school clubs or schools, including so-called pop-up maker spaces. Maker spaces are dynamic contexts where participants engage in creative activities while 'making' digital and non-digital artefacts. Such spaces have the potential to bring together creativity, design, play and deep learning (Marsh, 2017). In maker spaces, children are empowered as autonomous learners, and they share and collaborate with others and follow a unique personalised approach to learning.

Maker space activities are characterised by hands-on experimentation, improvisation, and problem solving while encouraging agency and self-efficacy. All participants draw on each other's expertise (Kumpulainen, 2017; Little et al., 2017), and maker spaces encourage play and tinkering. Most are multilingual spaces where indigenous practices and languages are also encouraged. The most suitable assessment practices for maker spaces are peer- and self-assessment. Marsh (2017) argues that maker space pedagogy is learner centred and is in line with early child education movements such as Montessori or Reggio Emilia, by virtue of focussing on holistic development, practical creativity, freedom to choose activities, integrating age groups, experimentation, enquiry and the use of technology. The connection between learning and researching is clear and very strong.

The main principles in the Maker Manifesto (Hatch, 2014) are:

- MAKE: making is fundamental to being human; we must create things to express ourselves; what we make are pieces of ourselves that embody our souls.
- SHARE: sharing what you are making and the methods you use makes you feel whole.
- GIVE: giving away what you made is selfless and satisfying.
- LEARN: you must always seek to learn more about making, pushing yourself to learn about new techniques, materials and processes.
- TOOL UP: you must have access to the right tools.
- PLAY: be playful with what you are making; you will be surprised what you can discover.
- PARTICIPATE: join the maker movement and reach out to others via seminars, parties, events, and classes with and for the makers in your community.

- SUPPORT: the movement requires financial, intellectual, political and institutional support; the best hope for improving the world is us.
- CHANGE: embrace the change that comes with making; you will become a more complete version of you.

Incorporating maker spaces into schoolwork requires teaching across traditional subject boundaries, acknowledging both school knowledge and everyday knowledge, and embracing flexibility and freedom that challenges traditional adult–child relationships. This requires a shift towards more open pedagogies and more equal and balanced relationships between teachers and learners (Jónsdóttir, 2017; Jónsdóttir & Macdonald, 2013), just like in research 'with' and 'by' children. 'The capacity of teachers to allow enough freedom, accepting the role of the flexible teacher in order to enhance learner agency and creativity within reasonable boundaries and in different contexts, seems to make the greatest difference' (Jónsdóttir, 2017, p. 24).

How is this relevant for research 'with' and 'by' children? Teachers working in open-ended and flexible ways across discipline boundaries can support child-led research and work alongside children in collaborative research promoting balanced, non-hierarchical relationships.

4.10 School Reform: Learner Consultation in Schools

One step that institutions can take towards embracing child-centred education is to take learner feedback seriously. The more systematically and deeply learner consultation is embedded into a school, the more likely it is that research 'with' and 'by' children can be accommodated. In fact, high levels of consultation are linked to child-led enquiry.

Learner consultation may be part of the school system's monitoring and evaluating strategies, a technique to support individual learners or a way of establishing a more democratic school system. School-wide processes of implementing genuine child or learner consultation that goes deeply into matters of teaching, learning curriculum and assessment is very rarely done in schools.

Schools today are dominated by targets, goals, performance indicators and league tables, and the drive for higher standards and accountability leads to a situation where few attempts are made to involve pupils as active participants in classroom-based research investigations (Flutter & Rudduck, 2004). Some important questions are almost never asked in classrooms, such as, for example, 'How do you learn best?', 'What helps you to learn?', 'What gets in the way of learning?', 'Why do you find it more difficult to learn certain things?', 'Do you

Table 4.3 Framework of pupil consultation (adapted from Flutter & Rudduck, 2004)

---

0 = pupils not consulted
1 = listening to pupils (source of data but otherwise not involved)
2 = pupils as active participants: teachers initiate and interpret data, but pupils are taking some roles in decision making + some feedback to pupils
3 = pupils as researchers: pupils are involved in the enquiry and have an active role in decision making and discussing feedback on findings
4 = fully active participants and co-researchers: everything is done jointly

---

learn better through particular styles?' and 'What encourages you to work harder?' (Flutter & Rudduck, 2004, p. 4).

Flutter and Rudduck (2004) make a convincing case for pupil consultation on the evidence that learners in both primary and secondary schools show remarkable capacity to discuss their learning processes. Opportunities for learners to participate in learning-focussed dialogues with adults/teachers have important tangible benefits for all, including learners, teachers and the whole school. Teachers report that listening to pupils helps them reconsider and adjust their teaching and make changes to their practice. Pupil consultation contributes to improving teaching and thus professional development. For learners, consulting with them also leads to better attitudes, enhanced self-esteem, confidence, stronger engagement and increased motivation to learn.

Building on Hart's ladder metaphor (in Chapter 3), Flutter and Rudduck's framework (Table 4.3) suggests that higher levels of consultation can be viewed as child-led research or enquiry (stage 3) or children working with adults/teachers as fully active participants and co-researchers (stage 4). It is interesting to note that in this framework child-led research is a lower-ranking activity in terms of participation than joint research with adults (teachers).

Approaches to consultation can take a so-called wide angle approach to identify general problems or issues, or a narrow angle putting the spotlight on specific issues and concerns, such as focussing on particular groups of learners who may need closer attention. If a school is taking student consultation seriously, participatory research projects or research 'with' and 'by' children may be more likely to be incorporated because of the systemic and explicit focus already placed on the importance of student voice.

Flutter and Rudduck (2004) give an overview of six themes that have emerged from their work in relation to concerns and ideas that children have brought to the attention of adults about their school life in the process of consultation (Table 4.4).

Table 4.4 Learner feedback: Summary of themes (adapted from Flutter & Rudduck, 2004)

THEMES
- TIME: allowing blocks of time; giving pupils greater autonomy in deciding their time on tasks; ensuring that pupils have sufficient time to answer verbal questions; offering more opportunities to work on longer-term projects; providing time and space for independent study; supporting the development of time management skills
- ASSESSMENT: effective feedback to pupils; active involvement in their own learning; adjusting teaching to take into account results of assessment; a recognition of the profound influence assessment has on motivation and self-esteem; the need for pupils to be able to assess themselves and understand how to improve
- CRITERIA FOR GOOD WORK: discuss these criteria as part of the ongoing dialogue; effective high-quality feedback
- FRIENDSHIP: powerful impact of social relationships on learning (not always positive); how teachers can support the link between friendships and learning; allowing some degree of choice in groupings
- SUSTAINING ENGAGEMENT: experiencing a sense of challenge but also being able to cope; offering variety and novelty; having a sense of ownership; pupils want more time to go into topics they are interested in; relevance to everyday life and future (frustration and boredom quickly set in when learning is obstructed); variety in lessons
- POSITIVE IDENTITY: receiving positive feedback and encouragement; discussions about self-perceptions, feelings, families and parents (can represent a surprising range of difficulties)

What is striking from this summary is that learners' desires strike a chord with the principles of child-led research and modern educational solutions such as maker spaces and twenty-first century approaches to education. In particular, they express their desire to have more ownership of their learning, have the opportunity to spend more time on longer, more meaningful projects and to work more independently while exercising more autonomy in both learning and evaluating themselves. All of this resonates strongly with promoting active child participation in research.

4.11 UNICEF Schools and Voice-Inclusive Practices in Schools

Internationally, the concept of child-centredness is also promoted by special schools created by UNICEF in an explicit attempt to put the principles of the United Nations Convention of the Rights of the Child into practice.

The so-called Child Friendly Schools (Phillips, 2016) operate in fifty-six countries and have been an international vehicle for promoting rights-based education for children. Typically established in areas where children did not have access to schools due to political disruption, these schools emphasise inclusiveness; effectiveness; healthy, safe and protective environments; and democratic participation. They prioritise making children's rights known to them. Parallel to this movement, UNICEF has also promoted Rights Respecting Schools, mainly in the UK and Canada. They also teach, promote and respect Convention rights and claim that the Convention is the heart of these schools' culture. In these schools less hierarchical relationships are cultivated between teachers and learners, leading to greater enjoyment of school and classroom conditions, which are more conducive to learning. In addition to these rights-focussed schools, many countries have appointed children's commissioners with the purpose of understanding children's concerns and respecting their rights. Based on the Convention principles, in some contexts voice-inclusive practices (VIP) are promoted with the aim of incorporating consultation with children into everyday practice, creating an ongoing dialogue between children and adults. VIP is defined as 'activities and practices that actively engage with children and their perspectives on matters that affect them…, particularly as relevant for their education' (Sargeant & Gillett-Swan, 2015, p. 181). VIP maintains that adults' voices matter too, but they do not stand in opposition to children's voices. Gillett-Swan and Sargeant (2018), based on Articles 12, 13, 23, 28, and 29 of the Convention, suggest that 'VIP offers the freedom for children to express their viewpoint and participate at a level of their choosing through communication modes that are accessible and materially relevant to them. Supporting, where possible, full participation, the implementation of pedagogy from a VIP perspective is inherently respectful and mindful of the child's perspective.' (p. 40).

4.12 Democratic Schools

Arguably, the highest levels of learner consultation happen in democratic schools, where there is genuine power sharing and dialogic negotiation between teachers and learners.

Originating from Dewey's work, where schools were seen as democratic communities with teachers and learners all working together to solve problems for the common good, democratic schools also exhibit high levels of compatibility with the principles of children's active participation in research.

Building a case for democratic schools, Beane and Apple (2007) suggest that in a democratic school all learners/children are active meaning makers, and education is to be directed towards problems, events and issues arising in the course of their learners' and teachers' shared lives. Learning in democratic schools is therefore organised around relevant and meaningful issues, with traditional subjects blurred. Instead, themes are selected for open-ended exploration. Power sharing between adults and children requires a completely different type of thinking for teachers. Children educated in democratic schools are likely to call dominant interpretations and teaching into question and reject sterilised versions of knowledge. Brough (2012), for example, describes a successful implementation of democratic principles in a primary school in New Zealand. The benefits were many, including enhanced achievements and engagement and increased levels of ownership of learning on the children's part. Challenges included initial lack of confidence on the teachers' part, peer censure and even student scepticism, but the study suggests that the initial gap between beliefs and practices can be closed by building a sense of community and gaining experiential evidence of the benefits over time.

Radical democratic schools embrace a person-centred approach to teaching and learning, centred around how to be/become a good person in an inclusive, caring society. This core principle sets these schools up in contrast to the neoliberal paradigm prevalent in educational institutions in many contexts around the world. In contrast, a radical democratic school is a living democracy, with both teachers and learners becoming researchers (Fielding & Moss, 2011) and engaging in collaborative dialogue and enquiry. A person-centred democratic approach to education sees individuals not as competitive customers but as relational beings who make choices within the context of 'deeper aspirations'. They ask fundamental questions, such as 'How do we become good persons?' And the answers are reached via dialogue with others that they respect and care for. A school where teachers and students ask such questions and work together to answer them sees itself as developing an 'inclusive, creative society through a participatory democracy which benefits everyone' (Fielding, 2011, p. 65). Students are listened to; they make decisions and take shared responsibility for current and future questions. The teacher–student relationships are characterised by dialogic learning that is emergent. The fellowship created between teachers and students is focussed on how to live a good life and how to co-create a good society and a

Table 4.5 Fielding: Six types of partnerships (with reference to Fielding, 2001, chapter 3; Hart, 1992; Shier, 2001)

Student as data source: staff utilise information about student progress or wellbeing	Research 'on' children
Student as active respondents: staff invite dialogue to deepen learning decisions	From weaker to stronger versions of research 'with' children
Students as co-enquirers: staff take a lead role with high-profile active student support	Truly balanced joint partnership is positioned as 'better' than either student-led or teacher-led enquiry
Students as knowledge creators: students take lead roles with active staff support	
Students as joint authors: students and staff decide on a joint course of action	
Intergenerational learning as participatory democracy: there is a shared commitment/responsibility for the common good	Teaching/learning (and researching) become one and the same process

better world. Where person-centred democratic education becomes particularly relevant to the ideas of research 'with' children and 'by' children is the emphasis on adult–child relationships in the pursuit of learning and researching together (see Table 4.5).

The fellowship dimension stands for respect and the way people regard each other (i.e. the practice of humanity). There is also the potential of transformation as a result of these experiences. Regular open communication is key, with egalitarian openness and mutuality. It is important to reaffirm freedom and pay close attention to each other or re-see each other every day. Teachers in communication with children/learners pay attention to using language that engages, encourages and excites. The highest level of partnership is where both students and teacher become researchers engaged in shared exploration for the greater good of all.

4.13 The Extended Framework of Researching with Children in Applied Linguistics

As we saw in Chapter 2, the alternative framework in a nutshell suggested that adults' own conceptions of childhood and their

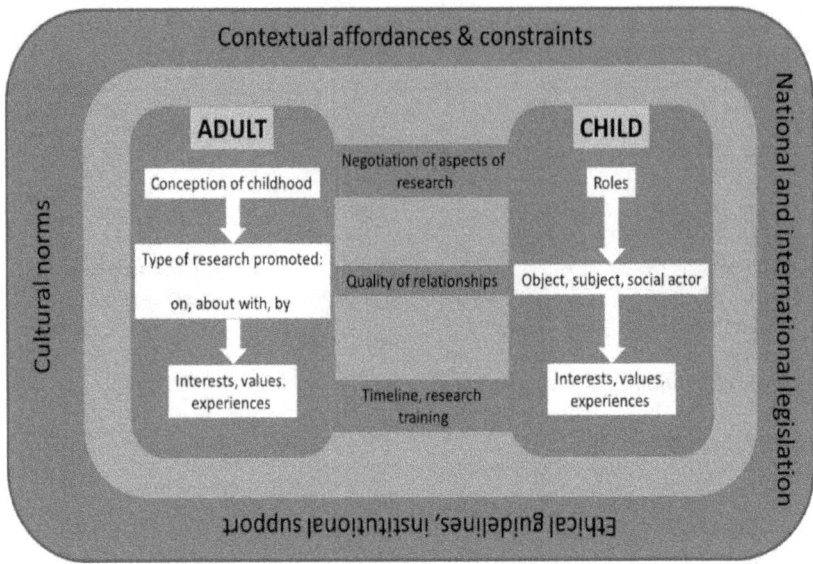

Figure 4.1 The key components of the extended framework

perspectives about what roles children can take in research such as objects, subjects or social actors, will be directly influenced by what type of research they decide to engage in (i.e. research on, about, with or by children). How adult researchers can plan, undertake and evaluate their research involving children will also be impacted by contextual affordances and constraints.

Having reviewed the key tenets of Childhood Studies and how those concepts can be translated into actual research 'with' or 'by' children (in Chapter 3), and having considered the educational philosophies and enabling institutional infrastructures (in Chapter 4), it is now time to flesh out the framework that was initially sketched out in Chapter 2 in order to explore what additional elements/questions might have to be added so that it becomes a more useful tool for researchers to consult as they plan their projects involving children in active roles. The key components of the extended framework are laid out in Figure 4.1.

Familiarity with this framework will allow the adult researchers to navigate their way through whatever their research focus, their background, their beliefs, values or epistemological stance might be, and whatever contextual constraints and opportunities they might face in their projects.

Additional elements/questions to consider:

The adult

What is the adult researcher's (the teacher or academic or member of larger team) conception of childhood?
What are his/her values, beliefs and epistemological stance?
What are his/her research interests, research questions and research experience?
What roles does he/she assign to the children? (Objects, subjects or social actors?)
What types of research is the adult familiar with and which will he/she promote? (Research on, about, with and by children?)
What is the adult's conception of ethical research with children?

The child

Who are the children?
How are they selected?
Are they volunteers?
What are their beliefs and understandings about the proposed research?
What are their conceptions of the adult researchers?
What is their previous experience of research (if any)?
What are their interests and concerns?

The quality and strength of relationship between the adult and the children

How important is the quality of the relationship in the research?
How will adult roles (teachers, outsider researchers, graduate students) impact on relationship building?
How can the adults navigate hybrid relationships? (e.g. both teacher and researcher)?
How much time and space is there for initial rapport and relationship development?
How do group dynamics in children's peer groups impact relationship building in any project?

Timeline for the project

Is the project short term or longer term? A few days? Weeks? Months?

The extent to which any negotiation happens between adults and children

All these questions could be considered in terms of whether negotiation applies or not:

- What is the main purpose of the research and who will benefit?
- Who is the funder? What are their goals and priorities?
- What are the goals/purposes? What will the research achieve?
- What are the main foci?
- What are the methods, approaches and tools used?
- What is the expected impact/outcome?
- Who is the audience for dissemination?
- How will the results be disseminated?

Is there any room for discussion and negotiation, or will the adults control or decide everything? If there is room for negotiation, further questions include:

- What aspects of the research (purpose, goals, methods, tools, outcomes) are open to discussion and negotiation, if any?
- Are the children involved from the beginning or are they invited to join the project once questions are decided?
- Might the adults have one purpose or goal while the children have another?
- If involved in an active role, what is the children's buy-in? (How far do they identify with the adult focus and purpose and if they do not, does this matter?)
- If participatory tools and methods are used, will these require training?
- What is the balance between the adult's and the children's contributions?

Research training (yes/no and for whom)

Is there any research training planned for the children?
If yes, what kind of training?
Who does the training, where, for how long, in what shape and form?
Do the adults need training?

Institutional support (micro-context)

Is there school support?
Will the project happen inside or outside of school hours?
To what extent are school structures conducive to undertaking the study?
Are the schools simply tolerant of the research and consider it separate/ additional extra? Do school structures and relationships support the

> research activities in a way that they are embedded to varying degrees into everyday practices?
> Will everyone in the school be aware that a study is happening?
> If the children are active participants (research with and by children), how have traditional hierarchical school structures been taken into account?

Legislation, guidelines, ethical procedures (macro-context)

Who are the stakeholders?
What roles do local educational authorities and school boards play?
What approaches and types of research are familiar/acceptable in the local context?
What ethical and legal requirements apply in the given context (e.g. consent procedures)?
Which guidelines or ethics boards does the study need to satisfy?
What cultural norms apply?

The extended framework proposes three different possible roles for children (objects, subjects and social actors) in four different types of studies (research 'on', 'about', 'with' and 'by' children). The additional elements and questions in the boxes have been drawn up to support researchers in appreciating the various possibilities and choices they have when planning their study.

While the contextual factors will constrain to some extent what might be feasible, the framework nonetheless represents an open-ended cluster of possibilities. If the study is 'on' or 'about' children, many of the additional questions will not apply. As someone is moving towards research 'with' and 'by' children, questions about relationships and opportunities for negotiation with the children about different aspects of the study become more important. Also, the time allocated for the study and whether the children will get any research training will become relevant. Finally, the way in which the study is supported by the school and all stakeholders is also more relevant in studies where children are collaborators, co-researchers or researchers. There are no recipes for best practice, but the framework intends to highlight questions for consideration for adult researchers working with children.

4.14 Conclusion

Starting from the image of the child as a capable social actor, the previous chapters have outlined the key principles and concepts promoted by Childhood Studies, such as voice, agency and participation. Examples of participatory tools and studies illustrating active child involvement in research have been briefly introduced, drawing on broad interdisciplinary input. Child-centredness as a concept has also been explored in various institutional settings. This chapter concluded with the extended framework, which proposes the incorporation of children's active roles into existing traditional frameworks. In the next chapter the focus will turn to the characteristics of existing applied linguistics research to take stock of the main approaches and methods and to examine the role and status of children in this literature. Chapter 6 will be devoted to examples of studies that move away from research 'on' children and showcase increasing degrees of active child participation in applied linguistics.

5 Children's Roles and Status in Applied Linguistics Research

5.1 Introduction

Having introduced some key concepts, tools and examples from the interdisciplinary literature of Childhood Studies (Chapters 2–4), and having argued at the end of Chapter 4 that a new extended framework is needed when engaging with children in applied linguistics research, this chapter will turn its focus to applied linguistics in order to examine children's status and roles in recently published work.

The scope of this chapter does not allow for a comprehensive overview of the field, so instead I will put a carefully selected 'slice' of the literature under the microscope to analyse the key features of empirical research involving child participants. The examples are taken from five applied linguistics journals covering the last ten years.

This review will confirm the claim made in Chapter 1 that applied linguistics is largely dominated by studies that carry out research 'on' children and 'about' children, with only a handful of studies identified that have pushed the boundaries towards research 'with' children, albeit only in a limited way. I refer to these as 'weak' forms of research 'with' children, where child participants take only modestly active roles.

In the first part of the chapter, the most important child development theories that have shaped the literature will be briefly outlined. Then, the main topic areas within the field of child second language education will be reviewed. Finally, studies illustrating children's roles in applied linguistics research will be reviewed.

5.2 Influences of Child Development Theories on Child L2 Education

The field of child second language education has its roots in SLA, which is an adult-focussed area of study (see Chapter 1). The exact boundaries of child L2 education are hard to define due to the multidisciplinary nature of this field and its close interconnections with neighbouring disciplines, such as, for example, bilingual acquisition in childhood or developmental psychology.

Over the span of childhood, significant physical, psychological, cognitive, emotional and social changes occur while children's relationships with both adults and their peers evolve all the time (Philp et al., 2017), and since learning and using a second/foreign language is embedded in all these processes, the field of L2 education for children continues to expand in all these directions.

Theories of child development have inspired research and pedagogy in L2 education, with three main theories dominating the field: Piaget (1923), Vygotsky (1978) and information processing theories.

In the early twentieth century, Piaget and his colleagues put forward one of the most well-known theories of child development, based on a vast amount of empirical data.

Using one-to-one interviews in their experiments, Piaget and his team posed questions to children of different ages about specific experimental problems. Based on the children's responses, they developed descriptors for four distinct stages of development (sensorimotor stage, pre-operational stage, concrete operational stage and formal operational stage), essentially describing the behavioural patterns of the 'average child' in a particular stage. All children go through these stages in the same invariable order, and their thinking changes and becomes qualitatively different as they progress from one stage to another. With close reference to these descriptors, researchers in applied linguistics have been able to adjust tasks, materials, tools and verbal or written instructions in research studies based on the assumed readiness of the children in question.

As a constructivist, Piaget believed children were active learners, always in the process of constructing their understanding of the world. By adapting to their environment and organising knowledge according to their developing schemata, children are believed to be in constant movement between assimilation and accommodation. Following explanations about new phenomena in the environment, the child gradually adapts their schemata by incorporating the new information, thus developing new levels of understanding.

Children in the early years (pre-operational stage, under 7 years of age) lack the mental operations to follow the rules of logic. Even though symbolic thought is present in play, such as in imaginative play or in drawings, children are closely tied to what they can see in the here-and-now and from their own point of view only. These characteristics were described as ego-centrism and demonstrated via the well-known 'three mountains tasks', where young children were asked to appreciate someone else's perspective. Typically, children under 7 were not able to do this. Other popular Piagetian tasks included questions about conservation, such as how the amount of water is changed after being poured into a taller glass. Again, children under the age of 7 struggled to appreciate that pouring water from one container into another does not change the amount of liquid.

In the next stage, the formal operational stage (between the ages of 7 and 11) all these difficulties relating to ego-centrism seem to resolve themselves. Children can appreciate reversibility, seriation, classification and perspectives others than their own. Finally, in the formal operation stage (from 12 years of age), children develop hypothetical-deductive thinking and scientific reasoning. They learn to appreciate many different angles to a problem or question and can think about these in an abstract way. Teenagers can understand how each variable contributes to a particular complex problem and thus become excellent problem solvers. They are able to reconcile seemingly contradictory information, and this ability has been linked to the development of creativity, which is an important characteristic of the teenage years.

Despite heavy criticisms, which were mainly levied at the manner in which the experiments were conducted with very little concern for whether the tasks, the language use of the experimenter and the contextual clues made sense or not (Donaldson, 1986), Piaget's legacy and influence is substantial, with many implications for educators working with and researching 'with' children. The vast amount of knowledge that has been accumulated about the way children's logical thinking develops going through the four developmental stages has been used to inform both teaching and research, from adjusting instructions fitting with the stage of development to designing language learning tasks that take into account to what extent the children in question can appreciate various angles and viewpoints of others when handling the task (such as in debates, collaborative tasks or information gap tasks).

Piaget's contemporary Vygotsky is an equally popular figure when it comes to theorising L2 learning processes with children. Vygotsky's emphasis on the way culture, context and social interaction play critical roles has been adopted in studies within child second language education. In particular, two key concepts have received most attention: the zone of proximal development (ZPD) and scaffolding.

According to Vygotsky, learning first takes place on the interpersonal plane (between people) before the knowledge is internalised by the individual (the intrapersonal plane) and becomes part of their independent thinking. Thus, the Vygotskyan approach has more interest in potentiality than in the actual response to a task or a question.

The focus is on what the child could become or be able to do rather than what the child can currently do on their own. Accordingly, the ZPD is defined as the metaphorical distance between the actual level and the potential level of a learner's performance during problem solving (i.e. between trying to do the same problem alone or with the help of an adult or an 'expert' helper).

Scaffolding (just like the structure around a building under construction) helps with the construction of the child's learning and understanding. Once the child is able to take a step on their own, the scaffolding is gradually withdrawn. This idea has important implications for teacher talk in general in any classroom, including the L2 classroom, but also for assessment. The Vygotskian approach invites a dynamic, interactive type of assessment where the interest is in the process of learning rather than giving correct answers to static questions. During scaffolding, increasing or decreasing levels of assistance are provided to the learner in their ZPD according to their individual needs (Poehner, 2007). Bruner (1983) suggests that scaffolding must start with inviting children to say what they already know and building on that as the foundation of learning. It is also essential to break down new information into bite-size chunks and encourage children to figure problems and questions out rather than simply telling them or teaching them the answer or explaining to them what to do. In research studies inspired by Vygotsky's work, qualitative work uncovered features of scaffolding and peer-to-peer and teacher–learner interaction using micro-linguistic analysis.

Information processing (IP) theories break down and explain processes of understanding information, such as how we acquire it, store it and retrieve it when needed. As the name suggests, IP uses a computer model or metaphor as an analogy, although more recently so-called connectionist or neural network models of learning have also been associated with IP. Accordingly, new information is connected to existing nodes in the network, and these connections get more and more complex as the child's brain matures. Information processing approaches have received a great deal of attention in illustrating how children process new input within the constraints of their maturational states and their ongoing experience with familiar materials and approaches. Studies that have explored children's memory capacities, metamemory, cognition and metacognition serve as important reference points for studies in child second language education, feeding into designing instructional strategies, materials or assessment tasks.

Younger children learn more slowly than older children since their encoding strategies in early childhood are weak and strategy training is not yet effective. Their executive function (i.e. higher-order ability to organise attention, memory and goal-oriented behaviour) is also weaker at younger ages. These abilities all develop across childhood as children learn to regulate their behaviour more successfully. The development of executive functions is greatly influenced by increasing levels of literacy and better self-control. The development of the 'theory of mind' is affected by these maturational processes but also by experiences; those with siblings, for example, develop these earlier.

In the early years, young children have limited attentional resources and are not yet capable of directing and sustaining their attention or ignoring distractions, although, interestingly, children pay attention more intensely to activities that they have chosen for themselves (DiCarlo et al., 2016). Attention also improves across the ages. In the Piagetian concrete operational stage, processing speed increases and children can rehearse and retrieve information better (e.g. Jarrold, et al., 2014), and they become better at using spontaneous strategies to aid their memory (Schneider & Ornstein, 2015). These developments explain why older children (e.g. Muñoz, 2006, 2014) learn second and foreign languages faster than their younger counterparts, with more ease and using more efficient strategies. The older the children, arguably, the more powerful cognitive and metacognitive strategies they can call upon during foreign language learning processes.

In the teenage years, self-concept and identity (including ethnic, racial and gender identity) become crucially important aspects of development, having an impact on self-esteem and the development of peer relationships. Teenagers become expert scientific thinkers with the ability to handle complex problems, but they have to learn to cope with increasing levels of stress and pressure at school, including peer pressure and exam pressures. Navigating life in school among popular children and bullies is challenging, especially when coupled with the largely negative impact of social media on self-esteem. Striving for autonomy and sustaining friendships are important ways of achieving appropriate levels of wellbeing (Shin & Ryan, 2014). In terms of emotional development, children's vulnerability to negative emotions and their changing needs with regard to relationships with peers and adults have been noted, with clear implications for setting up positive, comfortable environments where anxiety and pressure are minimised and where children feel confident in the company of adults and peers.

5.3 From a Narrow Focus to a Wide Range of Topics

According to Paradis (2007), originally child L2 research within SLA focussed on comparisons between L1 and L2 acquisition patterns for children and on how L2 learners compared with native speaking counterparts of their own age. These binary foci were of particular interest in the early naturalistic studies, such as those by Hakuta (1976) or Dulay and Burt (1972, 1974). This line of research aimed to document early L2 acquisition processes in childhood, and it uncovered both similarities and differences with L1 processes.

The 'universal stages' of L2 development have been described as nonverbal (the silent period) followed by formulaic and telegraphic periods. Studies have focussed on describing children's development of various aspects of the language system (i.e. phonological, lexical and morpho-syntactic acquisition). These are still key areas of research, but in addition more and more attention has also been devoted to the individual differences among children in terms of their motivation, aptitude, personality characteristics, first language typology, age or socio-economic status.

In contexts where young children switch to learning and using a new language quite quickly and with a need to make rapid progress, the processes of L2 acquisition have been researched alongside examining the role of young learners' L1, leading to theorisation of the relationship between L1 and L2 development. Cummins (2000) proposed the idea that children will have to tackle learning an L2 in context-dependent interpersonal situations first and then move to learning the L2 in context-independent, academic situations. This is referred to as a move from basic interpersonal communicative situations to situations where cognitive academic language proficiency is required. The time and effort that it takes for children to catch up with their peers in a new L2 and do well academically last many years. This line of research has attracted a lot of attention, not just in terms of the processes of learning the L2 to function well academically but also the question of what happens to the L1 development of minority children where the L2 is the majority language of the community. These are important questions in the current super-diverse, multilingual classrooms around the world. Researchers examining the processes of learning the dominant language in societies where immigrant children make up a sizeable proportion of classrooms have begun to document translanguaging practices (Leonet et al., 2017; Lin & Wu, 2015; Moriarty, 2017; Tai & Li, 2020).

Age as a variable within SLA has received a huge amount of attention in a quest to discover what might be the best age to start learning a second language in childhood and how exactly children's second language learning processes differ from those of adults (DeKeyser, 2012; Muñoz, 2006, 2014). This interest has inspired a huge literature, but despite the great efforts to establish the exact effects of age, research has instead uncovered just how complex this question is and

5.3 From a Narrow Focus to a Wide Range of Topics

how age alone as a variable is in fact impossible to isolate (Pfenniger & Singleton, 2017). Debates have revolved around the existence of the critical period hypothesis (CPH; Lenneberg, 1967). This line of research is interested in establishing whether there is a window of opportunity early in life (before puberty) to acquire second languages to native or near-native levels. Accordingly, studies have compared learners who were younger than 11–12 (puberty) with those who were older when they started learning a second language using a range of methodologies and tasks in naturalistic contexts. Overall, this literature indicates a clear advantage for older learners, with the caveat that in the long term some younger learners may catch up. Younger starters with earlier ages of arrival may show stronger effects for phonological production and grammatical knowledge (Huang, 2016), but ultimately, each individual's path is unique, as indicated by the patterns that have emerged from longitudinal studies such as Jia and Aaronson (2003) or Jia and Fuse (2007). Most studies examining the age factor have been conducted in ESL contexts, with relatively little research focussing on EFL programmes. The most well-known study in an EFL context, in Spain, the Barcelona Age Factor Project (Muñoz, 2006), also indicates beyond doubt that older learners outperform younger learners overall, with younger learners showing only modest advantages in pronunciation and listening. A more recent large-scale study in Germany (Jaekel et al., 2017, p. 654) also cautions not to 'blindly believe the myth that the earlier in life language learning commences, the better the outcomes of such learning will be'.

Nonetheless, policy makers and parents all around the world have ignored the messages about older learners' advantages by insisting that ever younger children start learning English as a foreign language with the expectation that the early start will lead to greater linguistic gains. At the same time, it is important to note that linguistic gains are not the only goals in early language learning programmes. Johnstone (2019) suggests that developing intercultural awareness, general language awareness, confidence, positive attitudes to others, cognitive and metacognitive skills, an international outlook and positive attitudes to languages are all worthwhile goals.

5.3.1 Areas of Research Activity

A number of scholars have written comprehensive, critical overviews of child SLA and child second/foreign language education. There are book-length analyses discussing key issues in more depth (e.g. Enever, 2018; Garton & Copland, 2019; Mourao & Lorenco, 2015; Murphy, 2014; Murphy & Evangelou, 2016; Philp et al., 2008; Pinter, 2011;

Rich, 2014) and key papers and chapters that offer meta-analyses of research overall or in a particular area (e.g. Butler, 2015; Collins & Muñoz, 2016; Copland et al., 2014; Nikolov & Lugossy, 2021; Nikolov & Mihaljevič Djugonovič, 2011; Oliver & Azkarai, 2017; Oliver et al., 2017; Philp et al., 2017). Helpful advice and guidelines about how to teach a second/foreign language to younger learners (as opposed to adult learners and older learners) have also been published in the form of handbooks and resource books (Cameron, 2001; Moon, 2000; Pinter, 2017; Scott & Ytreberg, 1990; Shin & Crandall, 2014; Slattery & Willis, 2001), with some of these making connections between theory and practice, tapping into the relevant literature on child L2 education or drawing out lessons for pedagogy.

All these authors draw out unique implications from the literature and put the emphasis in different places, but based on their overviews, the main themes laid out in Table 5.1 emerge.

5.4 Main Characteristics of SLA Research

Child second language education as a field relies on *dichotomies* and *comparisons*.

These dichotomies relate to

- Comparisons of younger and older child learners (i.e. studies focussing on detecting differences between learners of various ages reacting to the same task or prompt or the same sort of questions)
- Comparisons of adult and child learners
- Comparisons of native speaker (NS) children, bilingual learners and foreign language learners (a largely deficit approach to describing what language learners cannot do as compared to the norm, which is NS standards)
- Comparisons of different formal and informal contexts, such as those offering modest, significant and substantial time in the second or foreign language curriculum (Johnstone, 2019)
- Comparisons of children's performance on various elicitation tasks or their responses to questions about their language learning experiences across different country contexts.

When children are invited as participants, very little justification, if any, is given for why specific age groups might have been selected from particular contexts and why certain age groups are being compared with others. It appears that selection is quite random, based on convenience (i.e. whoever the adult researchers may have relatively easy access to). The majority of learners tend to be from urban, middle-class schools where both parents and headteachers are likely to

Table 5.1 *Broad areas of child L2 education*

Areas of research interests	Some illustrative sources
CPH and 'the younger, the better'	DeKeyser (2012)
	Genesee (2016)
	Granena & Long (2013)
	Lambelet & Bethele (2015)
	Muñoz & Singleton (2011)
	Muñoz (2008)
	Patkowski (1994)
L2 policy issues, including appropriate pedagogy and critical pedagogy	Enever (2014, 2018)
	Loópez Gopar (2019)
	López-Gopar & Sughrua, (2014)
	Sayer (2015)
The interaction paradigm, meaning negotiation, tasks and error correction	Azkarai & García Mayo (2016)
	Azkarai & Imaz Agirre (2016)
	García Mayo & Lázaro Ibarrola (2015)
	Lightbown & Spada (1990)
	Lyster & Ranta (1997)
	Mackey et al., (2003, 2007)
	Oliver (2000, 2002, 2009)
	Pinter (2006, 2007)
	Van den Branden (2000)
Translanguaging, multilingualism, the use of L1 and L2 and other linguistic resources	Bialystok (2001)
	Conteh & Brock (2011)
	Copland & Yonetsugi (2016)
	Cummins (2000)
	Leonet et al. (2017)
	Moriarty (2017)
	Murphy (2014)
	Prasad (2013, 2014, 2015, 2020)
	Tai and & Li (2020)
CLIL and other types of immersion	Barrios & Acosta-Manzano (2020)
	Ellison (2019)
	Ioannou-Georgiu & Pavlou (2011)
	Otwinowska & Foryś (2017)
	Pladevall-Ballester (2019)
	Wei & Feng (2015)
The use of technology, mobile devices, gaming and applications	Butler (2019)
	Dourda et al. (2014)
	Pellerin (2014)
	Phillips (2010)
	Segers & Verhoeven (2002)
	Sylveén & Sundquvist (2012)
Assessment and evaluation of L2 learning	Bailey & Carroll (2015)
	Butler & Zeng (2014)

(*continued*)

112   *Children's Roles and Status in Applied Linguistics*

Table 5.1 (cont.)

Areas of research interests	Some illustrative sources
	Hasselgreen (2005)
	Kormos et al. (2020)
	McKay (2006)
	Nikolov & Timpe-Laughlin (2021)
	Nikolov (2016)
	Papp (2019)
	Prosšicć-Santovac & Rixon (2019)
Individual differences, attitudinal domains, motivation, anxiety, learner identity	Butler (2017a)
	Carreira (2012)
	Lamb (2011)
	Lamb & Budiyanto (2013)
	Li, et al. (2019)
	Nikolov (1999)
Children's views about L2 learning	Aro (2012)
	Chik (2018)
	Millonig et al. (2019)
	Pfenninger & Singleton (2016)
L2 teacher development and education, role of parents and wider context	Copland et al. (2014)
	Emery (2012)
	Enever (2014)
	Hayes (2000)
	Rixon (2013)
	Sung and Padilla (1998)

appreciate the importance of research and have positive attitudes to it. In many countries, research universities have special relationships with specific primary and secondary schools where they send student teachers for their practicum and where there is already an existing research culture to tap into. The consequence of these trends is that certain types of schools and populations of children might never be selected for research.

5.5 The Selected Set of Studies

Having sketched out the broad areas of activity within the field of child second and foreign language education, this section is devoted to an overview of research studies involving children taken from five applied linguistics journals in the last ten years (2011–2021).

With the extended framework that I advocated at the end of Chapter 4, I argued that we needed more research 'with' and 'by' children, not just 'on' and 'about' children. To this end, the studies

5.5 The Selected Set of Studies

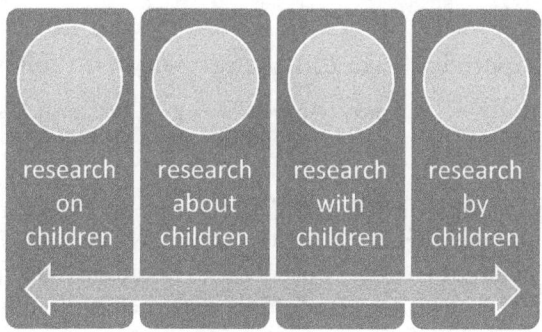

Figure 5.1 Types of research involving children

identified in the journals have been scrutinised as to what role they assigned to children on this continuum (Figure 5.1).

This 'slice' of the literature, which amounted to a total of 324 studies was drawn from *TESOL Quarterly*, *Applied Linguistics*, *System*, *Language Teaching Research* and *The Language Learning Journal* (please see Appendix on page 220).

The review in the Appendix includes empirical papers with child participants up to the age of 18. As discussed in Chapter 1, this broad age range does not comfortably fit with the most often used definitions of 'young leaners' in SLA or applied linguistics (e.g. Ellis, 2014). My reason to select this definition was justified in Section 1.5 as being in line with UN guidelines. This broad definition is further justified by the nature of the child populations that appear in these publications, namely, a very large number of studies include a mixture of different age groups in the same project (such as comparing learners aged 6, 8, 12 and 16). Sometimes comparisons are also made with adult learners. Such mixing of age groups in empirical studies means that had this review focussed strictly on 5–12-year-olds alone, a very large number of studies would have been excluded even though they reported on work which included these age groups.

In order to select the five journals for analysis, first of all, an international group of child second language education experts were approached to nominate and rank journals in terms of how influential and important they felt these journals were in our field. Based on the overall recommendations of this group, five key journals were selected.

The content of these five journals spanning a decade (between 2011 and 2021) was carefully reviewed, and a tabular summary was created listing all empirical papers involving children (all child participants up to 18 years of age). Articles with a focus on teachers, policy, corpora, classroom discourse, the development or evaluation of materials and meta-analyses or reviews were all excluded.

5.5.1 Focus/Area of Interest

The table in Appendix (page 220) is organised in the following way:

Author and year	Topic/key words	Country	Approach/ methods	Age	Child participant role (active or passive)

The table contains information about the author(s), the year of publication, the topic area and the specific focus explored. In addition, the country where the study took place is noted, as well as the main methodological approaches and tools together with the type(s) of analyses applied. Finally, the child participants' ages and their role and status in the study are recorded (stating whether these were passive or active, labelling the status as 'on', 'about or 'with' children). The labels were assigned following the categorisation established in earlier chapters (based on Kellett, 2010a; Mayne & Howitt, 2015). In the sample, studies mostly focus on English as an L2, although a small number of studies address other L2s.

While it is not possible to assign each study a single topic since many studies bring together several foci, such as individual variables and language growth in different types of teaching interventions, an overview of the content suggests that certain topics dominate the sample. *Vocabulary learning* is mentioned in the highest number of studies (more than 30 studies focus on vocabulary), with *literacy learning*, including reading and/or writing, being equally dominant (more than 30 studies in this category). *Motivation* is the third topic that appears in more than 30 studies across the five journals. *Focus on form and grammar learning* and *task-based learning* come next, with each topic appearing in more than 25 studies. Then, the category that I called *comparison of different types of interventions and instructional approaches* comes next with over 20 studies, and finally *learner strategy use and training* with about 20 studies. A sizeable portion of studies targets *CLIL contexts*, indicating that the appetite for research and publishing in countries that use CLIL tends to be particularly high, probably aided with funding available for research.

5.5.2 Age of Participants

As we can see from Table 5.2, out of a total of 324 studies, only about one third (122 studies) have been conducted with children under the age of 12 exclusively, while two thirds (188 studies) reported on work with children over 12 years of age (i.e. participants who were aged 12–18). This suggests that the majority of the work that is published is undertaken with secondary level learners rather than primary level

Table 5.2 Age distribution in the studies in the Appendix

Total number	Under 5 years of age	6–7 years old	8–9 years old	10–12 years old	13–14 years old	15–16 years old	17–18 years old	Studies that mix age groups
324	5	14	15	78	45	31	28	108

learners, although the exact age at which learners transition from primary to secondary varies across countries. Overall, it is clear that research with younger children (as opposed to older children) is underrepresented in this sample and in the research literature at large.

Within the under 12 category, the results are skewed in favour of the relatively older learners, with barely any studies targeting very young learners at the beginning of schooling or in pre-school years. Really young children under 5 years of age are almost completely absent from this sample (only 5 studies identified in the total of 324).

The most researched age group appears to be children between the ages of 10 and 12, with most studies focussed on the upper end (i.e. children who are 12 and in their first or second year of their lower secondary education). Only 78 studies out of a total of 122 involve any children younger than 12 years of age. This may signal that children under 12 are perhaps perceived to be more difficult to work with or to access for research. For the younger age brackets of 6–7 and 8–9 years of age, only 14 and 15 studies were identified, respectively. In the above 12 category, 13–14 years olds attracted the highest number of studies (45 studies in the sample), while there appears to be an almost symmetrical balance between two older teenage or youth groups, with 31 studies in the 15–16 years of age category and 28 studies in the 17–18 years of age category.

As discussed already, a large proportion of the studies is characterised by comparing age groups: 56 studies compare children aged between 13 and 18 years of age while 24 studies compare 5–12-year-olds, and a further 28 studies compare age groups including both primary and secondary years (i.e. participants whose ages range from 5 to 18 years). Some studies include students who are older than 18, such as college students, university students and adults of all ages, and these adult learners are compared with the child participants.

5.5.3 About the Contexts of Research

Some countries and research teams appear in the selected literature several times, representing their work in all of these journals. It is not uncommon for the same authors to publish an aspect of a larger study in one journal and another angle in another journal. There are clusters of research activity around the world, and looking at the geographical spread, Spain stands out as the best represented country with a total of 51 studies in the sample. This, among other things, may reflect the fact that more funding is available for applied linguistics research there than elsewhere, and that there is a healthy appetite for research fuelled by the popular CLIL policy in many primary and secondary schools. The next category of countries with noticeable presence are the USA (with 29 studies), the UK (27 studies), China (24 studies), Japan (22 studies) and Hong Kong (20 studies). Next, the Netherlands is represented with 10, Sweden with 9, Taiwan with 11, South Korea with 14 and Canada with 9 studies. Many other countries are represented with fewer than 5 studies, such as Australia, Norway, Germany, Chile, Iran, Türkiye, Poland and Singapore, and some countries appear only once or twice. Eleven studies compare research relating to children's L2 performances in different country contexts.

5.6 Studies Positioned on the 'on-about-with-by' Continuum

Unsurprisingly, while research activity in general has been buoyant, especially in the last few decades, children's roles remain almost completely passive, restricted to being data sources in research.

Almost all studies in the sample report passive roles for children (i.e. 311 out of a total of 324 studies, making up 96% of the total). Within the passive category, most (264 studies) were classified as studies 'on' children, while 47 studies were classified as research 'about' children. Modestly active roles were identified in 13 studies, all of these being 'weak forms' of research 'with' children, where children were responding to participatory tools rather than taking active roles as collaborators or researchers.

The majority of the studies in the sample report on short experiments where a set of tasks or treatments were administered to various groups of learners. In such studies children may only see the researchers fleetingly and may never have to interact with them beyond following minimal instructions, often conveyed by the teacher, to do the tasks, tests or otherwise contribute to a particular predetermined activity. In research 'about' children, the participating children may be more aware that research is going on because these studies tend to last longer, often with a variety of activities that children may be involved in over time. This way they have a chance to get accustomed to the presence of an outsider researcher and may also develop a better understanding of what the research might be about. They may be enthusiastically contributing their views, albeit to predetermined questions. While research 'about' children still attaches passive roles to children, in applied linguistics we still need more such studies to understand better what children think about language learning and how they describe their experiences, such as how they benefit from their learning. We need more studies because even within passive roles, research 'on' children dominates the literature with six times more studies in the sample than research 'about' children.

Even though these four categories (research 'on', 'about', 'with' and 'by') make up a continuum, there is a sharper, more significant divide between research 'about' children and 'with' children because this is where passive roles can turn into active ones. In the weaker versions of studies 'with' children, these roles are still limited and may just mean that children are responding to participatory tools that can help with data elicitation, for example by giving children *some* control over how they respond (what they draw or what photos they take), whereas a stronger form of research 'with' children will mean that participants have the opportunity to shape the research process, contributing actively to one, two, several or all the stages of the project.

There is a handful of studies (13) in the sample where either the authors explicitly labelled the children as active or such active roles can be inferred. The last category of research 'by' children, or child-led research, is not represented in the sample at all.

5.6.1 Research 'on' and 'about' Children

Research 'on' children usually follows experimental and quasi-experimental designs and approaches, where various groups of children are exposed to different treatments (e.g. different tasks, tests, input materials or different approaches to teaching/introducing the same material) and then their behaviour, scores or responses are measured, graded, evaluated and finally compared across groups to reach conclusions about the effectiveness of the treatment. Validated and standardised questionnaires are used to elicit responses for statistical analysis (with a focus on averages and trends), and sometimes additional interviews are used to triangulate numerical results or add detail to the data gathered in questionnaires. Interviews are seen as supplementary and secondary to the main data set. Whether the tools and approaches are appropriate for the given age groups does not tend to be discussed, even though it is likely that tasks and tests administered across a variety of age groups will disadvantage younger children.

Pre- and post-test design is most popular with experimental and control groups, and these are very often intact classes, which of course presents a particular ethical dilemma in itself, in that exposing classes of learners, even for a short period of time, to treatments that are suspected to be less effective can be seen as problematic. Most studies report on a range of tests and tasks and then compare the strength of different relationships, such as correlations.

Out of the 324 studies, only 63 studies (roughly 20% of the total) were found which did not follow some kind of an experimental design, with random groups or whole class groups, and with pre- and post-tests and some form of statistical analysis. Only 15 out of the 324 studies claimed to be longitudinal in their design, following learners over several months or longer. The rest of the studies were all short interventions.

A dominance of experimental studies which are largely quick interventions means that our understanding of the field is based on work that reports 'on' children in static and fragmented snapshots of performances from randomly selected groups. Groups of learners pulled from easy-to-reach urban school populations in research-intensive countries dominate. This body of research most definitely renders children as passive, unknowing participants and advantages academics with little consideration given to children's experiences and any potential benefits that the children and their teachers may or may not gain.

In the next section I will discuss three studies that belong to the passive categories of studies 'on' and 'about' children. These have been selected as illustrative examples. Then I will look at two examples labelled as weak versions of research 'with' children.

Studies that assign passive roles to children ('on' and 'about') are easy to identify. Those studies that represent a move away from totally passive roles are harder to pin down. The following two questions guided the categorisation:

- Were the children given explicit roles, that is, did the authors themselves assign an active role and evoke relevant literature?
- If these active roles were mentioned, did the children *actually* work alongside adults in partnerships (strong form of research 'with' children) or did they in fact still act as data sources, albeit working with participatory tools (weaker form of research 'with' children)?

The rest of the chapter will be devoted to exploring the examples moving from research 'on' and 'about' children towards research 'with' children.

A classic example of a study 'on' children is Tragant et al. (2017), which aimed to compare two intensive language learning contexts by measuring the learners' spoken and written performances both before

5.6 Studies on the 'on-about-with-by' Continuum

and after their courses in order to determine which programme may be more effective in driving language learning forward.

Example 1

Tragant et al. (2017) *Language Teaching Research*	Comparison of two domestic summer English programmes	Spain	Pre-test and post-test design/questionnaires, oral narrative task based on pictures/ written narrative based on comic strip and a dialogue task/ complexity, accuracy and fluency measures and lexical richness/ stats	11–13	Passive 'on'

Both groups of learners experienced an intensive language programme, with 58 learners in an informal summer camp and 47 learners receiving intensive instruction at a language school. The research questions were geared toward identifying similarities and differences between these two experiences in terms of which intensive programme helped learners to improve their L2 more effectively. Data gathered included interviews with the programme directors some observations, and questionnaires administered to teachers and other adults in both contexts. With regard to the learners, the emphasis was put on the pre- and post-tests to determine what changes occurred from the beginning to the end, while additional information about their learning histories, opinions, motivations and perceptions about their experiences was also elicited using questionnaires. Three tasks were used to measure the children's performances: a picture-based narrative task (oral task), a story-writing task and a dialogue-filling task (two written tasks). The analysis of the pre and post performances was based on comparisons of scores for fluency, complexity, accuracy and lexical richness. Repeated measures of ANOVA were used to determine any significant differences. Overall, the statistical data suggested that the summer camp had a slight advantage in terms of linguistic gains in the oral domain, but otherwise the results appeared to be quite comparable. The authors conclude that both programmes are beneficial since the 'post-tests tended to be significantly higher than... the pre-tests, both for the oral and written tasks' (p. 560).

While the differences between the variables can be summarised in neat tables and the numerical analysis of the differences is indisputable, it is interesting to note that comparisons of language programmes or treatments often do not produce results as clear-cut as we would like, with the consequence that in fact both programmes come out quite similar. With its elegant pre-post design, this is a classic study that can be categorised as research 'on' children.

The second example is a study by Shintani (2015), which also makes use of the pre- and post-test experimental design, but here the quantitative data is supplemented with extracts of interaction between the teacher and the children, analysed using conversation analysis.

Example 2

| Shintani (2015) *TESOL Quarterly* | Incidental grammar acquisition | Japan | Treatment/pre- and post-tests/stats/extracts from interaction | 6 | Passive 'on' |

The aim of the paper was to compare two treatments: FonF (incidental focus on form, when learners occasionally and spontaneously shift to form from meaning in a task) and FonFs (explicit focus on form, where the teacher introduces the same words using a present-practise-produce (PPP) methodology). Both types of instruction afforded learners exposure to and opportunity to use and understand plural 's' and the copula 'be'.

The research questions were:

- How did the interactions differ in the two treatments?
- How did they provide opportunities to notice the plural 's' and the copula 'be'?
- Did participation in both FonF and FonFs result in incidental acquisition of plural 's' and copula 'be'?

The participants were thirty Japanese children aged 6 who were complete beginners. They were divided into FonF and FonFs groups, and 30-minute lessons were repeated nine times over five weeks. The teacher focussed on a set of thirty words to teach (a set of twenty-four nouns plus six nouns in plural). The FonF group did three 'listen and do' tasks. The children chose a card and matched it with the teacher's commands by putting cards on the correct part of the map (zoo and supermarket). At the same time, the control group (i.e. the FonFs group) repeated words after the teacher and used game-like activities to practise the words in a PPP format.

5.6 Studies on the 'on-about-with-by' Continuum   121

Pre-test/post-test and a delayed post-test (one week before, one week after and six weeks after) were administered to measure the effects of these two distinct treatments. Two tests measured the learners' knowledge of plural 's': a multiple-choice comprehension test measured receptive knowledge, and the Wug test measured productive knowledge (Berko, 1958). A different test (i.e. the tell-and-do task) measured productive knowledge of copula 'be' (Shintani, 2015, p. 124). There was no evidence of incidental acquisition of copula 'be' in the interactions and tests for either group, but the FonF instruction resulted in a higher level of incidental acquisition of plural 's' than the FonFs instruction, though only for receptive knowledge. Conversation analysis was used to investigate the nature of the interaction between the teacher and the learners in the two types of classes, and the differences here confirmed the advantage of the FonF group. Qualitative data exploring the nature of the interactions between the children and the teachers in the two treatments was likely to reveal additional characteristics of the children's language use (albeit controlled tightly by the teacher), but such qualitative data in itself does not move the study along the continuum in terms of active roles. As long as the adult researcher is in complete control of the study, even fully qualitative studies that aim to uncover children's unique learning trajectories are still categorised as research 'on' children if the children's roles remain passive.

Still within the passive category, the next study is a good example of research 'about' children rather than 'on' children because the authors' primary goal is to find out from the children how they experienced some assessment tasks. The authors used traditional interviews to elicit responses from the children.

Example 3

Winke et. al. (2018) TESOL Quarterly	Young learner tests and their demands for NS and NNS children	USA	NS and NNS children took tests/interviews	7–8	Passive 'about'

Nineteen children aged 7–9, including both non-native speaker (NNS) and NS children participated in this study to give feedback about the Cambridge Michigan Language Test in both its Bronze and Silver versions. Even though these are standardised, validated tests, the authors suspected that hidden cognitive demands in the test items may mean that even NS children would sometimes struggle. In order to tease out any such cognitive difficulties, the participants were interviewed about their experiences immediately after taking the test, while it was still fresh in their minds. First of all, a parent questionnaire was given out to gather information about each child's background, then the children were videotaped while taking the test. After finishing the test, they were asked to draw a picture of the test-taking experience, and finally, one of the researchers (using the children's L1) interviewed them. They were asked which items in the test they found easiest and most difficult and why, and how they decided to choose a particular answer to these questions. This process revealed several items in the test that did indeed hide cognitive difficulties or problems for NS children as well. The incorrect responses stemmed from a lack of assessment literacy knowledge on the children's part or age-related cognitive limitations rather than deficits in English. The researchers commented that the results from the interviews provided insights that their quantitative data could not provide (which was reported in another publication), namely, what exactly the children were thinking while being tested, why they selected the responses that they did, and whether those selections stemmed from a true measurement of the construct or from construct-irrelevant issues. The researchers conclude that standardised language tests for children, even those already psychometrically reliable and valid, can be improved upon by interviewing child test-takers.

The researchers were genuinely interested in the children's views, but the children were invited to respond to specific adult questions only. The children were warmly welcomed, given a toy as a token of appreciation and asked to draw something first of all, presumably to ease them into the interview and have a chance to express their overall feelings visually. However, the scope of the interview was narrow in the sense that the researchers were only interested in the children's experiences inasmuch as those fitted with their own agenda. This of course makes perfect sense given the research questions, but it also illustrates the point that just because children were interviewed, it does not mean that their status has changed from passive to active.

Studies like this (research 'about' children) are still very much needed in our field because very little is known about children's views and perspectives in general. What could push a study like this more into the next category is the use of specific participatory tools which could be negotiated 'with' the children and which would allow the children's perspectives to come to the fore in a more spontaneous manner.

5.6.2 Towards Research 'with' Children

The next two studies are examples from the sample that pushed the children's status along the continuum towards research 'with' children. They still represent 'weaker' forms of research 'with' children, but they are definitely encouraging explicitly active roles for the participating children.

Both studies were initiated and conceptualised by the adult researchers and both aimed to gain insights from children (by giving them serious roles/tasks) to ultimately improve teaching/learning processes. The first aimed to improve learning processes by bringing the children and the teachers more closely together, while the second paper aimed to draw curriculum and material designers' attention to what children advise about effective learning materials, in particular online games. The second paper also involved a type of research training or targeted preparation for the task before the children were consulted about their views. This is significant in that appropriate training may help to elicit more meaningful feedback as opposed to ad hoc feedback where children may not have the chance to think more deeply about the questions they are presented with.

In D'Warte (2021) the children in an Australian multilingual classroom were asked to document and reflect on their own linguistic practices, both inside and outside the school context. Research 'with' children and the related literature are evoked in the methods section of the paper, and it is therefore a good example of a study where the author explicitly frames the research as one where children are assigned active roles. In fact, the author asks, 'What happens when young people are positioned as researchers of their own practices: studying the ways they talk, listen, read, write and view in one or more languages and or dialects inside and outside of school?' (p. 14).

Example 4

D'Warte (2021) *Language Teaching Research*	Working with culturally and linguistically diverse young people	Australia	Visual methodologies/ language mapping/ revisiting data from two classes from a larger study/linguistic ethnography/ design research/ observations/field notes and recorded lesson segments/student-produced language maps/ focus group interviews	10–12	Active weaker form of research 'with'

This paper focusses on group interviews and the content of fifty language maps created by the children. The map activity encouraged students to think about themselves as learners and language users, reflecting on their identities and cultural practices. The children were given the following prompt for creating the maps: 'Think about the ways you communicate every day, reading, writing, talking, listening and viewing in one or more languages inside and outside of school and use blank A4 paper and colouring materials to map out or draw what you do' (D'Warte, 2021, p. 19).

The author argues that the children were actively involved in exploring their own language use, practices and identities, producing interesting insights that fed into the adult's research questions. The map making indeed gave the children some space and control over how to respond to the adult's question. With close connections between pedagogy and research, this study feeds into improving everyday practice in these classrooms. The more the teachers understand about the children's multilingual practices, the better they can support these learners in their everyday teaching. The study encouraged students to share experiences and to validate their identities and languages, all of which can be an important source of energy for future learning. As a result of this project, teachers initiated dual language book reading programmes and encouraged multilingual story creation in different learner groups. While the children probably enjoyed this process and benefited in terms of their wellbeing, as far as the research design was concerned, it was the adults' research, their questions, their motivation to improve things and their ways of going about what they wanted to find out. Children had some control over the data, that is, they could choose what to say, what to draw or what to put the emphasis on. This is design fits with the weaker type of research 'with' children.

Finally, Butler (2017b) represents the strongest form of active involvement in the sample.

Example 5

Butler (2017b) *Language Teaching Research*	Motivational elements of digital games: children's game design	Japan	Mixed method: analysis of discussions, children's final game designs/peer evaluations	11–12	Active 'with'

The design of the project goes some way to incorporating the children's views to shape the study. Although it is still not a collaborative

5.6 Studies on the 'on-about-with-by' Continuum   125

research endeavour between adults and children, in the sense that the children did not participate in setting up the study and did not take part in all the stages of the research, they certainly played a serious role by offering consultation. Even though it was not explicitly labelled as training, the children did receive support and were prepared for the task of creating their own games by a professional game designer.

Eighty-two Japanese sixth graders (11–12-year-olds) who all played computer games were included in the study. The team of researchers included the author, two curriculum development specialists, a professional game designer, the students' classroom teachers and the children themselves. The children were invited to design computer games for effective vocabulary learning in English. First of all, they were asked to recommend features of games that they considered attractive based on their experiences. Then the children were given thirty-five new words to learn and asked to think about what the best strategies might be to learn these words. Their ideas for the strategies were discussed and recorded. Then the professional game designer drew storyboards to illustrate how to go about designing computer games. Having learnt about professional game design, in the next lesson, the children designed their own games in groups. They decided on the type of game and what elements they wanted to incorporate. Each group drew a storyboard for presentation and each class chose the best designs. These games then became the target of further exploration.

The games that children actually designed made use of elements such as having clear rules and goals, sounds and visual effects, speed and time limitations, and being cognitively challenging. Incorporating elements such as repetition and obstacles, and allowing the players to have greater control/autonomy, were also popular. Finally, children's peer-evaluations confirmed that game designs that utilized elements such as fantasies/stories, challenging, control, and feedback were important to them.

(Butler, 2017b, p. 746)

The children had a consultative role in the study since the adults asked for their views in terms of what design features they felt needed to be in an effective game task. But the children were not just consulted ad hoc; in fact, they were carefully prepared for their roles as consultants. Butler suggests that both teachers and curriculum designers might take note of children's voices more seriously as stakeholders in education.

Strong forms of research with children, where children closely collaborate with adults throughout the whole of the research study (by contributing to asking the questions, deciding the methods, collecting and analysing the data and disseminating the findings), were not found in the sample. Studies where children engaged in their own research or were being enabled to engage in their own research were also absent in the sample.

While 96% of the studies assigned passive roles to children, a handful of studies were found that showcased more active roles (moving from research 'about' to research 'with' children). The above examples illustrate gradually increasing degrees of active involvement on the part of the children, thus pointing to a direction where more research is needed.

5.7 Conclusion

Having looked at the roles and status of children in recent applied linguistics research, the next chapter will be devoted to these questions: What types of projects are possible or desirable in applied linguistics with children's active involvement? What kinds of partnerships are possible, and how can more research 'with' and 'by' children be implemented with benefits for the L2 classroom and beyond? Chapter 6 will follow the logic of this chapter in that gradually increasing levels of active involvement on the part of the children will be illustrated by suggesting studies that represent research 'about' children, moving on to weaker forms of research 'with' children and finally stronger forms of research 'with' children as well as research 'by' children in applied linguistics.

6 Filling the Gap: What Kind of Research Is Needed?

6.1 Introduction

This chapter will explore the immediate implications of the gap that was identified in terms of what type of research involving children is missing in applied linguistics. Seventeen studies, selected with a view to showcase a variety of possibilities, will be discussed to illustrate various opportunities to incorporate children's contributions by assigning them roles that are increasingly more active (i.e. from weaker forms of research 'with' children to stronger forms), including studies that are framed as research 'by' children or child-led research.

These studies have been drawn from a range of disciplines, including health education, climate education, social work and global citizenship education, with a few examples in L2 education. The variety of disciplinary backgrounds underlines one of the original aims of the volume, which is to encourage cross-fertilisations across disciplines interested in children and childhood. I will summarise each study and discuss the children's role and status as well as how the study could inspire work in L2 classrooms by applying various adaptations. Given that these summaries are brief and focussed on the children's status and roles, readers are most definitely also encouraged to read the studies in full and draw their own conclusions.

The intention is that researchers in applied linguistics can adapt these approaches, tools and ways of working with children to suit their own research goals, interests and needs.

There is no suggestion that these studies are 'better' than traditional studies 'on' children, or that the ones that involve higher levels of active involvement are the better than the less active ones. The studies have simply been selected to showcase a range of possibilities highlighting increasingly high degrees of active involvement with children of different ages to serve as an 'ideas bank'.

6.2 A Move from Studies 'on' and 'about' to 'with' and 'by' Children

As was discussed in Sections 2.8 and 3.4, the labels of research 'on', 'about', 'with' and 'by' children represent somewhat crude categories, meaning that individual studies can fall between two categories; in particular, within the category of research 'with' children, both weaker and stronger forms of participation have been detected. This chapter will discuss seventeen sample studies which have been listed in an *approximate* order of increasingly more active roles assigned to children and young people.

When we ask children to tell us about their language learning experiences, they are still passive respondents in that it is the adult researcher alone who is controlling the agenda. Nonetheless, by focussing on their views and listening to their concerns, it is reasonable to suggest that this type of research is moving away from being 'on' children towards research 'about' children.

When the adult researcher is taking steps to consider how certain tools and techniques, such as participatory action research (PAR) tools or arts-based, visual tools may help the children to express themselves more naturally, to communicate more readily, and if the children have at least *some* control over shaping the research by deciding what to draw or take a photo of (and what not to), we are beginning to work 'with' children, even if these are the weakest forms of active participation. Adults initiate the questions, but the intention is to facilitate children's potentially more active participation by attempting to diffuse inherent power dynamics (Truscott et al., 2019) and make the children feel at ease and ready to share their thoughts.

The next move along the continuum is when adults decide to share responsibility with the children for parts or the whole of the research, collaborating with them as partners in all stages or explicitly handing over tasks such as setting the research questions, sharing data collection and data analysis. If this is the case, training (Kellett, 2005, 2010a) or for younger children 'capacity building' (Lundy et al., 2011, p. 723) will often be incorporated to prepare children for their active roles. These are definitely projects that fall into the category of research 'with' children and likely to be labelled as stronger forms of this type of research. Finally, the adult researchers' ultimate goal may be to enable children to do their own research, in which case research training of some kind is a must before children embark on their own projects. Studies that aim to hand over to children in this way will be labelled as research 'by' children. However, even in studies that are labelled research 'by' children, the adult researcher's role is still crucial in overseeing the whole process and supporting the children from the background.

Table 6.1 is a summary list of seventeen studies, intended as examples of the kinds of projects that could be adapted or built on further in child second language education and applied linguistics.

- The first category (Examples 1–7) of studies attempted to elicit children's views about important matters. Some used traditional interview techniques while others used participatory tools and techniques with the aim of giving the children at least some control and choice over the research process. Where children's opportunities to shape or control the research process is minimal, the study is labelled as research 'about' children or a weak form of research 'with' children.
- The second category (Examples 8–15) includes studies where children have been explicitly labelled in roles such as advising and consulting the adults about the research, setting research questions, collecting and analysing data, and disseminating the outcomes. Some of the studies emphasise a close partnership with adults in all stages, while others focus on just one or two of these stages and roles. In this sense, even though all are labelled as research 'with' children, they still represent various degrees of active participation.
- The final category (Examples 16–17) of studies focusses on examples where children have been enabled to undertake their own research (i.e. research 'by' children, or child-led research).

The studies in Table 6.1 also represent a variety in terms of the ages of children involved (from 3–18 years of age), the aims of the adults, and whether the study was embedded in the classroom or seen as a separate activity outside the classroom. Some studies were on a large scale (involving multiple teams of researchers in several countries) whereas others were small-scale studies, involving just one teacher or researcher with a small group of children. Some studies are short in duration while others are much longer, with the longest example lasting several academic years.

6.3 Category 1: Eliciting Children's Views about Important Matters (Examples 1–7)

In applied linguistics, children are very rarely asked about important matters, such as teaching, learning or assessment, as these are considered adult territories. Yet, as the first study of our sample illustrates, insights from children can be enlightening, with the potential to feed into policy decisions, material development or building pedagogical

Table 6.1 Summary of studies: Increasing levels of active participation

Study	Aim	On-about-with-by	Tools	Child role	Research training	Classroom, community	Duration
Example 1. Butler et al. (2021) (with 9–12-year-olds)	Better understanding of children's needs; take them seriously as stakeholders	About	Semi-structured interviews	Passive, respondent to adult questions	No	Research project in school	Short
Example 2. Sargeant and Gillett-Swan (2015) (mean age 11 years)	Learner voice will enhance teaching learning; teacher education	About-with (weaker form of 'with')	Open-ended survey	Passive, respondent; minimal control	No	Research in schools, international	Short
Example 3. Griffin (2019) (with 8–10-year-olds)	Better understanding of children	About-with	Adapted interviews	Passive, respondent	No	Research project in school	Short
Example 4. O'Kane (2008) (8–12-year-olds)	Better understanding of children	About-with	PAR tools in interviews	Passive, respondent	No	Research in institution	Short

Example 5. Rouvali and Riga (2019) (3–5-year-olds)	Understanding children to feed into policy	About with	Multiple tools, visual, mapping, observation	Passive-active; flexible	No	Embedded into classroom; teaching/researching	Longer
Example 6. Pincock and Jones (2020) (10–14-year-olds)	Understanding needs and fostering wellbeing	About-with	Multiple tools, visual, mapping	Passive-active	No	Research project in community	Longer
Example 7. Kirova and Emme (2008) (with 9–11-year-olds)	Assist newly immigrant children to access school culture	About-with	Multiple tools, arts-based, visual and drama	Passive-active	No	Research project in school but not embedded into classroom practice	Longer
Example 8. Alerby and Kostenius (2011) (with 12-year-olds)	Understanding children's health	With	Survey	Active: consultants	No	Research project in schools	Short
Example 9. Niemi et al. (2015) (with 10-year-olds)	Teacher education	With	Action research	Active; data gathering; photos	No	Embedded in classroom practice; learning/researching	Longer

(*continued*)

131

Table 6.1 (cont.)

Study	Aim	On-about-with-by	Tools	Child role	Research training	Classroom, community	Duration
Example 10. Coppock (2011) (with 10–11-year-olds)	Programme evaluation, school improvement	With	Programme evaluation	Active: data collection, peer interviews	Yes	Research in school	Longer
Example 11. Porto (2016) (with 9–13-year-olds)	Intercultural citizenship training	With	Case study	Active: data collection and analysis	No	Embedded into classroom practice	Long
Example 12. Rout (2017) (with 13–14-year-olds)	Teacher education	With	Action research	Active: data collection and analysis	Yes	Embedded in classroom practice	Long
Example 13. Liebenberg et al. (2020) (with 12–18-year-olds)	Improving mental health and wellbeing	With	Action research	Active in all stages; focus on analysis	Yes	Research in community	Long
Example 14. Smit (2013) (with 6–16-year-olds)	Developing participatory school culture	With	Action research	Active in all stages	Yes	Research in school and museum	Long

Example 15. Cutter-MacKenzie and Rousell (2019) (with 9–14-year-olds)	Improve climate education	With	Ethnography/ maker space/ play space; para-academic	Active in all stages	Yes	School-based research	Long
Example 16. Wright et al. (2019) (with 7–11-year-olds)	Raise attainment in STEM	By	Surveys	Active in all stages	Yes	Embedded into school/ classroom practice	Long
Example 17. Pinter (2019) (with 9–10-year-olds)	Explore children's experiences as first-time researchers	By	Surveys	Active in all stages	Yes	School-based project but extra-curricular club	Long

theory. In Butler et al. (2021) semi-structured interviews were used to seek children's views about their L2 English assessment tasks. Though previous studies had already indicated that children can articulate their thoughts about issues relating to their assessment, the authors argue that these insights had not been taken seriously, that is, children's perspectives had not been incorporated into any existing language assessment literacy (LAL) models. This study makes recommendations that input from the children, as important stakeholders, should be incorporated into LAL models.

Example 1 Butler et al. (2021) L2 Learning (Testing, SLA, Applied Linguistics)

This study focusses on children's language assessment literacy (LAL), which is understood as stakeholders' knowledge and skills used to design assessment tasks and make use of the results. In most research LAL is studied from teachers' or test designers' point of view, but here the authors were keen to explore whether children could contribute to this traditionally adult topic.

The participants were twenty fourth- and sixth-grade children (aged 9–10 and 11–12) in China. After taking some mock English tests, which were similar to the kinds of test questions that children were exposed to in school or outside school English classes, the children were invited to participate in semi-structured interviews that aimed at exploring their understanding of relevant assessment issues and their views about the tests.

'The interview questions covered three major categories identified by previous LAL models, namely, students' understanding of the following: (a) assessment knowledge (their concept of assessment purposes and theories); (b) assessment skills (their views of assessment formats, procedures and content); and (c) assessment principles (their notion of fairness and feedback issues)' (Butler et al, 2021, p. 436).

The transcribed interview data were analysed using a qualitative thematic analysis method. The results suggested that the children already had substantial assessment literacy-related knowledge, and they were able to articulate their views, such as expressing a desire for more communicative tests rather than form-focussed tests. A lack of authenticity was noted by the learners, especially in listening tests. They also commented that they wanted more cognitively challenging and enjoyable assessment tasks and suggested that teachers should consult learners when it comes to test design and development. Students also noted that not everyone has a chance to learn extra English outside school, and therefore testing should take that into account.

Even though the adult-initiated interview questions rendered the children largely passive, using mock tests as a prompt was an important way of encouraging informed and meaningful responses. Having experienced the tests, the children were ready to tell the adults about them and were able to respond to the adult-initiated questions.

Conversations that encourage learners to think about the functions and the consequences of assessment can develop greater awareness of their own learning processes and help them understand about assessment criteria as well as how to make sense of assessment results. These are important gains from both the children's and the adults' point of view.

Many other aspects of language teaching and learning can be similarly explored using ordinary semi-structured interviews with children. For example, children may be asked about their views of various tasks, textbooks, games or other materials of all kinds. Just like in the study above, it is desirable to invite the children first *to experience* the tasks, games or materials in question before they are asked to express their views. These conversations may be conducted individually, in pairs or in small groups, inviting either unique individual or consensus views and leaving room for children's spontaneous comments and contributions in addition to the questions prepared by the adults. Paying attention to spontaneous comments and responses that take the adult away from the list of pre-decided questions can also be a conscious way of listening to the children beyond what we expect to hear.

In the next study, Sargeant and Gillett-Swan (2015) also set out to canvass children's views about important matters, but more generally about their school lives. The questions were decided by the adults, but they were designed to be open-ended, allowing for all kinds of different types of feedback from the children. It can be argued that such open-endedness invites feedback that is more unique to the children and less framed by adult priorities.

Data were collected from hundreds of children from both primary and secondary schools, with the ultimate goal of providing food for thought for teacher education (i.e. raising teachers' awareness about the importance of listening to learner voices). To promote the acceptance of more inclusive teaching and learning practices in classrooms for both pre-service and in-service teachers, information and insights from learners play an important role. In line with the first study (Butler et al., 2021) the authors argue that incorporating the views of all stakeholders in teaching and learning (i.e. including the views of the children) is the most effective way of 'supporting student wellbeing as well as educational success' (Sargeant & Gillett-Swan, 2015, p. 178).

Example 2 Sargeant and Gillett-Swan (2015) Teacher Education, Voice-Based Approach

This large-scale international study with many hundreds of young adolescent respondents (mean age 11) from several countries, including Australia, England,

Italy, Sweden and New Zealand, used an open-ended questionnaire that was designed to gain insights from children about issues that they wanted to flag up as important in their school lives. A range of open-ended questions were asked in the study, although this example focusses on just two questions.

- What is the one question that you have for adults?
- What is the one thing you would like the adults to know?

More than 400 responses were received for the first question and more than 800 for the second question.

The children were asked to give a free account, using their own words in their responses. Due to the fact that large numbers of responses from various countries were received, the authors suggest that their data reflected a compelling picture of young adolescents' overall experiences. A bottom-up inductive approach to data analysis revealed that the data sets from the different countries showed a great deal of similarity.

The children had a lot to say. They had a strong desire to seek acknowledgement from adults, and they were largely dissatisfied with the adults' lack of appreciation of their true capacities. They voiced concerns about schools being stressful places and wanted the adults to take children seriously. They expressed a clear desire to work with adults collaboratively and pleaded with the adults that they stop thinking they know everything! They also painted a picture that being a young adolescent means living through a period of your life that is full of change, with the ups and downs of identity development. In seeking to develop independence, they asked the adults to be more attuned to these processes.

The authors provide compelling evidence that children's voices need to be trusted and listened to, and that their capacities should not be underestimated. Any teacher and researcher will find student voice a useful resource. 'By suspending their pre-existing assessment of student capacity and engaging with their perspectives, teachers may reveal a positive resource that will enhance the learning and teaching process: the student voice' (Sargeant & Gillett-Swan, 2015, p. 187).

Inspired by this example, similar questions may be posed to children about their L2 experiences at school, outside school or both:

- What is the one thing you want to tell your English teacher?
- What is an important question you have for your headteacher?
- Is learning English or other languages important to you? Why or why not?
- Tell us how you think English/other L2 classes could be improved?
- What is the one thing you want to tell your teacher about using L1/L2 or other languages at home?

Naturally, once such responses have been elicited, it is important to take the responses seriously and feed the children's views into an action plan for change, no matter how small-scale. Data gathered from large numbers of students can be used to feed into continuous efforts to improve school performance but will also contribute to students' sense of wellbeing and a realisation that their views are respected. Asking for feedback in a systematic way, in a manner that does not automatically impose adult frames on the questions, may be a particularly effective way of exploring student voice.

The next two examples are still interview-based studies, but they explicitly highlight some ways in which basic interview techniques may be adjusted using movement or body positioning or by incorporating so-called participatory activities that require the hands-on manipulation of artefacts. These adjustments can make interviews more suitable and enjoyable for younger children and for children who feel less comfortable with providing verbal responses to adult questions.

Griffin (2019) was interested in talking to children about their reading habits but wanted to make sure that the children felt at ease and wanted to encourage even the shyest and quietest children to contribute.

Example 3 Griffin (2019) Education, Literacy Studies

Griffin worked with 8–10-year-old children in the USA, talking to them about their reading experiences, identities and their motivations to read. In order to make the interview process more suitable, the traditional question–answer routine was replaced by so-called shoulder-to-shoulder and mobile interviews, which both worked well because the pressure of 'eye contact' was eliminated and a more informal atmosphere between the adult and the child was naturally created.

The shoulder-to-shoulder interview is a simple technique involving both the adult and the child sitting on the floor, on the carpet or against the wall, with their shoulders together. The child is asked to bring along a toy, a book or some other artefact, which will be the starting point of the conversation, with both the adult and the child fixing their gaze on this object rather than looking at each other. According to Griffin, not all children will opt for the shoulder-to-shoulder interview when they are offered a choice between this and the traditional interview, but for some this is an excellent way of relaxing into a conversation with an adult.

In shoulder-to-shoulder interviews, it is important to let the child lead the conversation at the beginning about the object in hand, then continue with some small talk to create opportunities to smile or laugh together. As the interview progresses, some children may be ready for eye contact, while others may prefer to continue in the same way.

Griffin also recommends the so-called mobile or walk-around interview. This type of interview has many possible versions, but all share a feature of movement, which can be preferable than sitting down in a formal manner. When the adult researcher follows the child around (in the school, on the playground, in the classroom or in any other relevant venue or space), the child's movements can trigger meaningful questions. The adult researcher has the added advantage of observing the child's natural environment.

In these interviews children are still largely passive participants, but the difference is that they may feel more able and willing to contribute than in traditional interviews, which insist on eye contact and a certain level of formality. Talking to an adult (other than their own teacher or parent) may well be a novel experience for many young children.

Mobile and shoulder-to-shoulder interviews (which means sitting next to each other against the wall rather than facing each other) may be particularly useful tools if the adult researcher has limited time to strike up a relationship with the children and if the circumstances do not allow for multiple visits. However, these adjustments made to the conventional interview need careful planning in terms of the physical context. Griffin emphasises the importance of a suitable venue and space. Interviews work best in familiar places where the temperature, light, visual stimuli and noise and activity levels are all appropriate. Repeating back answers to check what was communicated and understood should be accompanied with positive non-verbal cues, such as nodding, smiling and relaxed body language.

In an L2 context, for a shoulder-to-shoulder interview a child might be asked to bring along a drawing or an artefact significant in their language learning or linguistic identity development, and the adult researcher can start the conversation based on this drawing (e.g. Ibrahim, 2021). Walking interviews might be useful in some contexts where children's language use or learning is associated with certain spaces.

The next example gives details of three classic PAR techniques, all of which, or any one of which, can be incorporated into conversations and interviews with a wide range of age groups. In addition to helping to reduce the reliance on verbal reports, these tools may go some way to softening the effect of the power distance between adults and children and may encourage some children, who might feel an initial reluctance, to talk more freely to the adult.

Example 4 O'Kane (2008) Social Work with Looked-After Children

This paper describes three PAR techniques which were used to understand the extent to which looked-after children were able to participate in decision making about their own lives in local authority care contexts.

The Decision-Making Pocket Chart
The decision-making pocket chart invites the child to draw a chart with two axes: 'what sort of decisions' and 'what people'. In this study, children (8–12 years old) in social care were asked about the decisions that they could make about their lives with regard to, for example, their clothes, their school holidays or their pocket money. The children were encouraged to connect each decision with certain people and then reflect on these connections.

The Pots and Beans Activity
The second activity, 'pots and beans', invites children to evaluate and reflect on ideas, statements or even abstract concepts. For this activity the adult facilitator brings along a jar of beans and several different pots, which are labelled. The labels are statements that the children are asked to evaluate. They are invited to decide how many beans (out of three) they would like to place in any pot. If you strongly agree with a statement, you can put three beans in that pot.

The Diamond Ranking Activity
This activity introduces a set of statements (usually nine statements) for the children to read and think about together in pairs or small teams. The aim is for them to rank these statements from most important to least important. The activity invites the children to discuss their thoughts and reach a compromise as a pair or a group. The statements can be written by the adult facilitator and/or can be based on previous input/discussion with the children.

The nine statements can be written on Post-it notes, and then a grid with nine squares is constructed in the shape of a diamond, with the most important statement at the top and the least important one placed at the bottom (Figure 6.1). Once a group reaches consensus they can feed back to the rest of the class and compare their responses with other groups' responses.

It is of utmost importance for the adult facilitator to make it clear to the children that there are no right answers, and the ultimate aim of the diamond activity is to spark discussion rather than find 'the answer'. Comparing one's own diamond with others' is a fruitful basis for further discussions between groups of children and the adult facilitator or researcher.

Using the three PAR tools (decision-making charts, pots and beans, and the diamond ranking activity) helped children in O'Kane's study

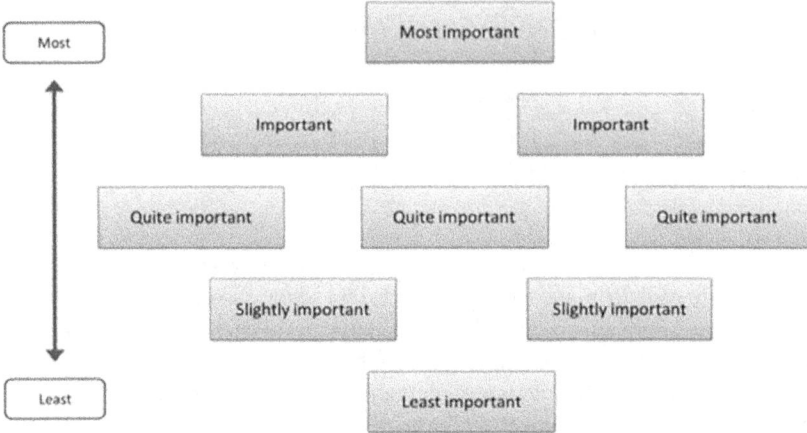

Figure 6.1 Diamond ranking activity template

to talk about their day-to-day challenges freely and flexibly rather than simply being exposed to narrow adult questions. They also enjoyed the hands-on element of doing things and moving things (i.e. placing beans in jars and moving Post-it notes around the diagram), which is described as a type of active communication. The author suggests that these PAR techniques also facilitated explanations about the research process, allowing the children to ask questions and make spontaneous comments on the tools and their usefulness. Since the tools allowed the children to control the process of data collection to an extent, mutual trust and a sense of partnership with the adults were created.

The three PAR tools can be easily adapted to focus on L2-related issues. In fact, some research in applied linguistics has made use of these tools already. Zandian (2015, 2021) used the 'diamond ranking activity' to understand Iranian children's real and imagined intercultural experiences related to their L2 (English). The children worked in groups and ranked nine statements about the importance of various strategies that they might need when they move to an English-speaking country. The children's choices of strategies and their justifications provided rich data that contributed to uncovering their understanding and views about intercultural issues. Similarly, Tabali (2017) asked young Chilean children to rank some L2 (English) communicative gap tasks according to how useful and enjoyable they found them (see Figure 6.2), and this provided important supplementary data when analysing children's performances on the tasks.

6.3 Eliciting Children's Views on Important Matters

Figure 6.2 Empty boxes representing different activities inviting children to place one, two or three beans to evaluate their experiences

The 'decision-making chart' could also be adapted to be used in L2 classrooms. The axes of the chart can be kept the same as above (what sorts of decisions and with what people):

- Who decides which languages I will learn?
- Who decides when I do homework?
- Who decides what books I read in L1 and L2?
- Who decides when I play English games online?

Depending on the context, alternative 'axes', such as 'what sort of activities' and 'with whom' (on my own, with friends, with parents, with teachers, in groups, in pairs, etc.) could be used to explore how children might practise English or other languages. Useful insights can be gained both at the level of the individual child and any larger cohort and the whole class.

Further ideas to exploit the diamond ranking activity can include:

- Most and least useful activities
- Most and least enjoyable activities
- Most and least useful resources
- Most and least useful mobile apps for learning the L2 and other languages
- Most and least popular activities outside the classroom
- Most and least useful practice strategies to remember new words
- Most interesting topics for projects
- Most difficult and easiest tasks
- Most often and least used learning strategies.

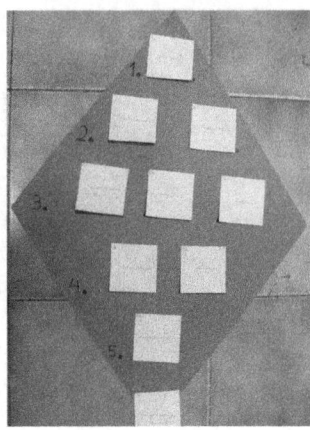

Figure 6.3 Diamond ranking tool (Zandian, 2021)

For all the above topics, nine statements or sentences are needed on Post-it notes (See Figure 6.3). Statements can be replaced or substituted by pictures, drawings or photos. It is also possible to enlarge the diamond to allow for longer texts to go into the various tiles, and the diamond can be extended (for certain types of questions) by adding further tiles (to make, say, 16 tiles), as long as the diamond shape is preserved. If consensus emerges (e.g. the children suggest that certain activities are disliked or unpopular), it is important to act on the outcome and adjust the classroom activities accordingly. Even if it is not appropriate or possible to drop an activity that the children do not like, it might at least be possible to adjust it or reduce the frequency of its use.

PAR tools such as the 'diamond ranking activity' can be used on their own, but in fact it is more common to use several tools together in combination, often in a longitudinal project to ensure that richer data are collected. The next three studies showcase the use of multiple tools.

Multiple tools allow children to have several chances to contribute and communicate their views, and if one tool does not appeal to them, it does not mean that they will be automatically excluded. There is also a cumulative effect resulting from the careful use of multiple tools in that such a design allows for the development of 'thick voices' (Carnevale, 2020, following Geertz, 1973), with messages and voices strengthening each other in the larger data set.

The next study by Rouvali and Riga (2019) utilised multiple creative and visual methods by implementing the 'mosaic approach' (Clark & Moss, 2001) discussed in Chapter 3.

6.3 Eliciting Children's Views on Important Matters

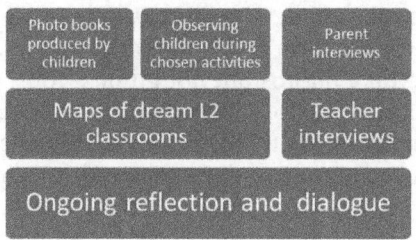

Figure 6.4 Possible components of a mosaic

The most important principle behind the mosaic approach is an active, flexible approach to listening, including not just listening to verbal messages but also non-verbal ones. This is reminiscent of the Reggio Emilia approach, which is described as a 'pedagogy of listening and relationships' (see Chapter 2). By promoting a flexible listening approach, adults can listen to the 'hundred languages' of children (Edwards et al., 1998, p. 344).

The mosaic is built up by combining data from child conferencing, observations, tours, mapping, role plays and the use of cameras (see Figure 6.4). In addition to the children's perspectives, parents', teachers' and researchers' perspectives can also be added to the mosaic. Once the mosaic is assembled and displayed, it is used for further reflection and stimulating ongoing dialogue.

To build a mosaic, Clark (2001) suggests that initial observations are conducted by the adults to prepare for the child conferencing interviews. Then, the child is asked to take some photos and is invited to take part in a guided walk around the classroom or school premises. These walks might be led by the child or a group of children, and the conversations during the walk are recorded. Walking with local guides while observing, asking questions, listening carefully and discussing points raised by the children can be a very rich source of data. Walking tours seem to work even with the shyest of children (see also Griffin, 2019).

Children can take photos during the walking tour and then choose some of these photos to make a map. The map serves as an end product, but it is also 'another vehicle for listening' (Clark, 2001, p. 337) as the children talk about them. Interviews with the child's parent and their teachers or key workers can also be conducted and included as data in the mosaic. The adults will be asked some of the same questions that are asked in the child conferencing interviews, but it is important to stress that adults' responses are complementary and that they are not to challenge the views of children but instead contribute to the richness of the mosaic.

The mosaic approach is flexible in that individual children can opt out and come back in when they are ready. For example, a specific child might like to take photos but not go on a tour, or the other way round, or might not want to participate one day but might another day. Such flexibility does not threaten the overall success of the project because of the large amount of data gathered for the mosaic overall. Clark and Moss (2011) suggest that it is important to commit to a process that will take a long time, and they warn not to draw conclusions too early. Once patterns in the data emerge, it is important to act upon the findings and initiate necessary changes in practice, such as adjusting everyday practice, improving learning spaces or enriching the curriculum.

In a Greek pre-school, Rouvali and Riga (2019) described how they implemented the mosaic approach, which allowed the teachers to become researchers to investigate their own practice by focussing on actively listening to the children. The environment in which the mosaic is implemented needs to embrace trust and care, and adults need to be committed to creating meaning and knowledge in collaboration with the children.

Example 5 Rouvali and Riga (2019) Pre-School Early Years Education

This study describes the implementation of the mosaic approach in a Greek pre-school with twenty-one children aged between 2 and 5 years and five teachers.

The study asked three questions:

- What do the children like doing in this pre-school?
- What are their favourite places?
- What are the most important things for them?

First, observations were conducted followed by adult-led interviews with the children. During this process, the children suggested child-led interviews (i.e. interviewing their peers), and these were incorporated into the flexible design. Digital cameras were given to the children to capture places, people and objects that were important to them in the environment. Every child had a chance to take over fifty photos and was given plenty of time to complete the activity. Then the children were invited to make maps individually or in pairs according to their choice. A basic map outline was given out, and the children were invited to draw places, incorporate some of their photos and complete their maps in their own ways. Finally, the maps were described by the children. They also led a tour of the facilities describing their favourite spaces in the pre-school, both indoors and outdoors. Finally, parent questionnaires and teacher questionnaires were distributed to gain insights from the adults, focussing on the same sort of questions that the children were asked.

The results revealed that children had strong feelings about which places they liked and why, and some of this came as a surprise to the adults. The children were able to reflect on their own experiences deeply and explored their own understandings about life in the pre-school, while the adults gained unique insights into the child's sense of the place. At an institutional level, the children's views were taken into account when budgets for school renovations were allocated.

In L2 classrooms, the mosaic approach offers excellent opportunities to initiate dialogue with children as well as with parents and teachers about topics such as the curriculum, the materials in use or the L2 learning environment. For example, children might be asked to take photos of activities in books or classroom tasks that they particularly enjoy, think they learn from and want to recommend for use. Such photos can be supplemented by talking to children while touring the resources, the school or the library, observing and documenting what the children comment on. The mosaic could be displayed on the wall, and parents as well as teachers can put forward content or recommend interpretations.

The next activity is reminiscent of the mosaic approach in that it combines multiple tools, but this study was conducted with older learners, aged 10–14 years. Pincock and Jones (2020) worked with marginalised youth in Jordan and Ethiopia.

The authors suggest that their tool kit, containing four flexible PAR tools, which were 'my favourite thing', 'community mapping', 'body mapping' and 'friendship circle', helped to address power relationships between the researchers and the children and created spaces where the voices of these children could be heard.

Example 6 Pincock and Jones (2020) Sociology, Wellbeing

This study focussed on exploring children's wellbeing. Four different activities/PAR tools were used, and each participant was invited to contribute to all of these.

My Favourite Things
The process started with asking children to think of a favourite object which they could bring along to the first meeting. The subsequent conversation then used this object as an entry point to explore the significance of it in the children's lives. The object directs the conversation to children's own concerns and interests

and can instigate poignant conversations. This step was followed by an exercise where the children were asked about their worries and accomplishments and invited to talk about their future aspirations. This again allows them to direct the conversation to a large extent.

Community Mapping
Community mapping is an activity allowing the children to define what matters to them in their communities and what services and spaces they have access to. The dialogue about the maps can spark the development of new insights by the children and candid discussions may reveal important factors that the adult was not aware of. Community mapping undertaken in small groups can also lead to new ideas and perspectives emerging in the group and create spaces for collective discussion and an expansion of the children's ideas and concerns.

Body Mapping
Body mapping further contributes to the exploration of the children's lives and wellbeing. The aim is to draw connections between body, mind, feelings and experiences. It starts with a blank outline of a human body and enables the children to raise questions and comments about various body parts and express experiential states such as happiness, excitement, nervousness, anger, frustration or discomfort. A fictitious character might be drawn, or participants can reflect on their own feelings and experiences. If the former is chosen, this can reflect experiences in a striking way but still carry anonymity. This activity can be therapeutic, exploratory and reflective.

Friendship Circle
In friendship circles, children or youth are encouraged to bring along one or two friends with them to the interview. Talking together with a friend can embolden children because they are speaking in front of others with whom they enjoy a high level of trust. This discussion has the potential to reveal interesting insights about peer networks and how peers shape children's views and interactions. Having friends present can also help with readiness or willingness to share ideas and views.

Overall, the authors report that these highly flexible tools were appreciated and enjoyed by the adolescents because they felt at ease in the conversations with adults. The longitudinal design means that the children are not asked just once but encouraged to participate in several activities over time, and they come to see that their views are respected and appreciated. Combining these tools can result in rich data, although 'the quality of data generated will often depend on the researcher's probing skills, their being cognizant of the assumptions the children bring to the table, and ensuring that findings are interpreted

Figure 6.5 Body map–inspired identity text produced by a Polish–English bilingual EAL learner and a Vietnamese–English bilingual EAL learner in England

within a detailed understanding of multi-layered contextual factors' (Pincock & Jones, 2020, p. 9). Adults may have to be trained to work with PAR tools to maintain high-quality conversations.

In L2 classrooms, these tools or a version of them can be used to explore children's perspectives. Significant objects and artefacts can be used to prompt conversations about identity and what different languages may mean or represent for learners. Mapping can be adopted to explore how these languages are used in the community and to illustrate how, when and with whom L2 (or other languages) are used. Body mapping is a further tool to explore language identities in creative ways and explore how various body parts might be associated with children's emotions about different languages (see the responses by English as an additional language (EAL) learners in Figure 6.5).

Finally, in this category, another study by Kirova and Emme (2008) is discussed. They used PAR tools but combined them further with arts-based and drama-based techniques. Arts-based and drama-based approaches encourage emotional and creative responses, further enhancing the potential richness of the children's contributions. Kirova and Emme's study involves several stages of data collection over a longer period of time, which means that the children had the opportunity to think about and reflect on their experiences again and again, while the creative element shapes the design in an unique and emergent way.

The study was conducted in a Canadian school with a large immigrant population. The aim of the adult researchers was to assist newly immigrant children to gain access to their peers' majority culture. The project revolved around creating a fotonovela, which the authors define as a form of arts-based research. A fotonovela 'can best be understood if viewed as a studio in which all participants are involved in a creative process that has the potential to bring them deeper level of insights and knowledge' (Kirova & Emme, 2008, p. 38).

Example 7 Kirova and Emme (2008) Education, Multilingual and Multicultural Schools

A group of twenty-eight children volunteered to be involved in the study. They were invited to join a photo club at lunchtime to explore the idea of a 'fotonovela'. The children were told that the whole project was aimed at creating something useful for future students like themselves.

First, the children were asked to become reporters of school life and take photos in classrooms as well as playgrounds, focussing on anything important that they felt was going on. They were encouraged to take as many photos as possible. All the photos were collected, printed and displayed on the wall. Next, they were asked to comment on their photos and were invited to move them around, arranging them into different categories according to content and intended messages.

At the next stage, with some of the children who were still genuinely interested in exploring school life further, the adults began negotiating possible stories that could be assembled based on the photos that had been arranged into categories. Groups of children began to work on constructing photo-comic style stories using carefully selected photos from the collection. They also superimposed thought and speech bubbles on the photos. Once these stories were ready, the children and the adults agreed to act out these stories, using their bodies, in other words, showing with their bodies what happened (embodied experiences). Some of the stories were about the importance of friendship ties, peer exclusion, rejection, isolation or loneliness; others were about exploring desires, hopes and other feelings and emotions. Dramatisation became a tool for exploring what the children knew about and felt about situations their stories were communicating. The story creation allowed the children to weave in some imagination and convey ideas that were somewhat removed from reality but still had important implications for it.

The final products were shared with others in the school, and the participants developed a well-deserved sense of accomplishment and pride and a sense of belonging to the school (p. 52).

This whole process is described as 'open-ended, playful and spontaneous'. The children felt they were doing something really useful for future students. The authors comment that 'helping others who, like the children who participated in the study, were from another part of the world, to understand the school rules and the peer culture not only gave purpose and focus to their photo club activities but also helped them reflect on and understand their own experiences as newcomers' (Kirova & Emme, 2008, p. 52).

Although the adults designed and managed the study and came up with the research plan, the participatory and creative tools gave the children a great deal of freedom about what story to tell, which pictures to use in which order, what characters to animate and what thoughts and words to give these characters in the comic version of the story. Fotonovelas open up new spaces for dialogue, for resistance and for representation of a new way of knowing (p. 53).

Fotonovelas could be creatively adapted to document language learning experiences (e.g. with a view to explore ideal lessons) to tap into changes in language learning motivation, identities or anxieties. For example, in step 1, children could be asked to take photos of places and activities when they use English and other languages. In step 2, all these photos can be displayed and then categorised to make stories. Then stories can be acted out and written up to share with wider audiences. The actual authoring experience using children's available linguistic resources in a creative way will potentially be a motivating and empowering experience.

So far, the studies in this section have used a variety of PAR tools to explore children's and young people's perspectives and views about various aspects of their lives. The children's roles so far, even though increasingly active, still have not been labelled explicitly as 'co-researchers' or 'researchers'. The Kirova and Emma study with its multiple PAR tools and additional creative tools gave the children perhaps the most amount of freedom to shape the research so far and thus appears to be closest to the category of active participation (research 'with' children). The next category (with eight studies) will showcase some examples where children were given explicitly active roles, working in partnership with adults in the research and (nearly always) explicitly labelled as co-researchers or researchers.

6.4 Category 2: Children in Active Roles (Examples 8–15)

In this category of studies, children are involved in asking research questions, collecting and analysing data, and taking responsibility for disseminating research outcomes. Such participatory research with children holds great benefits in terms of 'promoting the wellbeing and flourishing of children throughout the research process as well as generating knowledge that is more coherent with how children view their wellbeing' (Montreuil et al., 2021, p. 12).

150 *Filling the Gap: What Kind of Research is Needed?*

As discussed in Chapter 5, I categorised these studies as 'research with children' if the children were taking up genuinely active roles in the studies. The following questions were asked before assigning studies to this category:

- Are the children given explicitly active roles?
- Are they working in balanced partnerships with the adults?
- How do the authors label and define the children's roles, if at all?
- Do the authors embed the study in the relevant voice-based, rights-based Childhood Studies literature?

A close scrutiny of children's roles in these studies suggests that some authors label children as co-researchers even when their roles are quite limited, while on the other hand, some children do take active roles but the authors do not explicitly refer to these roles as co-research. For example, children probably shaped the research project a great deal in the Kirova and Emme study discussed in the previous category, but the authors did not label the children as co-researchers and did not give them specific roles as 'data gatherers'. Hence, the study was listed in the previous category although it was acknowledged that the level of active participation was high compared to the other studies in the same category. With these caveats, I now turn to the studies showcasing children in active roles from consultants to co-researchers.

The first study (Alerby & Kostenius, 2011) proposes the idea of inviting children as consultants. This is a minor role but an explicitly highlighted active one in that the adult researchers are seeking insights and guidance from the children before they finalise the design of their research tools aimed for other, comparable child populations. The adult researchers will adjust their draft tools and methods in view of feedback from the children themselves.

Example 8 Alerby and Kostenius (2011) Health Care

The need to consult children about survey construction and sharing the results with them grew out of the research Alerby and Kostenius conducted in Sweden, working with 12-year-old children. The questionnaire that they distributed to large numbers of children in Sweden and several other countries was focussed on children's health indicators.

This study does not discuss the results relating to these health indicators but instead raises concerns about the methodology, and in particular about the problems children faced in filling in the survey.

The researchers found that a large number of questions were unanswered, crossed out or left blank, and at the same time many children chose to write comments on the margin of the pages. The authors refer to these as silent messages or messages that are being silenced. Anything written on the margin is unlikely to be noticed and noted by those undertaking a traditional analysis of the data. Unanswered questions are usually just ignored and discarded, even though they may hide important insights. The authors suggest that despite the designers' efforts to create a child-friendly questionnaire, with so many extra notes on the margin and so many unanswered questions, the creators of the questionnaire did not take the life worlds of the children into account.

Adults who want to use questionnaires with children can invite and involve children in the process of construction in order to have a greater chance of fitting with the intended participants' life experiences. Inviting children to consult with adults at the beginning of the study can engage children deeply and genuinely with research. The willingness of the participating children to fill in the questionnaire is likely to increase, too, when they discover that the survey instrument was designed with significant input from their peers.

After the questionnaires are administered, the child consultants can be informed about the results in follow-up meetings. These can serve as the first step in the analysis, giving adults validation and a better understanding of children's experiences.

In L2 research children can also be invited as consultants to give advice about adult-created tools and activities (Zandian, 2015). Zandian consulted a group of children about the draft questionnaire she designed for a group of 10-year-olds in Iran about intercultural encounters. The children who acted as consultants spotted some wording in some of the items that they felt was difficult to understand and suggested alternative phrases. They also recommended a few additional questions which the adult researcher included in the final instrument. In this way the children actively shaped the adult plan.

The next few studies all position children as data collectors or data gatherers.

In Niemi et al. (2015) the authors describe an action research project in Finland. In this context, when teachers are undertaking action research projects to deepen their own understanding of their classrooms and the children are explicitly labelled as active partners, children as co-researchers document evidence in the classroom so that their teacher can make continuous improvements to their classroom practice.

In the Finnish school system exploring student voice is a priority. Teachers are committed to develop children's skills, using democracy as a tool, which means encouraging children to speak out and make suggestions about practices which are taken for granted. They also promote enquiry-based learning, which starts with the learners' questions and perspectives to build new knowledge, and pupils are encouraged to participate in the evaluation of everyday teaching and learning processes in classrooms as a matter of routine. Listening to children's voices is thus an essential ingredient of everyday teaching.

The adults (one of whom is the teacher) raise the following research questions in the paper:

- What constitutes meaningful classroom pedagogy from the children's point of view?
- How does understanding these experiences contribute to the development of teachers' practical theory?

Example 9 Niemi et al. (2015) Education, Teacher Education

At the start of the study the children were 10 years old. Twenty-five pupils participated, and there were two cycles of data collection.

In cycle 1, the children took photos of their meaningful learning experiences during two learning projects over a period of several weeks. They could take photos any time. About 240 photos were taken, which were described and discussed in videotaped group interviews. Each interview started by pupils explaining their photos.

In cycle 2, three further projects were covered, and photos were taken again but this time mainly in the student teachers' classes. These teachers were taking the classes as part of their practicum, supervised by the class teacher. A further 113 photos were collected.

Following the photo documentation and the group interviews in the first cycle, the teacher conducted a holistic content analysis of the photos, whereas in the second cycle the student teachers were asked to think about the photos and identify any patterns. Finally, the first cycle and the second cycle outcomes were compared and combined.

The children, the teacher and the student teachers all reflected on the photo evidence. The children highlighted mainly positive experiences. Important themes about how the children experienced time and space, belonging to the class and helping each other were noted.

Pedagogical action research of this kind considers all individuals as co-researchers. Photography as a tool was used to make connections between experiences and the reflective stories children were able to tell.

Participatory pedagogy that invites the children as partners in the teaching and learning process can transition seamlessly into participatory action research. Teaching and learning in the classroom and researching become the very same process, blurring these boundaries.

Being fully embedded in everyday practice means that the distinct roles of teachers, learners and researchers also become blurred.

In participatory pedagogy and action research, when children voice their opinions and say that they do not like something, teachers are encouraged to re-think their plan. The children's feedback and consistent documentation of classroom learning give the teacher a new lens to see their own pedagogy through the eyes of the children. Discoveries and surprises allow the teacher to revisit and adjust their practical theories. Such ongoing documentation of learning through the children's eyes could be adopted in L2 classrooms as well, with the commitment to adjusting pedagogy in line with learner feedback.

While Niemi et al.'s study explored ongoing action research relying on the children's documentation of their experiences as data gatherers, in the next study by Coppock (2011), the children also acted data gatherers, but this time they collected data from their peers in another school in an activity that took them outside the walls of their own classrooms.

Here the children were trained to interview other children. They were working in pairs, with one child asking questions and the other one acting as a scribe, supporting each other as a pair of data gatherers. Some scholars have highlighted the fact that children gather different data from their peers (Kellett, 2010a) as compared to adults because of their different relationships with peers and the special dynamics of their peer networks. Although collecting data from peers carries its own challenges (see Chapter 7) in some contexts, this may be a good way to induct children into research as it is often a manageable first step and an enjoyable and satisfying experience.

Example 10 Coppock (2011) Education, School Programme Evaluation

As part of a school emotional literacy programme evaluation, 10–11-year-old children's views were sought. Children were trained to interview others and collected data from peers in another school.

In this study a complex set of tools were used to evaluate an emotional literacy programme, which included data from teachers, parents and children. The children's peer data collection was just one set of data in this complex mix. In one of the schools, the children in year 6 had already completed the emotional literacy programme in question, while in the second school a group of year 5 children were just at the point of getting ready to start the programme. The study was designed to connect these two groups.

First of all, focus group meetings were organised with the year 6 children to explore their experiences of the emotional literacy programme and to discuss their ideas about how to prepare the children in the second school for the same experience. Just before the programme started in the second school, the year 6 children visited the year 5 children and talked about their experiences informally, as well as demonstrating how the emotional literacy project had worked for them. Then the year 6 children interviewed the year 5 children about their hopes and fears. After the emotional literacy project was completed in the year 5 classroom, the peer researchers from the first school came back and interviewed the children again in pairs (one child asking the questions and the other child writing down the answers) to get their views and insights and to record some of what they had learnt. The adult researcher prepared the children for the peer interview by getting them to role play these interviews in advance, and she worked with them on constructing a list of questions to ask. After data collection the peer researchers worked together on analysing and making sense of the responses, and they wrote up short reports to incorporate into the adult researchers' final report.

A project like this can teach children rudimentary research skills which can be called upon again and again and which can be built on in subsequent projects. Some might argue that the children's participation was rather tokenistic, but this is perhaps not that surprising if this was the children's very first opportunity to participate actively in a research study. With more experience, more training and more opportunities to participate actively, children will progress on the continuum of becoming more accomplished researchers. In L2 contexts, children may be able to interview their peers in parallel classes using the L2, and this can be a very satisfying and authentic experience. Peer interviews could focus on anything related to language learning, and role playing while rehearsing as well as actually conducting these interviews with peers in L2 would make for excellent language practice, too.

The next study by Porto (2016) also involved children as data gatherers, even though this role was not explicitly emphasised. The project described by Porto was embedded into English as an L2 classes in two countries, Denmark and Argentina. The children participated first and foremost in this project as L2 users of English tackling important environmental questions, a topic chosen by their teachers. They acquired a range of research skills and took some genuinely active roles in the research, such as interviewing people in their community. And yet, no reference was made to the child-led research literature. Instead, the study was linked to the global intercultural citizenship education literature (Myers, 2006), which aims to develop civic knowledge, skills and attitudes so that learners can develop awareness about global issues and contribute to building a better world. This type of transformative, action-oriented view of education associates itself with discourses of hope (Andrews, 2010; Webb, 2010) and a political stance which suggests that learners need to act upon the world to improve life for themselves and future generations. This deep view of education encompasses the dimension of justice, care and compassion for all, and here in particular the shared struggles for a greener world (Budd, 2013; Dobson, 2003, 2007).

Example 11 Porto (2016) L2 Intercultural Education and Global Citizenship Education

This paper describes an online project relating to ecological and intercultural citizenship in the primary EFL classroom between two schools in two countries, Argentina and Denmark.

The children were aged 9–10 in Argentina and 12–13 in Denmark. The project's goals were to encourage children to explore and reflect on environmental issues both locally, in children's homes, schools and communities, and globally, across countries.

A range of activities were used, such as documenting local green crimes, sorting rubbish at home, at school and in the community, sharing children's drawings and other findings on local environmental issues, analysing texts and media images, engaging in dialogue with others about environmental matters, and making and sharing posters. There were important linguistic aims for the children to communicate their ideas with their peers in another country using English, but all three languages (Danish, Spanish and English) were used throughout, and important products and texts, such as shared posters, were created in all three languages. Students worked together on exploring a range of environmental issues, and during their longitudinal engagement they interacted with each other sharing local concerns and discussing solutions. They analysed and challenged their own assumptions, developed new ways of thinking and engaged in critical thinking skills.

The schools initiated this project because they were interested in the children's voices and trusted them to take interest and ownership of this important topic. The activities transcended the boundaries of the classroom and culminated in taking civic action locally. The children designed street banners to communicate key messages to the local community. They were interviewed by journalists and published their posters in the local paper.

The project was framed as a case study, and the data were analysed using content analysis. Both conversational and documentary data were analysed.

The children developed key skills such as comparing, contrasting, analysing, observing, interpreting, critical thinking and reflecting, and they also undertook surveys and interviews with people in their communities (i.e. collected and analysed data). Even though this was not framed as child-led research, the children's engagement, framed from a different perspective, could in fact represent an example of co-researching.

Intercultural projects with a focus on global citizenship can tap into important content in L2 curricula, especially in immersion and CLIL contexts. This project was originally planned in the L2 classroom with L2 English serving as a lingua franca between Danish and Argentinian children, but it quickly outgrew the classroom as the children engaged in activities that took them into their local communities. They continued their discussions with their peers from another country, deepening their awareness about global citizenship. Even though the children's L2 English proficiency was relatively high in both Argentina and Denmark, it is noteworthy that all their linguistic resources were made use of, and all shared products, such as posters, were created in all three languages.

Despite these very positive outcomes, the author suggests that the project took an extremely long time to plan and execute, required the full commitment of the participating schools and teachers, and was seen as 'extra work' and something that could not be sustained in the current school structures and curricula.

Examples so far have illustrated how children might be involved and positioned as data gatherers documenting their own experiences and eliciting data from peers and others community members. The next study showcases an example where children were involved in all stages of the research from the very beginning of deciding what to explore to the final stages of analysing and disseminating the data they collected.

Rout's (2017) study is a classroom action research project that was undertaken by a teacher in an L2 English class in an Indian primary school (Pinter et al., 2016). Rout (2017) facilitated a research partnership in his own classroom with the children. The goal was to encourage children to participate in all parts of the project, from deciding the focus and the questions to gathering the data and analysing the outcomes. Working with children in this way helps to deepen the children's awareness about their own learning processes. The children's co-researcher activities were embedded into everyday teaching and learning and lasted for several months.

Example 12 Rout (2017) L2 Teacher Education, Action Research

Rout's learners (13 years old) had been involved in diary writing about their experience of reading English story books selected from a mini library. This was a focus the learners chose themselves for the investigation.

After several weeks of reading story books and diary writing, the teacher asked the students to go through their diaries and take note of important points that indicated learning new things. These points were collated, and the class decided to design a questionnaire to evaluate the learning that happened relating to their story project.

First of all, the teacher demonstrated how to write good questions, which was a type of training, and then the learners were trusted to write questions relating to the points that emerged in earlier discussions. The students helped each other to brainstorm and edit the questions. Then the teacher invited a group of learners to design the questionnaire by selecting the most important questions and sequencing them. When the questionnaire was ready, the teacher asked a few volunteers to try it out first. Following the feedback from the trial run, the same group of students finalised the questionnaire before the whole class filled it in.

This allowed the whole class to reflect on their learning experience and to discuss the results.

Figure 6.6 is an extract from the survey the children designed in the class to get some empirical data about how story reading helped them to learn English.

Similar projects to investigate L2 learning-related issues in any classroom could be initiated in partnership between teachers and learners. For example, vocabulary learning strategies, game playing habits or extra-curricular English activities could be explored. The teacher can explore opportunities for training and piloting tools created by the children. Results from the project can be incorporated into presentations and school exhibitions and may serve as the starting point for the next investigation.

It is sometimes suggested in the literature that children enjoy data collection but that data analysis is seen as more laborious and challenging and children as co-researchers often lose interest after the data collection stage is over. The next paper by Liebenberg and colleagues (2020) is an example which discusses how data analysis (a specific stage in the collaborative research partnership) can be undertaken with the active involvement of the children in a way that is both enjoyable and meaningful.

> **Questionnaire**
>
> Read the following statements and circle the answer from the choices given. 5 is the highest and 1 is the lowest.
>
> | | | |
> |---|---|---|
> | 1. | I learnt new words by working on this research project. | 1 – 2 – 3 – 4 – 5 |
> | 2. | I learnt to guess the meaning of new words in the stories. | 1 – 2 – 3 – 4 – 5 |
> | 3. | I learnt to speak English. | 1 – 2 – 3 – 4 – 5 |
> | 4. | I gathered new knowledge and information. | 1 – 2 – 3 – 4 – 5 |
> | 5. | I have become a better thinker. | 1 – 2 – 3 – 4 – 5 |
> | 6. | My memory has become stronger by working with stories. | 1 – 2 – 3 – 4 – 5 |
> | 7. | It gave me motivation and confidence to learn English. | 1 – 2 – 3 – 4 – 5 |
> | 8. | It enhanced my judgement ability. | 1 – 2 – 3 – 4 – 5 |
> | 9. | It gave me the ability of self-assessment. | 1 – 2 – 3 – 4 – 5 |
> | 10. | I learnt how to create new stories. | 1 – 2 – 3 – 4 – 5 |
> | 11. | I learnt how to write new stories. | 1 – 2 – 3 – 4 – 5 |
> | 12. | I got pleasure by working with the stories. | 1 – 2 – 3 – 4 – 5 |
> | 13. | It enhanced my grammatical knowledge of English. | 1 – 2 – 3 – 4 – 5 |

Figure 6.6 Can stories develop our language proficiency? Child questionnaire from Rout (2017)

Liebenberg et al.'s study (2020) was undertaken outside formal classrooms, in the community, with indigenous child participants in Atlantic Canada. The aim of the project was to explore indigenous youth's informal community engagement and wellbeing. The young people were involved in all the stages of the research project in a balanced partnership with the adults. This paper, however, is devoted to the detailed discussion of the data analysis process alone, which many childhood scholars suggest is the hardest and least enjoyable role for children and young people to take on. Yet the authors suggest that children's input into data analysis is important because leaving it to the adults may well distort original voices, even if unintentionally. The young people in this study focussed on making sense of their own data first before comparing their impressions with each other, and then they learnt to use a thematic approach in a creative way based on Braun and Clarke's (2006) guidelines.

6.4 Children in Active Roles   159

Example 13 Liebenberg et al. (2020) Mental Health Research, Wellbeing

The project 'Spaces and Places' explored the role of formal and informal community structures in the engagement of indigenous youth in Atlantic Canada with 12–18-year-old participants. The aim was to understand their engagement in order to support their wellbeing.

The study used visual elicitation tools (i.e. the children took photographs of places where they felt they belonged) before interviews were conducted with each participant, exploring their photos. Data were collected in three communities. Once the data collection stage was over, the adults were keen to find an alternative, creative approach to 'participatory data analysis' without putting too much pressure on the children and youth so that they did not have to code a massive amount of data.

The paper breaks down how the authors included the youth participants in the data analysis process, which they call the participatory thematic analysis. The six steps by Braun and Clarke (2006) were followed. These steps are 'familiarization with data, generating initial codes, identifying themes that reflect collections of codes, reviewing data to understand and explain the meaning and dynamics of themes, maintaining rigor through inter-coder agreement and producing the final report' (p. 4).

First of all, the participants were familiarised with the data set. They listened to their own data (i.e. their own recorded interviews) and looked through their own photos to select material that best described their experiences. They were also told to think about what aspects of their own data they were most comfortable sharing in the group. As a next step, participants made analogue Facebook pages on large sheets of paper, with their photographs and their selected key information displayed in the workshop. Once these posters were up, the participants were able to walk around, read and comment on each other's information. This process allowed them to familiarise themselves with their own and their peers' data sets. This stage concluded with a focus group-style discussion group where they explored the similarities and differences of their data sets.

Once they were all familiar with their own and each other's data, initial codes were assigned to the data set. To facilitate this, two mapping activities (community maps and body maps) and a card game were organised by the adult facilitators to mimic the processes a researcher goes through when undertaking initial coding. The mapping activity was done individually first and then in pairs. This helped participants to identify overlaps and begin to generate some initial codes. Community maps indicated places of safety, meaning and belonging, and the body maps indicated what a healthy, happy young person would look like. Then these two types of maps were connected. During the discussion focussed on the different maps, adult facilitators collected potential codes relating to places, people and activities. These codes were then transferred to cards. Codes from the cards were used to make links with the participants' data. Participants were selecting cards that they felt best described their data, explaining their justification. Initial codes on cards were then grouped together while the participants discussed their reasoning behind what constituted a category. Then themes were generated and coloured strings were used to connect the themes together visually so that these were as clear as possible for further reflection.

Through all this, participants shared further anecdotes and stories which helped with the deeper understanding of the data. All discussions were recorded as the analysis progressed.

Involving children and youth in data analysis ensures that the collective child voice remains central to the process. The discussions recorded in the sessions allow for a deeper appreciation of the data.

The whole process brought the participants together and strengthened their commitment to the research. Findings were shared with local service providers.

This approach to data analysis mimicked what the adult would have done, and yet it was manageable and fun for the children and did not require previous experience of coding. The participants, who learnt to work with an adapted version of the Braun and Clark (2006) approach to analysis, were referred to as co-researchers. Similar creative approaches to data analysis in L2-related projects might be possible to experiment with if the children are willing and interested to take on the challenge of making sense of the collected data. Focussing on one's own data first of all and comparing and contrasting it to other data in the group is a good foundation on which to start this process.

The next study by Smit (2013) describes a research partnership between adults and children where the children were invited to take part in every stage of the project. The student–adult teams (children with academics external to the school) worked collaboratively, exploring teaching and learning matters while the teachers were involved as observers. The unique feature of the study is that the project was moved into a museum in order to avoid the problems resulting from the tension between rigid hierarchical school structures and the democratic processes needed in true collaboration between children and adults.

The museum as a place for learning is seen as a less problematic option than exploring learning and teaching processes within the school, although the authors admit that their long-term goal was to understand adult–child collaborative research better so that it could be incorporated into school life at some point in the future in order to develop a more participatory school culture.

Example 14 Smit (2013) Education, School Development

The project was conducted by teams of teachers and students from several schools working together with museum educators. The focus of the project was about student learning in an external educational setting (i.e. a museum).

Ten teams of students and teachers from both primary and secondary schools (ages 6–16) took part, facilitated by an external educator. The teams worked collaboratively, designing and conducting the investigation and formulating proposals for improvements to the learning processes in that setting. The proposals could refer to the design and organisation of the setting, but also to the teaching methods, educational goals or educational relationship between pupils, teachers and educators. The study was longitudinal, lasting several months, altogether half a school year.

The children received some training in social research. After this preparation phase, the research teams collected data in the museum by means of photographs, video clips, drawings, notes, observations and interviews with staff. Back at the school peers were consulted about how to improve learning conditions further. At the end a research fair, which was like a conference, was organised for the teams to share their data.

The project involved external academics and groups of children working together with museum educators, with the teachers in the background as observers. It is noteworthy that the teachers were impacted by the project in positive ways, and after the completion of the project many of them continued implementing and expanding student participation practices in their classrooms and kept on promoting them among their peers. Domains of teacher change included relationships with students, student motivation and enthusiasm and letting go of controlling everything in classrooms.

It may be an option for some adult researchers to explore collaborative research processes relating to second language learning in venues outside formal school contexts, such as in school clubs, museums or summer camps, thus bypassing some of the immediate structural issues in school contexts. L2 summer camps, for example, can be devoted to child-led projects that are planned and undertaken in small groups into specific areas of interest selected by the children. The more relaxed atmosphere and the fact that longer periods of time might be available to engage in sustained project work can make these less formal contexts particularly suitable for engaging children with research.

162 *Filling the Gap: What Kind of Research is Needed?*

The next study by Cutter-MacKenzie and Rousell (2019) also describes children and adults as co-researchers working together in a third space, a so-called maker space (see Chapter 4). Maker spaces combine serious work with tinkering and fun and are conducive to collaboration and creative experimentation. This longitudinal study encouraged children to engage with research by inviting them to take part in a project focussed on climate change. Since the maker space amalgamates traditional research training with playful artistic expression, the children had the chance to explore a range of creative tools and methods to develop their knowledge about climate change issues and create powerful messages to tackle local issues as well as actually take action.

The maker movement literature discusses the importance of establishing concrete physical spaces where children and adults who share an interest, such as teachers, academic researchers, parents and even siblings and other children of different ages, come together and create things, both physical and digital. The participants in this study had the chance to share, explore, discuss and experiment with different ideas in a 'research maker play space'. Material resources were provided, such as computers, mobile devices or cameras, as well as art and craft materials.

Rather than training children to think and work like conventional academic researchers, in the co-research play space children's development as para-academic researchers was fostered, encouraging them to actively disrupt the conventions of academic research (Cutter-MacKenzie & Rousell, 2019).

Example 15 Cutter-MacKenzie and Rousell (2019) Climate Change Education

In this study, 9–14-year-old children in Australia were invited to join a 'co-research play space' (maker space).

Children were first of all trained in ethnographic interviews and visual approaches and encouraged to interview people about climate change in their schools and communities, including parents, peers, siblings and teachers. In addition to the traditional research training, the children were encouraged to experiment with more artistic ideas, which were playful and broke the conventional rules about traditional qualitative research in social sciences in line with activities associated with maker spaces and play spaces. For example, some children interviewed trees and created imaginary scripts based on such interviews, while others acted out a future world populated by avatars, creating cartoons and blogs and inventing new modes of co-creation. Much of the output

6.4 Children in Active Roles

produced was artistic and playful with political and aesthetic messages that illustrated children's passion and understanding about climate change. The authors labelled the child researchers as 'para-academic researchers' who were encouraged to disrupt normative research protocols and adult expectations by experimenting with artistic media.

The children were given tablet devices to use in the process of their research to make films about climate change. Some of these openly revealed what the children might be thinking and doing when adults were not there controlling the process. The tablet devices acted as a window onto their imaginations, and play spaces offered an excellent medium for experimentation and creative play.

The whole project described by the authors lasted three years and culminated in organising a public exhibition of the data viewed by tens of thousands and radio interviews given by the children.

Authentic external audiences who viewed the children's work made the project even more meaningful in achieving its goal of impacting their community, raising awareness about the climate change agenda.

In schools where staff and children are interested in undertaking projects like the one described above, it would be possible to create research maker or play spaces. For example, in order to explore L1/L2/L3-related issues, children, teachers, researchers and parents can all come together to promote multilingual practices in their communities. Traditional research training would need to be supplemented with artistic opportunities inviting children to explore the use of materials in their artistic collages, self-portraits or family portraits. Children could interview parents and grandparents in the community about their languages, and data analysis could be approached using either traditional or arts-based methods: thematic analysis versus posters, paintings or poetry. In order to make the work that emerges in maker spaces more meaningful, children would also be encouraged to think about the implications of their research work, how it all translates into making a difference or making a change. Local exhibitions and write ups in local newspapers are good ways in which such research can be disseminated. Research maker or play spaces in a school could also encourage projects that focus on issues beyond the L2 classroom.

In the field of second language education, Prasad's work (2013) resonates strongly with this approach. Prasad worked with culturally and linguistically diverse students in Canadian schools while encouraging the children to collaborate with her as co-ethnographers. The children produced linguistic portraits and family language maps which were also supplemented by creative collage work and identity texts containing expressive, artistic and aesthetic messages about their multilingual lives, both real and imaged. These tools allow creative meaning making and encourage reflection, and children can take their time to express their views and recount their stories that seem relevant to the topic of the research exploration, which is the children's bilingual and multilingual identities and lived experiences. These spaces, dialogues and reflections with adults can lead to a transformation of thought and experience.

While the various studies in this section have illustrated various collaborative research endeavours between adults and children, the last section illustrates the possibility of promoting child-initiated and child-led research where the adult explicitly wishes to stay in the background rather than continue in a balanced partnership. In child-led research children are enabled and encouraged to undertake their own projects, asking their own questions, selecting their own topics and collecting as well as analysing their own data. Both examples described here address work that was undertaken with first-time child researchers, that is, children who were trained step by step while undertaking their own studies.

6.5 Category 3: Child-Led Research (Examples 16 and 17)

The first example is a study conducted in an educational centre, while the second study was undertaken in an after-school research club.

Wright et al. (2019) aimed at raising the educational attainment of young Tasmanians in Australia. The project was to be embedded into teaching science by carrying out science investigations linked to the curriculum guidelines in Australian primary schools.

Example 16 Wright et al. (2019) STEM Education in Primary

This paper describes a project where the adult facilitators aimed to introduce children aged 7–11 to conducting survey-based research. The children were introduced to the concept of research and then enabled to do some research on their own.

Fifteen children participated in five two-hour sessions over the course of a two-week period. The children were taught about the role of a researcher, ethics, basic descriptive statistics and how to construct an online survey.

In the introductory session the children learnt about scientific research, familiarised themselves with important research terminology and discussed posters made by previous child researchers. Then they completed a mock survey and discussed any difficulties in filling it in. In groups of three they were given the results of a particular survey question, and they had to think about how to summarise or re-present the information. Each group presented some ideas, and all ideas and solutions were fully discussed.

After this the children began to work on their own surveys with the help of the adult facilitators, who guided them through inputting their questions. The questions ranged from preferred football players, time spent on electronic devices and getting evidence to test the hypothesis that younger children spend more time watching TV than older children.

Once they had their questions ready, they were guided to use the free online platform SurveyMonkey. Then a selection of the survey questions was sent out to students in the school. Approximately ninety students completed the survey. Before analysing the results, game-like activities were used to illustrate various ways in which data could be represented from a survey. The children were then asked to comment on the results of the survey questions (i.e. describe the graph; what does the data tell you?; did anything surprise you?; what were you expecting to find?; tell me a story from the data).

Through the posing of questions, the collection of survey data, the creation of graphical representations, the analysis of the data and then the sharing of stories drawn out of the data, the children experienced collecting evidence to explain phenomena and making data-based decisions.

A session was organised to brainstorm ideas about how to disseminate the results, and the children's suggestions were taken up.

The authors comment on the success of project and claim that the research experience motivated the children to engage in science enquiries and increased their enthusiasm for future research. 'The children actively engaged in the development of science inquiry skills, and effectively communicated new understanding and skills through storytelling. It is anticipated that the larger Tassie Researchers project will foster other children's enthusiasm for data-based scientific research with the goal of promoting future generations of scientists' (Wright et al., 2019, p. 19).

The context-appropriate research training was carefully embedded into the process of researching, and the children's ideas and initiatives were supported with ongoing help, training and discussion. Particular emphasis was put on making sense of authentic data by introducing multiple ways of summarising findings.

The second example (Pinter, 2019) is similar as it describes the steps taken by the adult to guide the children through their first ever piece of research. The participants were a small group of mixed-ability learners (aged 9) from a UK primary school.

The children learnt about research, got inspired by previous child researchers' work, then learnt about features of surveys before creating their own questionnaires, some individually and some in pairs. The real high point of the process was when the children's questionnaires came back with data, some filled in by teachers and some by students in the same school.

Example 17 Pinter (2019) Extra-Curricular Research Club

This study was conducted in an after-school club in a small primary school in the UK, with 9-year-old children who were a mixed-ability group of eight students. Half of the groups were EAL leaners who used an L1 other than English at home.

The project started with bespoke research training which guided the children through the steps of planning, implementing and analysing survey-based research. The whole project ran for only six weeks, once a week on Friday afternoons.

Having sorted out permissions, and after getting to know the children, the first training session introduced some examples of summaries of child-led research from the Open University website to inspire the children and get them thinking about what they might be interested in researching.

Then these same materials (i.e. presentations by previous child researchers) were also used to teach research terminology, which was practised using games.

Then the children were introduced to an authentic survey to familiarise themselves with different question types and provide them with the experience of answering survey questions. The different question types were recorded on posters, and suggestions about writing good questions were elicited and discussed. These posters stayed on the wall for the whole duration of the project.

Then the children began to think about their own topics. They were helped in the process of identifying their research question by filling in this skeleton sentence: 'What do... think about...?' The children arranged themselves into pairs to work together, with some preferring to work on their own. They helped each other, and the adult facilitator also offered help drafting the questions.

Next, all the questionnaires were typed up, decorated, printed and distributed in the school, either to teachers or other students. Topics included what games younger and older children played, what school subjects younger and older children liked and what teachers believed about homework or uniforms (Figures 6.7 and 6.8).

Hi! We are Sonia and Clara. We are in grade 5 at Gray Cloud Primary school. We like to know what you think about 'real games and computer games'. Will you please help us by answering this questionnaire?

Name: ....

1. Are you a girl or a boy?

☐ Boy    ☐ Girl

2. Are you
☐ Year 3
☐ Year 6

3. What are your favourite games?
   1._____
   2._____
   3._____

4. What games do you like best?
☐ real
☐ virtual (on computer)
☐ don't know.
☐ both real and virtual
☐ neither

3a. If you like real life games, how much

   ☐ 😄 I really like it

   ☐ 🙂 I like it

   ☐ 😐 it's fine

Figure 6.7 Example of a questionnaire from child-led research (Pinter, 2019)

3b. If you like virtual (computer) games, how much

☐ 😃 I really like it

☐ 🙂 I like it

☐ 😐 it's fine

5. Do you have access to a computer/console
☐ no
☐ yes

6. Have you ever paid for a video game?
☐ Yes
☐ No

7. Do you like walking/ running?
☐ Love it
☐ like it
☐ fine
☐ in the middle
☐ don't like it much
☐ really don't like it
☐ Hate it

8. How do you like to play?
☐ on your own
☐ with others
☐ both

9. Did you enjoy doing this questionnaire?
_____.

Figure 6.7 (*cont.*)

The completed questionnaires were collected and returned to the children for analysis. Some had as many as sixty responses. The children were very keen at this stage to work on tallying the responses and creating graphs in Microsoft PowerPoint.

Once the data were analysed and represented using pie charts and bar charts, the children completed a presentation on the school computers, telling the story of the research.

At the very end, after the last session, the children were also interviewed about their experiences, having just completed their first research project as child researchers.

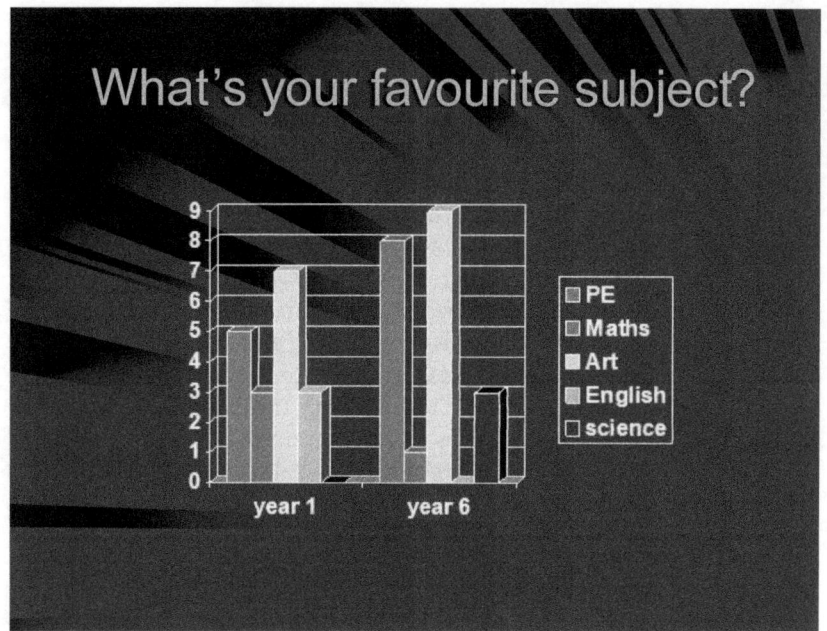

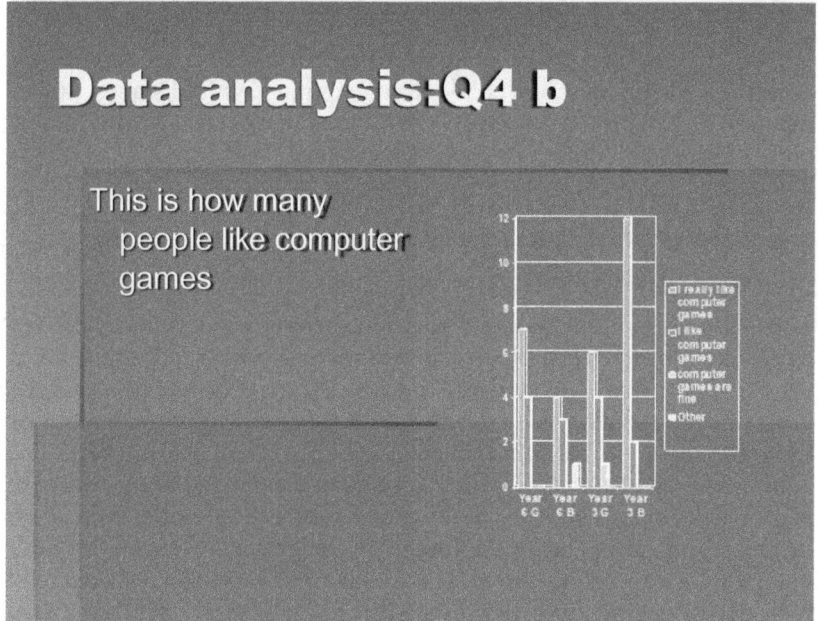

Figure 6.8 Examples of children's data analysis slides from the child-led project (Pinter, 2019)

In Pinter (2019) the children recorded their presentations on tablet devices, and these were uploaded to a website for external audiences to view. The children were proud of their achievements, surprised themselves as to how much work they were able to do on their own and really appreciated working on their projects autonomously. They all said that they wanted to do another project straightaway and had good ideas about how to do better next time.

Dissemination in these projects is crucial. In the Australian study the children wanted to send their results to the local paper and inform others in their school and beyond, whereas in the UK study the children's presentations were displayed at school and were uploaded to the academic facilitator's research website. These appeared to be very attractive ideas, and the children were motivated by these outcomes to complete their work to a high standard.

Pinter's study offers a skeleton of steps to follow whatever the focus of the study might be. In L2 classes children can be enabled via training to undertake their own studies in these topics:

- What do English teachers think about assessment?
- What do teachers think about language learning games/apps?
- What do children think about using drama techniques?
- What L2 activities do third graders and sixth graders like?

Both these papers describe child-led research in its initial stages, unfortunately without the next steps. If more time had been available, a new cycle of research could have been undertaken.

6.6 The Focus of Research 'with' and 'by' Children in Applied Linguistics

The focus or topic for research with children in active roles in applied linguistics will start from issues, questions and points of interest relating to L2 (English) learning processes and experiences, but it has the potential to spill over the L2 class and continue within the school or the community (Table 6.2).

In terms of content, a logical start would be a focus on the 'self' before broadening the focus to other topics of interest in the immediate context and then beyond. Initial investigations, especially with younger children who are not yet experienced with research, will typically centre around questions such as 'who am I as a language learner?', 'who are my peers, my family and community?', and then gradually with more experienced children it will be possible to explore topics that are more distant, more abstract and more complex.

6.6 The Focus of Research 'with' and 'by' Children

Table 6.2 Topics of interest for research with and by children in applied linguistics

TOPICS		
L2 (and L2 learning/teaching) as a topic of interest – L2 as a vehicle to communicate research		
ABOUT	Views about aspects of L2 learning, perspectives and opinions about self as a language learner, about English, textbook, curriculum and others	Investigations into own and others' learning processes or issues of interest such as views and perspectives of others, peers, teachers or members of the community; exploring topics of interest beyond L2 classroom and beyond the topic of language learning
WITH		
BY		

Researching the self and language learning in the immediate context:

- Exploring interests, strategies, learning styles (relating to children's own L2 learning skills and experiences)
- Exploring vocabulary knowledge, my favourite words and why I like them, easiest words to remember and how to remember them; reading habits, game playing (L2 learning experiences and awareness)
- Exploring what learning a foreign/second language means (relating to understanding about language learning)
- Exploring what is difficult, boring, motivating and enjoyable (best ways of learning an L2; feeding into teaching materials and policy decisions).

Researching topics going beyond the self:

- Exploring topics of interests in L2: topics usually covered in L2 but also stronger links with content-based approaches such as CLIL
- Topics of interest to the learners and teachers in their own communities, such as looking after the local environment, local climate education topics or global citizenship-related topics.

The use of L2 as the medium of communication may be appropriate in certain contexts whatever topic is being investigated, but it is more likely that children will be using their full linguistic repertoire.

6.7 Conclusion

This chapter aimed to present some possibilities for research 'with' and 'by' children that could be translated into projects in applied linguistics. The intention was to whet researchers' appetites to explore what type of active participation might be possible. While I tried to dissect the studies according to what roles the children were given and whether the research was 'about', 'with' or 'by' children', active participation is also seen as a continuum of possibilities of child–adult partnerships (Fielding & Bragg, 2003).

7   Ethical Issues and Dilemmas

7.1 Introduction

This chapter is devoted to questions of ethics in research involving child participants. The main aim is to encourage adult researchers to reflect on their own ethical stance, principles and practices in relation to their current and future work involving children. I will cover some general background and then focus on a selection of internationally available codes of ethical practice relevant to research with children in applied linguistics. Bringing together ethical requirements mandated by institutional ethical boards and local, 'in-situ' concerns that arise from the day-to-day interactions with children and other stakeholders presents ever more complex challenges in research involving children. The chapter considers ethical challenges associated with different adult and child roles in research, including a focus on active roles for children.

7.2 Origins of Research Ethics with Children

In order to protect participants (all participants, not just children), research ethics guidelines have been traditionally based on four main principles which originally emerged from medical ethics, including autonomy, non-maleficence, beneficence and justice (Beauchamp & Childress, 1979).

- *Autonomy:* participants must be able to consent through free choice, without fear, worry, or any negative consequences if they decline.
- *Non-maleficence:* participants must not suffer any harm in the research process.
- *Beneficence*: the overall benefits to the participants should outweigh the potential risks in the research study.
- *Justice*: all participants must be treated fairly and equally.

The above principles are aimed at protecting participants in all kinds of research, both adults and children. However, with the realisation that children need specific attention, child research ethics (which is a sub-field of human ethics) was established with the Nuremberg Code (1947) and then the Declaration of Helsinki (1964), which examined children specifically as research participants. This latter document stated that if the child/minor is able to give it, informed consent should be sought from them as well as from the parent/guardian. Parents' and guardians' consent is usually sought first, and once these permissions are in place, children's assent or consent is added. Gaining consent from both parents and children is, of course, far from unproblematic in practice because they may disagree, but still including children was an important step towards recognising children's rights to have a say about their own participation in research.

Alderson (2014) suggests that there are three main frameworks to describe ethical research with children, including principles-based, outcomes-based and rights-based frameworks. The principles-based approach rests on the idea that children need to be respected as dignified human beings, including their personal integrity, autonomy and beneficence by avoiding harm and attempting to do good. The outcomes-based system focusses on how to avoid harm, reduce negative consequences and inform practice and policy to promote effective child services. Finally, the so-called rights-based frameworks, such as the UN Convention on the Rights of the Child framework, focus on participation rights and insist on gaining informed consent from children. It is this last rights-based framework that scholars promoting children's active participation in research are most concerned about.

7.3 The UNCRC and Rights-Based Research Ethics with Children: A Compromise between Children's and Adults' Rights

The Convention is considered to be the most important document defining and outlining children's rights even though the interpretation of these rights can vary, and so can the importance assigned to the rights of adults whose main task is to protect and seek the best interests of the child.

The most often cited articles (Articles 12 and 13) underline the child's right to be listened to and consulted:

Article 12
States Parties shall assure to the child who is capable of forming his or her own views the right to express those views freely in all matters affecting the

7.3 The UNCRC and Rights-Based Research Ethics

child, the views of the child being given due weight in accordance with the age and maturity of the child.

Article 13
The child shall have the right to freedom of expression; this right shall include freedom to seek, receive and impart information and ideas of all kinds, regardless of frontiers, either orally, in writing or in print, in the form of art, or through any other media of the child's choice.

Additionally, Article 17 has also been referred to as key to establishing children's rights to information (i.e. in the case of research to the outcomes of research).

Article 17
States Parties recognize the important function performed by the mass media and shall ensure that the child has access to information and material from a diversity of national and international sources, especially those aimed at the promotion of his or her social, spiritual and moral well-being and physical and mental health.

From these articles, what is widely accepted is the unequivocal endorsement of children's voices and that they have to be heard, and that children have the right to give their views and opinions about all issues that matter to them. For those wishing to work with children as active participants in research, such rights naturally extend to research as a matter of importance. What seems to be more challenging to reach agreement about is quite how to interpret the role of adults in judging children's competence and maturity.

Article 3 addresses children's 'best interests', which underscores the role of adults (parents, guardians and others) in judging what is right for the child and thus potentially curtailing the child's wishes and views.

Article 3
In all actions concerning children, whether undertaken by public or private social welfare institutions, courts of law, administrative authorities or legislative bodies, the best interests of the child shall be a primary consideration.

Ennew (2009) argues that Article 3 should be interpreted as a requirement that high professional standards must be adhered to by adults at all times when working with children. In this sense the best interests of the child are still to be determined based on the wishes of the child but in dialogue with an adult. Kellett (2010a, p. 58) makes a similar point when she suggests that children have the right to 'quality research' about their lives. This means that research should be exploitation free and quality assured.

Article 36 specially concerns children's protection from exploitation, and it has been interpreted in research as the children's right to be 'properly researched' (i.e. according to ethical principles that respect children as individuals just like adults).

Article 36
States Parties shall protect the child against all other forms of exploitation prejudicial to any aspects of the child's welfare.

In some interpretations, Article 5, which addresses parental guidance, can be extended to researchers as members of the community, pointing out the importance of facilitating children's developing competence to exercise their rights through participating actively in research.

Article 5
States Parties shall respect the responsibilities, rights and duties of parents or, where applicable, the members of the extended family or community as provided for by local custom, legal guardians or other persons legally responsible for the child, to provide, in a manner consistent with the evolving capacities of the child, appropriate direction and guidance in the exercise by the child of the rights recognized in the present Convention.

Looking at the key tensions in the text of the Convention, one of the most pressing issues is related to the conflicting rights assigned to children and their parents/adults. The Convention suggests that parents have rights too and they are also responsible for the correct implementation of children's rights. On the one hand, the Convention thus promotes a paternalistic view of the child needing protection; on the other hand, it emphasises the empowering view, referring to children as active persons encouraged to shape their own lives. Behind these two principles lie two contrasting philosophies of rights: the liberationist and the reformist views.

7.3.1 A Balance between Protection and Participation Rights

The liberationist perspective declares that the denial of rights to children is analogous to the oppression of minority groups, such as women or ethnic minorities. Children are entitled to civil rights and the autonomous exercise of those rights. Liberationists propose to grant the same rights to children as adults on the basis of equality of all people (Verhallen, 2000). At the other extreme is a view that denies firmly that children can be bearers of rights at all, claiming that they do not meet the qualifying criteria for autonomy and rationality. This so-called reformist perspective maintains that although children might be generally capable of taking responsible decisions earlier than once thought (e.g. Donaldson, 1986 nonetheless, it is still the adults' task to protect children, make decisions for them and speak for them. Granting the same rights to children as to adults would overestimate children's understanding and wisdom (Purdy, 1994). Instead, scholars such as Simon (2000) suggest that the emphasis should be on adults' obligations to protect children from harm and, while participation rights are important, protection must always come first. The most sensible approach lies somewhere in between, and it is precisely this delicate balance between the two extreme views that needs carefully calibrating in any study involving children in active roles.

Those who remain sceptical about children's rights and a rights-based approach justify their position by citing children's lack of competence. Lacking competence and autonomy, of course, is not a matter of either/or but a matter of degree, and children can only hope to acquire these capacities if they are allowed to exercise these powers regularly. If they are always denied the right to act autonomously and are always spoken for by adults, it will be impossible for them to learn to be more independent, responsible and autonomous.

In addition to the two extreme views (i.e. those that reject children's rights altogether and those who want to assign the same rights to both adults and children), a range of other pragmatic views sit in the middle. For example, many believe that *some* children should have rights, such as older children or adolescents, while others have endorsed a view that children may share some rights with adults but not all. Children may have rights but only 'rights-in-trust' which are essential prerequisites to develop into adults, such as the right to an open future (Feinberg, 2007).

The most widely accepted pragmatic view is that researchers need to balance protection rights and participation rights in unique proportion as judged appropriate in any one study. In particular, the age of the children and the type of activity they are involved in should be the basis for determining what kind of balance is needed. Freeman (2011, p. 387) refers to this middle road as 'liberal paternalism' by talking about a 'vulnerable but competent' child. Lowden (2002, p. 103) suggests that 'maintaining a balance between protection and self-determination rights may help to overcome conflicts, confusion and problems between the diverse approaches to viewing children's rights'.

According to the argument that a compromise between protection and participation needs to be achieved, the right to participate should function as a starting point for opening up a dialogue between adults and children. Ideally, spaces need to be created to explore how children's rights are understood and implemented in each context, and these discussions should involve both adults and children. Children's views and understandings about the meaning of rights should also be sought as they can offer insightful bottom-up perspectives to feed into adults' understandings and eventually into policy and practice. This requires time and 'intentional space for dialogue' (Harcourt & Hägglund, 2013, p. 22). Even very young children (4–5-year-olds) can successfully communicate via drawings and photos about what rights mean for them. Adults can use these insights for reflection and seek validation from the children on their initial interpretations as well as reflect further on the children's comments. Older children may have more sophisticated understanding of the concept of rights, but adult researchers still need to open up spaces for dialogue to share these understandings.

A rights-based approach to ethics has had an overall positive effect on research with children. Even though the Convention on the Rights of the Child has sparked criticism and debate, as Archard (2013, p. 757) comments, it is still a celebrated document and 'even those persuaded that it is fundamentally mistaken to think of children as possessed of rights, or who believe that the Convention misrepresents the rights that children do have, may nevertheless think that the Convention needs to be defended'.

While rights-based research and rights-based ethics with children are broadly accepted as good starting points for research with children, critical voices have been suggesting that some have gone 'too far' in their interpretations of the Convention. These interpretations include the belief that participatory research is always more ethical than other types of traditional research and that research with children is only ethical if they benefit from the research process directly. Hammersley (2015) refutes these ideas and argues for a more careful and balanced assessment of rights-based approaches. Indeed, ethical research does not absolutely have to be participatory or undertaken 'with' children as there remain various research questions that call for methods that cannot be turned into a participatory format and should not be. These types of studies must not be labelled as unethical just because they are not 'with' children. Hammersley (2015) also maintains that depending on the research questions and the context, a great deal of research undertaken with children does not directly serve them or benefit them.

7.4 Codes of Practice Relating to Applied Linguistics

Given the already interdisciplinary nature of research within applied linguistics, there exists no single set of official guidelines that researchers can turn to when working with children.

A range of guidelines and ethics frameworks exist internationally, but none of these is an obvious match for studies in applied linguistics that focus on children, especially children in active roles. The most well-known guidelines in the UK are issued by the British Association of Applied Linguistics (BAAL, 2016), with similar equivalents existing in other contexts. However, guidelines from institutions with a focus on general education or psychology research might also be consulted, such as those issued by the Australian Association for Research in Education (AARE, 1993), the British Educational Research Association (BERA, 2011), the American Educational Research Association (AERA, 2011), the American Psychological Society (APS, 2017) or The British Psychological Society (BIPS, 2018).

When working with younger children, the International Charter and Guidelines for Ethical Research Involving Children (ERIC, 2016) or the European Early Childhood Education Research Association (EECERA, 2015) guidelines may be consulted. Some researchers prefer one or another of these, or work with local or regional equivalents, or follow the recommendations of the institution they are affiliated with (which may reflect the principles in one of these frameworks).

In the UK, one of the most often consulted guidelines or codes of ethical practice is offered by BAAL (2016). Advice specifically regarding children is overall scarce in the document, but the section devoted to child subjects does explicitly encourage researchers to work with children in such a way that they play more active roles, as it states that 'it is possible for even younger children to be involved effectively in the planning, conduct and dissemination of research' (p. 6; see Figure 7.1). It also addresses the need to seek children's consent, not just their parents', and warns against different types of overt or covert exploitation.

For those working with children in applied linguistics, an alternative code of practice is BERA (2011), and many prefer to work with this because it gives more detailed advice (Figure 7.2).

The BERA code of practice specifically refers to the UN Convention on the Rights of the Child and advises researchers to balance the welfare concerns and the participation rights of child participants according to their local contexts, considering the specific needs and interests of the individual children they are working with, paying particular attention to vulnerability.

Typically, while most codes refer to children and caution educational researchers to take special care with vulnerable populations such as 'children, youth, special needs students or recent immigrant

> All of the above points apply to research carried out with children as well as adults; it is possible for even young children to be involved effectively in the planning, conduct and dissemination of research. However, particular care may be needed with certain aspects of research when working with children, for example in providing explanations and consulting at all stages of research, including consultation about the outcomes of research. Informed consent may be obtained even from young children, but researchers need to spend time ensuring children understand, to a degree commensurate with their capacities and interests, what they are agreeing to when they give consent. For children under 16, consent also needs to be obtained from parents or other adults acting in loco parentis. Researchers should be aware, however, that in some cases, particularly with internet research, it may not be easy to determine informants' ages.
>
> Children may be in a relatively powerless position vis à vis researchers and other adults: it is important that care is taken to ensure they do not feel under undue pressure to participate in or continue with research; it is also important not to exploit children's enthusiasm, and to ensure they do not undertake activities that may be against their own interests. Researchers planning to work with children may be required to obtain clearance from the Disclosure and Barring Service (DBS).

Figure 7.1 Extract from Code of Ehtics (BAAL)

populations' (AERA, 2011, p. 151), the advice they offer is rather generic. Typically, most detailed discussion is devoted to the specifics of gaining informed consent and the need to judge the level of risk involved carefully. AARE (1993, p. 4), for example, states that when 'minors are too young' to consent, research should not carry any risk', which is a rather vague piece of advice.

A recently developed alternative code of practice that is particularly appropriate for researchers working with children, including those working with young children, is the International Charter and Guidelines for Ethical Research Involving Children, referred to as the ERIC guidelines (Truscott et. al., 2019; see Figure 7.3). Basin their work on comprehensive empirical research, the ERIC team have developed what they refer to as the emergent conceptual framework for ethical practice in research with children, which rests on three key concepts: rights, relationships and reflexivity ('the 3Rs'). The framework has been developed out of a survey study of hundreds of expert respondents engaged in child research from forty-six countries worldwide, as well as a critical exploration of

Children, Vulnerable Young People and Vulnerable Adults

16. The Association requires researchers to comply with Articles 3 and 12 of the United Nations Convention on the Rights of the Child. Article 3 requires that in all actions concerning children, the best interests of the child must be the primary consideration. Article 12 requires that children who are capable of forming their own views should be granted the right to express their views freely in all matters affecting them, commensurate with their age and maturity. Children should therefore be facilitated to give fully informed consent.
17. The Association considers that the spirit of Articles 3 and 12 above should also apply in research contexts involving young people and vulnerable adults.
18. In the case of participants whose age, intellectual capability or other vulnerable circumstance may limit the extent to which they can be expected to understand or agree voluntarily to undertake their role, researchers must fully explore alternative ways in which they can be enabled to make authentic responses. In such circumstances, researchers must also seek the collaboration and approval of those who act in guardianship (e.g. parents) or as 'responsible others' (i.e. those who have responsibility for the welfare and well-being of the participants e.g. social workers).
19. Researchers must ensure that they themselves, and any collaborators or research assistants and students under their supervision, comply with legal requirements in relation to working with school children or vulnerable young people and adults.
20. Researchers must recognize that participants may experience distress or discomfort in the research process and must take all necessary steps to reduce the sense of intrusion and to put them at their ease. They must desist immediately from any actions, ensuing from the research process, that cause emotional or other harm.
21. Researchers must recognize concerns relating to the 'bureaucratic burden' of much research, especially survey research, and must seek to minimize the impact of their research on the normal working and workloads of participants.

Figure 7.2 Extract from Code of Ehtics (BERA)

an extensive literature (Powell et al., 2012). The large number of countries involved makes this a particularly robust internationally accepted document.

The ERIC guidelines emphasise the fact that all children are entitled to fair treatment in research and that consent needs to be carefully

The ERIC framework:

International Charter for Ethical Research Involving Children
As a research community working with children, we are committed to undertaking and supporting high quality ethical research that is respectful of children's human dignity, rights and wellbeing. The following seven commitments guide our work:

Ethics in Research Involving Children is Everyone's Responsibility
We, the research community, including all who participate in undertaking, commissioning, funding and reviewing research, are responsible for ensuring that the highest ethical standards are met in all research involving children, regardless of research approach, focus or context.

Respecting the Dignity of Children Is Core to Ethical Research
Ethical research is conducted with integrity and is respectful of children, their views and their cultures. Involving children respectfully requires that researchers recognise children's status and evolving capacities and value their diverse contributions.

Research Involving Children Must Be Just and Equitable
Children involved in research are entitled to justice. This requires that all children are treated equally, the benefits and burdens of participating are distributed fairly, children are not unfairly excluded and that barriers to involvement based on discrimination are challenged.

Ethical Research Benefits Children
Researchers must ensure that research maximizes benefits to children, individually and/or as a social group. The researcher bears primary responsibility for considering whether the research should be undertaken and for assessing whether research will benefit children, during and as a consequence of the research process.

Children Should Never Be Harmed by their Participation in Research
Researchers must work to prevent any potential risks of harm and assess whether the need to involve the individual child is justified.

Research Must Always Obtain Children's Informed and Ongoing Consent
Children's consent must always be sought, alongside parental consent and any other requirements that are necessary for the research to proceed ethically. Consent needs to be based on a balanced and fair understanding of what is involved throughout and after the research process. Indications of children's dissent or withdrawal must always be respected.

Ethical Research Requires Ongoing Reflection
Undertaking research involving children is important. Ethical research demands that researchers continually reflect on their practice, well beyond any formal ethical review requirements. It requires ongoing attention to the assumptions, values, beliefs and practices that influence the research process and impact on children.

Figure 7.3 ERIC Guidelines

negotiated and monitored throughout any study, and if possible, the research should bring some benefits to the children. They stress that the highest possible ethical standards are everyone's responsibility (i.e. all adults working with children).

The 3Rs framework works alongside a fundamentally 'rights-based' understanding of ethics with children (Bergum & Dossetor, 2005; Noddings, 1984), which underscores the approach promoted by the Convention as a starting point. In addition to a rights-based principle, however, the importance of local relationships (between child and researcher but also peers, parents and teachers) is emphasised since it is within the web of interconnected relationships that children's participation needs to be negotiated. This is also referred to as relational ethics. What is right and ethical to do depends on the circumstances, and the solution will always be generated within specific relationships. In this web of relationships, the rights of all parties are important (including parents, children and researchers), and this creates a messy interconnectivity. Relational ethics and children's rights need to work together. Relational ethics invites a closer consideration of the relational contexts where children's rights are applied (Herring, 2013).

'Hence, relational ethics positions research ethics as an ongoing social practice, with emphasis placed upon mutual respect, engagement, embodied knowledge, attention to the interdependent environment and uncertainty' (Truscott et al., 2019, p. 46). Going back to the 3Rs framework (rights, relationships and reflexivity), the last component of the framework is reflexivity, the critical engagement with the power dynamics inherent in the context, which can encourage researchers to challenge their own assumptions (Powell et. al., 2016) and to recognise their own values and the fact that research is taking place in a context of broader social relationships and personal connection (Abebe & Bessell, 2014). Such reflexivity is referred to as ethical mindfulness (Warin, 2011) or a way of being and an overall attitude (Probst & Berenson, 2014).

Parallel to the ERIC guidelines, another set of guidelines developed by EECERA (2015; see Figure 7.4) has also been influential in promoting ethics-related discussions, especially among early years researchers. This set of guidelines deserves its place here because of its commitment to a detailed description of the highest ethical standards relevant to working with children and their families, and it includes details relevant to all stages of the research project from planning to dissemination. The EECERA ethical guidelines have been developed by a working group of EECERA trustees through a collaborative process with the involvement of the *International Journal of Early Years Education*.

Summary of EECERA Guidelines

1. <u>The child, the family, the community and the society</u>: always seen as subjects and not objects throughout childhood, no matter how young; always situated in families and communities; everyone to be treated without any prejudice
2. <u>Democratic values</u>: fair sensitive treatment of all participants irrespective of age, religion, language, disability, health condition, gender identity, sexuality, race, ethnicity, class, national origin, culture, social economic status, marital, domestic or parental status; deep respect for voice; acknowledge the right of others to hold different views and attitudes to those of the researcher; be sensitive to cultures, strive to eliminate bias, and distribute power so that all can contribute equitably
3. <u>Justice and equity</u>: actively promote democratic values and social justice; respect for plurality in paradigms, disciplines, theories and methodologies, illuminating complexity, prismatic approach; respect different voices and realities
4. <u>Knowing from multiple perspectives</u>: promote original research while respecting existing work; aim to extend knowledge from all perspectives, such as participant learners, educators, policy makers and the public; acknowledge the legitimacy of diverse views
5. <u>Integrity, transparency and respectful interactions</u>: make public the ethical principles which guide research practice; ensure researcher does not knowingly jeopardise the welfare of others; ensure all research is transparent and fully documented ready for critical review; acknowledge all contributions fairly in all outputs; ensure findings are communicated in straightforward fashion; make results public unless to do so would cause harm; researchers never compromise ethical behaviour in favour of collegiality
6. <u>Equality and rigour</u>: design of study serves the objectives; choices in design fully acknowledged; highest ethical standards to respect participants; highest standards of presentation and dissemination
7. <u>Academic scholarship</u>: all contributors listed as authors; status and power should not determine the order of authors; obligation to attribute external sources of support, including financial support and sponsors; authors disclose publication history
8. <u>Social contribution</u>: research embodies an awareness of social responsibility towards communities; research serves the public good, advances scholarly knowledge; ensures research has utility, contribution to wider community in a spirit of constructive criticism, generating impact on policy, practice and knowledge creation

Figure 7.4 EECERA Guidelines

7.4 Codes of Practice in Applied Linguistics

The EECERA guidelines draw researchers' and practitioners' attention to the unique complexities that are difficult to untangle in any one project and encourage adults to accept rather than fight this complexity full of dilemmas. Working out the most appropriate course of action may take time and effort. Working with the families of young children brings its own additional challenges and compromises.

Even though there is a tendency for ethical guidelines to be standardised internationally, in some countries codes of ethical practice for researchers working with children are not yet readily available, and there is a great deal of uncertainty with regard to how to follow best ethical practice. In addition to professional organisations (such as BAAL), ministries responsible for research with human subjects and universities will set their own ethical guidelines and procedures, overseen by institutional ethics committees. In research-intensive universities a great deal of formal research is initiated by undergraduate, masters and doctoral students as well as academics, with the intention to undertake research internationally. Graduate students, for example, who wish to work with children as part of a masters or doctoral research project need to apply for ethical clearance in their institution where they study. At the same time their project has to be workable, feasible and ethically appropriate as seen by the local stakeholders, such as parents, educational authorities, teachers and other gatekeepers in another country context where the field work takes place. Ethical practices are deeply entangled with cultural, social and historical practices that need careful unpacking.

In the everyday practice of ongoing fieldwork, the adult researcher has to become the 'ethical tool' (Mortari & Harcourt, 2012, p. 239) who can navigate between ethics of justice and ethics of care. Ethics of justice refers to the codes, protocols and guidelines, while ethics of care concerns the beneficence of the individual. Both of these angles are needed. Ethics of care is relational (see also relational ethics by Truscott et al., 2019), and it is not just about the two separate individuals but the experience of interconnections. The essence of ethics of care is about responsibility, respect and feeling 'obliged' towards the other, to appreciate that the other has intrinsic value as a person and to search for what is good for the other. This orients to developing a 'giver' posture. Acting ethically is also an emotional investment and requires cultivating positive sentiments such as kindness and tenderness (Noddings, 1984). Such approaches founded on 'ethics of care' become even more important in the case of very young children (Gilligan, 1982; Held, 2006; Noddings, 2003). With a focus on care, compassion and relationship building with the children, such relational focus in ethics emphasises feeling 'with' the participants (i.e. empathy or emphatic attunement; Carnevale, 2009). The adult researcher not only tries to tune into the emotional state of the child but also puts themselves in the child's shoes (as much as possible) in trying to understand their situation. Even though ethics of care is emphasised in the work of adults who conduct research with young children, the concept is also relevant to older children because the quality of the relationship and mutual understanding between adults and children in collaborative research are crucially important.

Christensen and Prout (2002) promote what they call 'ethical symmetry' in research with children. Ethical symmetry between children and adults is founded on ongoing dialogue throughout the research process, and it means that the researcher takes as their 'starting point' the view that ethical relationships between the informant and adult is the same whether the informant is a child or an adult. Each adult right has a 'counterpart for children', and any differences between adults and children should arise from the context 'rather than being assumed in advance' just because the participant is a child. Practices need to be in line with children's experiences, interests, values and everyday routines (Christensen & Prout, 2002, p. 482). Christensen and Prout also emphasise the importance of local cultures of communication (i.e. paying attention to the children's social actions and their language use as a basis for establishing a meaningful dialogue). They argue that 'ethical practice is tied to the active construction of research relationships and cannot be based on presupposed ideas or stereotypes about children or childhood' (2002, p. 484). There cannot be stereotypes about methods either, as all methods are contingent on the frames of cultural references of those involved (Fraser et al., 2014).

Researchers must consider the choice of physical spaces where the study will take place, whether it is an office, a classroom or a playroom where children may feel able to relax and participate more readily. Some researchers may not have a choice about the venue, whereas others can proactively secure the best possible venue for their research. School structures, with their rigid setup and traditionally arranged furniture, are rarely ideal for the kind of studies that invite children to work alongside adults. Rearranging the furniture can certainly help, even if just on a symbolic level. The room needs to be quiet and private, with no access to those who are not part of the study (such as teachers or other staff).

Some researchers decide to work with children in their home contexts, hoping that this will be less problematic than school-based research. It may well be the case that access can be granted more quickly, but of course home contexts are just as fraught with ethical dilemmas as schools. Parents or siblings may overhear or even interrupt the research process, and all kinds of domestic routines may have to be worked around when trying to undertake research. Finding a space within a home is also difficult as some parts of the house are seen as communal, whereas other parts are too private. The right level of privacy is somewhere in between but not always possible to find. Careful thought must be given to the advantages and problems likely to emerge in different venues, and the adult researcher must be prepared to compromise. (Barker & Weller, 2003; Valentine, 1999).

7.5 The Debate about Consent

In research 'with' children, since children are respected as individuals in their own right, it follows that they should give their own consent. This is an ethical imperative accepted by many and yet, legally, it is the parents' and caretaker's consent that matters; without this consent, children, typically under the age of 16 but sometimes under the age of 18, cannot in fact participate in research of any kind.

Debates about children's informed consent can be traced back to the key concern and about how to judge/measure competence. Traditionally, children used to be silenced in research because their ability to report their experiences was questioned. Their actions were deemed to be irrational and unreliable and their accounts untrustworthy or even incoherent, so it was their parents', guardians' or other adults' role to speak for them. This conviction – based on insights about lack of competence at younger ages established by some studies in developmental psychology (see Chapter 2) – led to the situation whereby it used to be acceptable for children to be volunteered for research by adults without their own consent or even assent.

Such beliefs are strongly contested by researchers working in the New Childhood Studies paradigm, which promotes an argument that competence is in fact a social construct, and therefore how it is viewed, articulated and measured is a product of a social and historical context rather than a matter of static and abstract level of ability in exercising one's judgement. Given that competence is contextually situated, even young children in some contexts can begin to understand the meaning of consent if it is explained and presented in a way that they can relate to it and, crucially, if their willingness to participate is revisited frequently. Offering children opportunities to discuss and negotiate consent and even change their minds about it (i.e. giving it first and then withdrawing it later or the other way round) is seen as an important cornerstone of good practice.

A milestone event that (at least in the UK) has had a major influence on the ongoing debate as to whether children could be considered competent and thus give their own consent to participate in research, even in the absence of parents' consent, was related to a high-profile legal case, *Gillick vs West Norfolk and Wisbech Area Health Authority*, in 1985. This case is noteworthy because for the first time a judge decided that children younger than 16 years of age could in fact give their own consent for medical treatment without their parents' agreement or even knowledge of the treatment. In the final decision Lord Scarman, the judge, declared that a child could consent if they were deemed to be fully able to understand the medical treatment that was being proposed. 'As a matter of Law the parental right to determine whether or not their minor child below the age of sixteen will have medical treatment terminates if and when the child achieves sufficient understanding and intelligence to understand fully what is proposed' (cited in Morrow and Richards, 1996).

When researchers refer to the 'Gillick competence', they contend that it is 'not age' per se that determines whether someone is competent, but instead competence relates to achieving sufficient understanding of what is being proposed. Armed with this argument, researchers working with children, even young children, have set out to gather evidence to illustrate that children can make sense of what is expected of them in research and therefore should be considered competent to consent. Even though the Gillick case had nothing to do with academic or classroom research-related consent, as it was about a medical issue and constituted a legal judgement, nonetheless the outcome has had a lasting influence on researchers' and other professionals' beliefs, practices and judgements regarding children's ability to consent.

7.5.1 Challenges with Consent

What is in fact the definition of consent? Consent is one of the main foundations of ethical research and refers to participants articulating their voluntary informed decisions as to whether they want to be involved in a particular research study. Participants need to understand the nature, purpose and likely consequences of the project. This is quite a demanding set of conditions because, for example, with regard to the consequences, it may be impossible to foresee these, especially in certain types of exploratory studies that tend to evolve organically over time.

The first challenge for adult researchers is to consider how best to explain their research and its overall purpose to the children they would like to invite to work with them. This initial phase of getting to know each other, having opportunities to talk informally about the research and the children's potential roles, is a time-consuming phase but one that cannot be compromised. With younger children in particular, various opportunities should be given to the potential participants to ask questions, make comments and share any concerns. Children need to take their time to decide whether they would like to participate, and thus it is good practice not to press them for an answer in the first meeting. A two-way transparent discussion about the project is needed (Alderson & Morrow, 2004) facilitating genuine negotiation. A common challenge is to judge just how much information is needed not to make the introduction too overwhelming, which then might lead to boredom or confusion.

At some point during the consent negotiation process, a signed consent form might be required with a static signature. This contract-like approach may not work well with all children, and instead a more dynamic process may be preferred, such as revisiting consent every time the children and the adult researchers meet. The adult researcher can take just a few minutes at the beginning of each new meeting to check that the children are still all happy to continue with their participation. Even with a dynamic approach, withdrawal can be difficult to manage and negotiate. Children might not know how to say 'no' to an adult, or they might worry about the researcher's reaction or feel guilty about letting the researcher down. The better the adult researcher knows the children, the easier it will be to spot any signs of doubt, unease or reluctance to continue. There is a fine line between coercion and encouraging participation, particularly in school contexts where interdependence on peers, teachers and generally on institutional hierarchies is magnified.

Consent is always more 'complicated and ambivalent' in practice than it looks on paper; the 'researcher may explain what a research project is about, and the participants might seem to understand and perhaps genuinely believe that they do – but none of this guarantees that they both share the same conception of the project' (Gallagher et al., 2010, p. 474).

In a study by Pinter and Zandian (2015), for example, it was clearly demonstrated that children's interpretation and understanding of what they consented to at the beginning radically changed by the end of the study. The children in this study were asked to talk about their experiences of communicating successfully with newcomers to their school who had limited language competence. Since the adult researchers lacked such insights, the children were positioned as knowledgeable experts and were invited to share their experiences with regard to what strategies they thought worked best. In the briefing sessions at the beginning, the children seemed to understand what the study was about and what their roles were in it, but at the very end they reported that their actual experiences turned out to be different from how they had imagined it at the beginning. They simply did not realise at the beginning that their views were to be quoted word for word without adult 'corrections'. Such small yet important revelations illustrate that understanding is always messy and incomplete, and as the project progressed the children were gaining deeper and deeper understanding of their roles. Through this process of comparing their initial expectations and their summative reflections, the children were able to develop new understandings about research in general and their own roles in it. As this study illustrates, getting children to understand fully what they consent to at the beginning is a challenging if not impossible task.

Children may sometimes consent just to please adults but expect the adults to tell them what to do and what to say. Children know from experience that adults normally control all aspects of their lives, and therefore in situations where they are invited to participate in research actively and adults suddenly suggest that the status quo is turned upside down, children might be puzzled and may refuse to believe it. Consequences for teacher researchers, who know the children well, and academic researchers, who do not have an existing relationship with the children, will vary, but in both cases the social status and the authority of the adult will carry inevitable weight. Hence, building trusting relationships and creating spaces for genuine dialogue over time is essential in preparing the ground for high-quality research with children.

Children may also simply refuse to participate because they want to distance themselves from a group of peers or indeed agree to participate simply because their friends have agreed to it. Gallagher et al. (2010) also note that stigma may be attached to not understanding initial instructions (especially in school contexts) and that children might simply not admit to this. Research in schools is always laden with problems around peer pressure and institutional constraints, and adult researchers need to become familiar with the complexities of relationships that impact on children's willingness to participate. David et al. (2001) go as far as to suggest that believing that children have the right to choose to participate in school contexts is simply naïve because of adults' and peers' overwhelming influence on any one child.

In the case of younger children, Harwood (2010) emphasises that it is particularly important to build trust and rapport not just with the children but with the parents/guardians as well before negotiating consent. Young children may be less able to verbally express their doubts about the research or may only show subtle physical signs of wanting to opt out, such as looking bored or distracted. Researchers therefore need to attend to both physical and verbal aspects of children's consent and stay in touch with family members throughout the project. With older children the use of technology to mediate the process of gaining consent has proven to be successful. Parsons et al. (2016) suggest that technology can enhance the research process, especially at the beginning stages of sharing information about the research via videos, for example. Delivered in a mode of communication (such as via social media) that is more familiar and comfortable, some groups of children may feel more confident to negotiate details with the adult researchers at their own pace. Added to that, communication with the adult researchers may be more private (i.e. not shared with the whole group), thus affording children more privacy and personal autonomy.

A dynamic approach to negotiating consent with children is a solid ethical principle in the sense that such practice attempts to ensure that children understand as much as possible about the proposed research and their roles in it. However, this process typically takes a long time, and in the case of large-scale studies where hundreds of children are involved, this is not always seen as feasible. For example, García Mayo (2021) reports that in L2 task-based research with children working with five schools at a time (i.e. hundreds of children), it is simply not feasible or practicable to get individual consent forms from children in addition to their parents. A range of considerations are relevant to justify the decision not to ask for the children's consent directly. First of all, since parents are asked to discuss the details with their children at home before they themselves sign the consent forms, the children are already aware and must have agreed with their parents about participating in the study. In García Mayo (2021) teachers work with the academic team collaboratively, and this means that the boundaries between what is everyday practice and what is research become easily blurred. The teachers are keen to implement findings from the study, and since classroom practice is closely related to research and the children do not have a free choice about their English classes, by extension it makes sense for them to participate in the research as well, as long as the parents sign the consent form. It must be noted though that not all parents consent for their children to be involved in the research, despite the carefully worded leaflet and the school's as well as the teachers' enthusiastic endorsement of the project. Many parents are worried about the accidental exposure of their children's data on the Internet and decline their children's participation. Finally, in studies where researchers are interested in children's spontaneous interactive talk elicited by various communication tasks, explaining to the children too much about the purpose of the study (e.g. explaining that the researchers are interested in the specific ways they can correct each other's English output) would mean that the elicited data are no longer spontaneous as the speakers could intentionally focus on aspects of the output that were identified and highlighted in the introductory briefing.

Thus, an approach where the researchers carefully camouflage the actual purpose is necessary to yield the type of natural and spontaneous spoken interaction the researchers are trying to capture. The question arises, though, of how the children can be better informed and whether there are any ways in which they can have some space in this research to have their voices heard. In large-scale experimental studies, even though the transcribed interactive data resulting from the tasks will provide the core evidence to answer the research questions, it may still be feasible or desirable to talk to the children to get a sense of what the experience was like from their point of view. This can usefully inform future studies and the design of actual tasks. Such open-ended dialogue with the children may give the researchers unexpected insights into the children's performances, possibly explaining aspects of the performance that they could otherwise only speculate about.

What type of consent is required will depend on the types of roles children take. Children in less active roles will need only one consent form, while children in more active roles, such as co-researchers or researchers (or in child-led research), will need to be approached first of all as participants working with an adult who is facilitating their work, but at the same time they also need to consider their role as a researcher working with other children. Kellet (2010a) talks about a 'hierarchy of consent', meaning that in all cases the first step is to secure the parent's or guardian's consent and then negotiate further with the children according to their roles. When working with more vulnerable children, such as children with special educational needs or refugees, Kellett recommends the use of a 'circle of consent', where the circle involves people who are close to the child and can support the child to help them to decide whether they want to participate.

7.5.2 Practical Difficulties Relating to Wording Consent Forms

In our field to date there is limited empirical evidence about what happens when adult researchers attempt to negotiate consent directly with children. In a recent study (Mourão, 2021) post-graduate student teachers who undertook small-scale action research projects in Portuguese EFL classes decided to record their consent negotiations with their child participants. In her role as the teacher educator, Mourão describes the challenges that student teachers faced having to explain the research and ensuring that children were informed. The first challenge was having to explain what consent meant. This took an unexpectedly long time, with the consequence that precious time was lost from the actual research project. This is a concern in the sense that access to children for research is often limited by gatekeepers, and adult researchers may be tempted to rush through consent negotiations in order to be able to move on to the main study phase as quickly as possible.

The student teachers were creative in their endeavours to invite the children to participate in their studies, but Mourão draws attention to the fact that even very minor differences in the wording of the consent forms could inadvertently lead to real or perceived coercion.

The following are examples of possible unintentional coercive strategies, as expressed by a certain choice of words, taken from information sheets shared with the children (Mourão, 2021):

'What do you say? Interested? Can I count on your participation?'
'I would really like it if you accepted to participate in my study.'
'I would really like it if you helped me get a good mark!'
'Thank you for being part of my research. Your parents have already agreed to your participation.'

Added to this, the use of emoticons was problematic, such as, for example, the use of happy and sad faces. Circling the sad face to say 'no' may have implied that the child was going to make the researcher sad or upset. The overall conclusion of the paper is that creating information leaflets and consent forms is a more challenging exercise than expected. On the positive side, the student teachers reported that the children felt proud and really appreciated being asked about their participation and hence were fuelled with enthusiasm to help and get going with the projects.

Taking time to introduce children to the research, taking great care in wording initial information leaflets and consent forms, and having the opportunity to discuss the research and what it means, can begin to build awareness about research with children who have never experienced it before. Several student teachers in Mourão's study took time at the end of their project to return to the children to share with them the findings of their studies. In some cases it became clear that the children took interest in the outcomes as well. One of the student teachers in this study (Cravo, 2019, cited in Mourão, 2021, p. 237), described her experience like this:

I told them that only after all my analysis I fully understood how much they had become aware of why they played games and worked in pairs: 'in the beginning you said that we played games mainly to have fun. With time we realised that you played games not only to have fun, but to learn English'. I also pointed out that in the beginning they didn't seem to fully understand why they worked in pairs, but later their answers showed me that they realised that when they are working in pairs they are also learning from each other, not only from the teacher. I pointed out that in the beginning they didn't always understand what 'speaking' meant. I told them that they had told me they had done a speaking activity when they had simply said 'hello', but with time they realised that speaking activity meant participating in a dialogue or making a presentation. Then I asked them what means I used to help them achieve our results, and several students were able to say that I had helped them to reflect upon the work carried out in class.

Cravo also commented: 'I think that [in] the same way [that] asking the children's consent is a good introduction to our work with the children, sharing the results is a good conclusion of the same work, and the two elements are totally related' (Cravo, cited in Mourão, 2021, p. 237)

7.5.3 Consent across Local and Global Contexts

Recent calls within the social sciences have questioned the status quo regarding consent. Darian-Smith and Henningham (2014), for example, note that even though protection and participation rights are equally important, authorities/gatekeepers tend to give more prominence to protection, sometimes to the detriment of participation rights. They comment:

We are concerned that the regulatory environment for academic research with children may, through a focus on protection, have the unwanted consequence of denying children the right to participate in research of interest to them. An unintended outcome of protection may also be to silence and limit the input of particular groups of children, including those for whom action arising from the research outcomes may be the most pressing.
(Darian-Smith & Henningham, 2014, p. 331)

Research with children is automatically considered a 'high-risk' activity by gatekeepers and institutional ethics boards, yet in reality much social, educational or language learning–related research is reasonably low risk. The increasing over-bureaucratisation of ethical procedures leads to a situation whereby children can be excluded from potentially empowering research because parents can override children's wishes

7.5 The Debate about Consent

to participate as they might not fully understand the complicated information leaflets that use legalistic language and run into several pages.

Darian-Smith and Henningham (2014) reported that in their study the information package provided to parents ended up as a six-page document. The complexity of the documentation gave the unintended impression that the parents in fact ought to protect their children from the research rather than support the project. Some parents also speak a language other than the language of the consent forms or simply lack appropriate literacy skills to understand the relatively complex language of the documents. The difficulty is balancing the complexity of these documents against the conviction that a proposed study should be inclusive, maybe even potentially empowering, and therefore easily available to all. Currently, it seems that the tendency is that complex regulatory requirements lead to a situation whereby 'we are in the danger of administering children out of their right to participate?' (Darian-Smith and Henningham, 2014, p. 334).

A further complication is that ethical guidelines in some countries simply do not match the priorities stated in guidelines that were originally created based on Western examples. In some of these contexts, individuals (especially children) are unlikely to be able to decide about important things as it is the central role of the family to decide things for the individual, including even some of the adults in that family. Oral consent may be more binding than written consent, with the consequence that written forms are simply rejected. Complex gatekeeping and the way power hierarchies function may mean that permission, once granted, may still be withdrawn at a higher level (Abebe & Bessell, 2014; Shamim & Qureshi, 2013). Parents may not expect to see a letter about research at all and may feel that it is the school's discretion to approve and handle research. In fact, they may even be alarmed to see a letter asking for their consent, assuming their children are in trouble. Demand for a signature on an official letter might also put parents off in some contexts where they have had negative experiences with signing documents that they did not fully understand (Kuchah, 2013; Pinter et al., 2016; Murphy, 2021; Skelton, 2008; Zandian, 2015).

It is universally accepted that parents or guardians can decide for children about their participation in research in their capacity as protectors. Yet parents' roles and competence to consent can be brought into question (Coyne, 2010). Adults and parents in particular may also be prone to using coercion one way or another when it comes to consent, and they themselves may base their judgement on questionable knowledge and experience about research. The need to consult parents and guardians of all minors under 18 is often reported to be problematic in studies such as, for example, by Skelton (2008), who worked with teenage girls in the Caribbean, all of whom identified as adults and did not understand why parents' permissions were required.

In sum, regarding consent, Gallagher et al. (2010, p. 479) suggest that just as researchers need to think about their beliefs and conceptions regarding children and childhood, they also need to think about their own position regarding children's consent. Do they believe it is possible in their study to achieve informed consent from the children? What is the children's understanding of consent? How will consent processes operate exactly in practice? What strategies will be used to harmonise consent processes for parents and children?

7.6 Adult Roles in Research

Research undertaken with children can happen in schools led by teacher researchers or by academic researchers who are outsiders. However, there is a whole range of other possibilities in between the simple insider–outside positions. In addition to teachers undertaking action research, which can be more or less formal or informal and can involve collaboration with their colleagues, research can also be a collaborative effort between the class teachers and academic researchers. Outsiders can also include various groups of people, such as university academics and their teams, or undergraduate and post-graduate student teachers collecting empirical data for their projects under the guidance of an academic supervisor or teacher educator. The status of adult researchers matters because in order to involve children in active roles, relationships need to be built between children and the adults. In the case of outsiders, a particular difficulty may arise because of the conflicting relationships of these researchers with other adults versus the children. Wyness (2019, p. 98) argues that 'the alliances that researchers are trying to develop with children are often in conflict with the professional and collegiate relations that they have with the teachers'. If the researchers are teachers (insiders), other types of challenges arise. For example, 'good' teachers may be undertaking informal investigations in their classrooms as part of their normal practice all the time. In terms of where the boundaries lie between a research/inquiry stance to everyday teaching and a more formal action research undertaken by an insider seems blurred; in fact, sometimes 'an activity that starts as informal experimentation may evolve into a more formal research undertaking' (Mathew &

Pinter, 2021, p. 212). Such a shift will require some important changes to one's ethical practices.

Whether insiders or outsiders, it is the adults' responsibility to select the child participants, and while there might be good reasons for selecting some children rather than others, an ethical issue also arises about who gets to participate and who is left out. Not surprisingly, it is usually high achievers with superior communication and social skills and those who come from a certain socio-economic background that tend to be invited to participate. The consequence of this is that children who are shy, less confident or less able or ready to contribute may be systematically sidelined. Children with learning difficulties are almost never selected, even though there is evidence that these children can contribute as well, given extra support. When working with learners with special educational needs or other difficulties, Urbach and Banerjee (2019) suggest that having several people, including those that the child is most comfortable with, explain the project and ask for assent is a good starting point. It is possible to elicit help from a communication partner that the child is comfortable with, and non-verbal techniques such as the use of photo-based data may also serve as a useful springboard for discussion. There is a careful balance to achieve between providing them with a voice versus invading their private worlds, and the researchers have to trust their own judgement on this.

Outsiders such as university academics coming into schools rely almost entirely on the judgements of teachers or other adults when it comes to the initial selection of child participants, whereas teacher-led research can attempt to be more inclusive. In promoting an approach that encourages giving children opportunities to undertake small-scale research in schools whereby they can familiarise themselves with research and practise with it in a sustained manner, many explicitly endorse a view that it should be every child's right to take on active roles in research as long as they are interested (Pinter, 2019; Pinter et al., 2016).

Privacy and Confidentiality

One of the cornerstones of research ethics is to protect the participants by promising confidentiality. However, in research with children there is an important caveat to the promise of confidentiality. It cannot be maintained where children disclose issues such as abuse or bullying. In such cases it is ethical to breach confidentiality to prevent further harm happening. However, the children may interpret this as betrayal of their trust, so care must be exercised to handle this delicately.

Unless all school staff and parents are specifically trained or briefed about issues of privacy and confidentiality, they may feel they have the right to have access to the information and the data (i.e. what the children said or did). These adults (such as school staff) may interfere by simply ignoring the children's right to privacy. This needs to be avoided by securing a private physical place as well as an agreement between participants and the adult that all stakeholders are aware of.

Privacy concerns arise about who owns and keeps photos and drawings or other artefacts created as part of the project. Lipponen et al. (2016) contend that we very rarely consider the life cycle of the digitally created visuals, that is, how are they produced, consumed, preserved and re-used, and if selected for use in research, what happens to them after the research project is over. Leith (2007) suggests that children should be appropriately informed about who will use their drawings and how these will be used. Images need to be handled with care when they are touched, moved or changed to avoid causing any harm unwittingly.

7.7 Challenges in Studies Where Children Play Active Roles

Children working in co-researcher roles are both participants and researchers. Such a complex relationship with the adult facilitator is delicate, and it will only work as long as children feel they are doing a worthwhile job, feel enthusiastic about the topic and the whole process and stay motivated to continue. If, for whatever reason, children lose interest in their roles as co-researchers, a careful negotiation process has to take place to move forward, either to support the children to re-engage or to help them exit their roles. Since becoming a co-researcher can only happen if the children have a trusting, secure relationship with the adults (teachers/researchers), which is usually built up over time, the challenge is to develop this relationship to a point where the children are working with the adults on an almost equal footing. Bucknall (quoted in Kellet, 2010a) recommends that children need training in this area because their usual stance towards adults is that of listening passively and unquestioningly obeying instructions.

If and when children are enabled to undertake their research on their own, the support of the adult facilitator is still essential and the relationship still matters, even though the adult can step back and may only be consulted from time to time. Child researchers who work largely on their own usually come with experience of working as co-researchers or have had other relevant experience and training. Adults can scaffold children's initial attempts of engagement with research by guiding them towards easy small-scale projects.

Kellett (2010a, p. 111) suggests that to be meaningful for children, particularly young children, research undertaken must emanate from their own experience, be very small scale at first and involve simple analysis techniques: 'If small research projects were carried out by large numbers of children in large numbers of locations, this would create multiple cultural snapshots and soon build into a rich canvas of knowledge about children's perceptions on our world.'

Child–child relationships, power dynamics and possible conflicts can come to the fore when children are working as researchers in their peer groups. Kellett (2010a, p. 92) suggests that operating as a child researcher can be a challenging role and that some children may have negative experiences, such as becoming overwhelmed with the prospect of interviewing a popular child or someone older than themselves. The adult facilitator's role and support is crucial in these situations, and it is the adult's responsibility to carefully monitor and check how the child researchers are getting on. School-based research with children acting in co-researcher and researcher roles can be difficult to achieve because of the hierarchical power structure and low levels of real autonomy afforded to children. After all, becoming a researcher comes with autonomous decision making, choices and responsibilities that do not fit easily with the traditional role of listening and following strict instructions.

Even if children act as co-researchers or researchers, it is almost always the adult who ends up re-presenting and writing up the study in academic publications, and this carries risks of misrepresentation, even if not deliberate. Although member checking is a useful tool, this is not always feasible. Another dilemma is whether children's time and effort in a research project, especially when they play important roles and invest their time, should be compensated. There is a debate about what shape compensation might take, and the answer is always to consider what is ethical, acceptable and feasible in the given context. Should children be paid? How much time do they invest? They may be giving up something else for the sake of research, and they may miss out on earning some pocket money elsewhere. An alternative view is that children benefit because they learn new skills, which is seen as their reward.

Working with children (whatever their roles might be), adults need to develop a 'reflexive approach' to their research practice. Graham et al. (2015) suggest that reflexivity in research with children involves a process of questioning decisions as they are made before and during the research, but also questioning one's own stance, attitudes and assumptions about children and childhood. During actual field work, Ritterbusch et al. (2020) recommend using the 'Window on the World' activity as a tool to enhance researcher reflexivity. In this activity, individual adult researchers are prompted to think through their own personality strengths and weaknesses as data collectors and about the relationship between their own life histories and the research agenda, trying to notice possible prejudices, stigmas or preconceived notions that may affect the research process. The adults are asked to draw a window on large poster paper, with each section of the window containing information about the researcher's interpretive lens regarding personality, life history and prejudice or stigma surrounding the research community. Then they are asked to imagine children living in the given contexts, standing on the other side of the windowpane. The objective is for the adult researcher to return to this image of the window as an interpretive lens after each day of fieldwork and each day of data analysis, and to reflect on the ways the windowpane may have distorted the data.

7.8 Conclusion

Once a study is decided upon, ultimately, what is ethical practice with children in research is a personal understanding and commitment which cannot be separated from the researcher's own conceptions of childhood and children or their own deeply seated ethical and political persuasion and epistemology. What is ethical is also the product of the context, with its unique complexities. It is often the case that gold-standard principles that look solid when stripped of any concrete context suddenly seem in conflict with local priorities that emerge from the children's perspectives.

Building up a knowledge base through case studies in child second language education research about ethical dilemmas when researching with children in active roles, including enabling children to undertake their own research, would serve us all well in our continuing work with young language learners.

8 Towards Children's Active Engagement in Applied Linguistics Research

8.1 Introduction

This last chapter aims to summarise the main arguments developed in the book and suggest that our field, applied linguistics, and more narrowly, child second language education, will benefit from more diverse approaches of researching with children.

Embracing diverse approaches in research with children will go some way in addressing the current lack of balance in our field. Raising awareness about the extended framework and opening up opportunities to move along the continuum towards research 'with' and 'by' children is a real possibility in any context, working with children of all ages, from pre-school to secondary school.

My hope is that the volume will encourage researchers to think critically about their work with children and young people, and that whatever their research focus or interest might be, they will find some inspiration from the ideas discussed in the volume.

8.2 The Relevance of the Extended Framework for All

As a largely adult-focussed discipline, applied linguistics has to date not engaged with the concept of child-centred or child-focussed research in earnest, and the status and roles afforded to children in research have been left implicit and vague. In response to this, in this book I have attempted to focus explicitly on children's status and roles in research. I have pulled together key arguments in favour of a broader research framework, which claims that children (and young people) could take up more diverse roles from passive to active, from objects to subjects and from data sources to participants who can and will shape the research process alongside adults by becoming partners or researchers themselves. Accordingly, the extended framework (see Section 4.13) envisages research in applied linguistics not just 'on' and 'about' children but also 'with' and 'by' children. It is the move away from research 'on' children that this book has devoted a great deal of attention to by unpacking how such research (especially research 'with' and 'by' children) can work in practice.

The ideas discussed in this book are relevant to all adult researchers interested in working with children in applied linguistics. As an untapped resource, the active participation of children is certainly a panacea that all need to implement, but raising awareness that such possibilities exist and can become reality is important for all L2 teachers and researchers working with children in applied linguistics.

The promotion of active roles for children is linked to children's rights and has the potential to improve children's wellbeing and raise their awareness about their own learning processes. Some researchers may wish to elicit children's views and perspectives about a particular aspect of their second language education and decide to incorporate participatory tools into their interviews or conversations (research 'about' or 'with' children). Other adult researchers may go further. They may design projects where children can take active roles as partners in research by inviting them to contribute to one or several stages of the research (research 'with' children). Yet others might be interested in enabling child-led research by providing training and supporting some children on their journeys to become researchers (research 'by' children).

Engaging children in active roles will also be relevant for those adults whose studies follow a traditional design, that is, where children have passive roles. In these studies, to complement the statistical results, children's perspectives may be interesting to elicit before, during or after the main data collection because such insights may throw further light on the quantitative data. Looking at the study through the children's lens will mean that the adult researchers might benefit by discovering new insights about the study and its tools. However, the adult researchers have to be open to this potential, take time to listen carefully to children's feedback and above all take the children's comments, anecdotes and questions seriously, even if this requires extra effort (e.g. Kuchah, 2013; Pinter & Zandian, 2015).

The extended framework does not suggest that there is one best or a prescribed way of working; instead, it implies that there are always possibilities that individual adult researchers can explore if they are familiar with the complexity of the framework.

The extended framework for children's involvement is envisaged as a flexible, non-linear, open-ended system of possibilities, a bit like a 'rhizome' of entangled possibilities (Deleuze & Guattari, 2004), where an adult researcher embarking on a study has many possible avenues

8.2 Relevance of the Extended Framework for All

to consider. Many different types of engagement can be imagined, with one decision or idea sparking off new possibilities, such as the children's unsolicited responses, comments or questions emerging from open-ended dialogues with adults. Much will depend on local constraints and even more on the levels of awareness, belief systems and intentions of the adult who is working with the children in any one context. The framework can encourage adults, whatever their role, background or research interest, to reflect on and rethink their own previous practice. In their future research they may be inspired to add new elements to their practice, such as opening up more opportunities for talking to the children, spending longer to familiarise themselves with the children before the study starts, or getting useful feedback from the children at different points in the study.

Studies that aim to collect thick data to understand and evaluate children's linguistic output can benefit from a more active involvement of children, moving the study on a continuum from research 'about' to research 'with'. In longitudinal studies the possibilities of involving children in active roles become even more feasible and meaningful because there is more time for training, relationship building and dialogue, and for negotiating and piloting various tools with the children.

A rather sharp dichotomy of traditional and alternative approaches to working with children in research can be attributed to the enthusiastic early scholarship in Childhood Studies, which exaggerated this divide. Today, most would agree that the dividing line is not quite as sharp as was originally argued; indeed, it is more a continuum, and many studies fall somewhere between the traditional ('on' and 'about') and alternative paradigms ('with' and 'by'). While this book aims to promote active participation, it does not intend to suggest that the more active the participation, the better the quality of the research. The aim of this volume has been to open these possibilities rather than push them at all costs. It is duly acknowledged, here and elsewhere, that active participation of children is not always possible or feasible, and sometimes it may not be appropriate. Accordingly, Thomas (2021, p. 13) argues:

> It is hard to see how anyone could seriously claim that all children are competent to conduct all kinds of research; or conversely that no child is competent to conduct any kind of research. The questions have to be about which children are competent to conduct what kinds of research, in what circumstances and conditions; and which children might want to conduct research and whether it would be to their benefit, also in the context. But competence in conducting research does not come with age; most adults do not have those skills. It comes with experience, reflection on that practice and learning from others with greater experience.

The extended framework is, of course, also relevant for children themselves. All children who want to should be entitled to have research experiences where they take active roles as part of their schooling, not just because it can be a powerful positive learning experience but because it fits with their rights to have their voices heard.

8.3 Bringing Together Arguments for More Active Participation

Even though my own interest in active participation and the alternative paradigm goes back to the key concepts of Childhood Studies, and I acknowledge this field as the foundation on which I based this book, the key principles have resonated more widely and found support from a range of literatures. To bolster the key argument, *that children and young people should be and could be considered in some studies in more active roles in research in applied linguistics,* a wide range of philosophical, legal, psychological, ethical and critical arguments have been woven into the discussion to strengthen the call for the new angle and to encourage cross-fertilisation of ideas from several largely discrete areas of enquiry.

The idea that children should be able to participate in research in more active roles is fully supported by international legislation such as the UN Convention on the Rights of the Child (1989) and further consolidated by more recent documents by the UN and UNICEF. Accordingly, 'rights-based' and 'voice-based' approaches to researching with children have been justified by suggesting that children as right-bearing citizens need to be enabled to make their voices heard in all important areas of their lives, including matters in their schooling (i.e. teaching, learning, curriculum and research).

Child-centred (and learner-centred) philosophies and theories of education promote the idea that in order for any learning to be effective, learners must feel engaged, interested and invested in their learning processes. They need meaningful tasks that encourage experiential learning and open-ended enquiry. Recent developments in general education that emphasise the open-ended nature of learning include the 'maker movement' or the 'twenty-first century skills' movement, both with a view to cut across traditional school subjects and promote individualised learning. Psychological principles and theories that cultivate synergies with child-centredness, such as the self-determination theory (Deci & Ryan, 2012) or the theory of education as happiness (Noddings, 2003), underline the importance of readiness to learn, the need for autonomy, competence, mastery motivation, a positive emotional disposition to learning and the cultivation of a personal interest rather than coercion or pressure. Such open-ended approaches to teaching and learning are conducive to encouraging child-led research and working in partnership with children in research.

Via the use of participatory techniques, children can be enabled to communicate their insights since these tools can make the process more meaningful and less reliant on conventional verbal data. Going further, many believe that offering opportunities to work in research partnerships with adults or being enabled to do their own research can also be empowering to children because they enjoy the process, gain confidence, learn new transferable skills, feel accomplished and develop their self-esteem. Those who embrace critical transformative pedagogy principles might not talk about research 'with' and 'by' children, but they certainly go some way in empowering children by respecting them as active learners through focussing on their ontologies and material lives. These adults encourage children to focus on relevant enquiry that is personal and meaningful, tapping into themes such as health, social justice or climate change (López-Gopar, 2016; López-Gopar & Sughrua, 2014). In these classrooms children develop positive identities and take active roles in their own learning. Such classrooms, therefore, can be fertile grounds for cultivating research skills and promoting joint research involving children or child-led research.

So-called democratic and radical educational principles also represent a clear link with the ideas of research 'with' children and 'by' children. Democratic education sees teaching and learning as the enactment of true democracy, where every child and every voice is equally important and where learning is always open-ended, motivated by and undertaken in the service of the community and its needs. This means that children take active roles in navigating their learning journeys in partnerships with adults. In fact, learning, teaching and researching become three aspects of the same process.

Bringing together such a variety of literatures from more elite ideas and concepts, such as twenty-first century approaches to learning to critical pedagogies introduced in marginalised communities, may not sit together comfortably at first glance, but the point of the book is this: *giving children and young people opportunities to take more active roles in research and in everyday teaching–learning processes is a realistic possibility in any context. Children can be invited to share their views, consult and collaborate with adults or indeed do their own research in any context, whether it is resource rich or poor.*

8.4 Research in the Vacuum versus Incorporated into School Life

Most children who have the chance to participate in research in active roles will do so accidentally and completely unexpectedly. One day an academic researcher turns up at the school, and the teacher in charge selects some children who will be invited to participate.

Even if such an opportunity turns into a project where the children will become co-researchers or are enabled to undertake their own child-led research, such isolated experiences are unlikely to have a lasting effect. After the project is completed, the children are expected to forget all about it and seamlessly slot back into their everyday school experiences, where they no longer take active roles. When such projects are undertaken in the 'vacuum', with children returning to the status quo after the project is concluded, there is an inevitable gap and a sense of loss or disappointment at the end because it is difficult to reconcile the active roles in the project with the passive roles assigned to them in everyday teaching and learning. Closing this gap would mean promoting pedagogic approaches within second language education that are more in line with participatory and active research experiences. Pedagogic approaches that cultivate autonomy and take learner-centredness and the learners' needs and identity as the foundation for planning teaching and learning can certainly prepare the ground for child-led research and collaborative projects between adults and children.

Schools can intentionally incorporate the opportunity to learn about and undertake research for everyone who is interested. Some scholars have consistently argued that all children should have the right to participate in child-led research projects while they are at school, as well as become familiar with the messages of the Convention on the Rights of the Child. Schools that decide to take closing this gap seriously can consider how to bring teaching and researching in alignment. One piece of advice offered by Fielding and Bragg (2003, p. 42; see Figure 8.1) is to run multiple 'student as researcher' groups at any one time, appoint a teacher coordinator in charge of child-led research and organise regular training for both adults and children.

8.5 Benefits and Challenges of Children's Active Participation

Evidence has been reviewed in previous chapters about how children's voices and views make a difference to how adults understand their reality and how they can influence service provision, materials development or school improvement in a positive way.

8.5 Benefits and Challenges of Active Participation

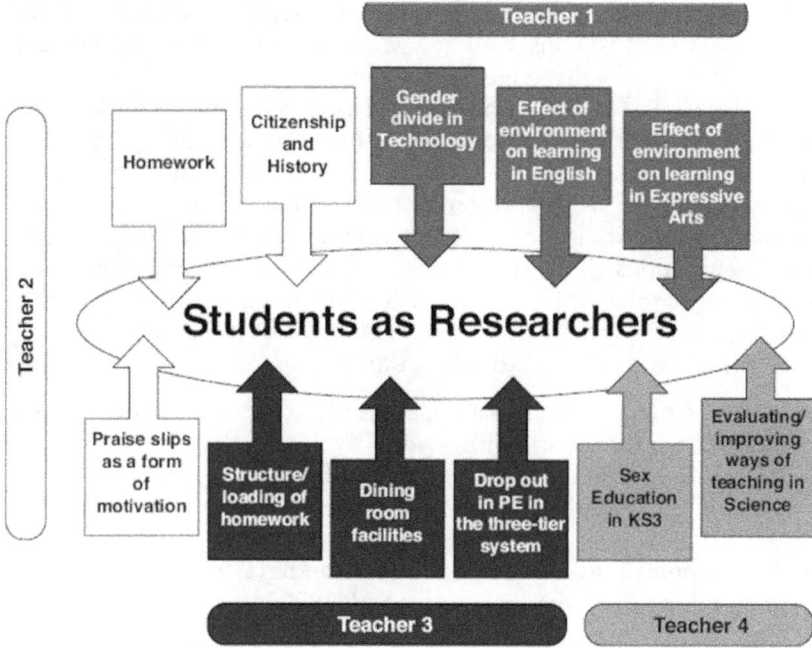

Figure 8.1 An example of running multiple child-led research projects in a school (Fielding & Bragg, 2003, p. 42)

Numerous examples have also illustrated how certain approaches and tools in different contexts can enable children to express their views and perspectives more confidently. Various types of active participation can be encouraged with multiple benefits. Some of these possibilities include children working as co-researchers or consultants or becoming researchers in their own right. While none of these options will be inherently better or more successful than traditional tools and approaches, in certain contexts under certain circumstances they have the potential to uncover unexpected insights from the children. These opportunities also give children the chance to develop their confidence, self-esteem and a range of transferable skills, to reflect about their learning and to discover research.

In research which invites children to be more active in the process, ethical dilemmas have the potential to become much more complex and difficult, so researchers working in this way need to be prepared to manage the ethical maze by following their individual path of good practice (Pinter, 2022) in an ongoing effort to work towards the highest ethical standards, keeping in mind what is best for the children while combining both macro- and micro-ethical concerns. Adult researchers need to constantly juggle what is fair, right and feasible. Warin (2011) calls this ethical mindfulness.

A great deal of discussion has covered aspects of ethics in this volume, suggesting that ethical approaches and decisions are highly dependent on the roles, beliefs and understandings of the adult and their paradigmatic assumptions. Facilitation and letting go of control but taking ultimate responsibility makes for a complex task. Challenging one's own assumptions all the time and staying mindful of inadvertent coercion must be the cornerstones of reflexivity alongside a disposition of 'humility' and respect for children (Prasad, 2021, p. 123).

Adult researchers need to reflect on:

- What their role and status as an adult researcher is and how they see the children they work with
- What child-centred research means to them
- What international legislation and guidelines mean in their contexts
- What ethical research with children means to them
- What opportunities and constraints they have in listening to children, taking their views seriously and acting on these views.

Alderson and Morrow (2020) remind us that it is also essential to think about whose interests are being served with any new study proposed, namely, who funds the research, in whose benefit, and whether the research is really necessary. 'All research is influenced by certain agendas, vested interests and stakeholder groups, which will influence the scope of the research and the research outcomes. The interests or agenda of an organisation, researcher and children and young people may be very different and have different implications for outcomes for each group' (Water, 2018, p. 39).

Any new study must also be eco-ethical, that is, it must consider ways in which steps can be taken to reduce the impact of the study on the climate crisis. Yet another piece of research undertaken in the interests of an adult group that will simply repeat previous findings might be harder to sell in the future as necessary and eco-ethical.

When children become co-researchers or researchers in applied linguistics, a key question arises about the *focus* and the *content* of their research and the language(s) they might use while engaging in the research. This is a particularly challenging issue because in many contexts children's L2 proficiency tends to be limited, and they may only be at the stage where they are developing initial steps in learning basic phrases and elementary grammar and vocabulary. In other contexts, or after learning an L2 for several years, proficiency levels will be higher, but still it is likely that children will have to fall back onto using their stronger or dominant languages when undertaking research, although even in these contexts it will often be possible to deliver outcomes such as presentations, posters or other summative documents in L2, or using a mixture of the L1 and L2, or indeed in multilingual contexts using the children's full linguistic repertoire in a holistic way. Especially in contexts such as CLIL or other types of immersion programmes, bilingual or multilingual practices and products will be both desirable and meaningful to the children. Engaging in research can be an excellent vehicle to tap into children's full linguistic repertoire.

8.6 Future Directions and Challenges

8.6.1 The Future of Childhood Studies

Since the main inspiration of this volume comes from Childhood Studies, it is important to pause and consider how the future of Childhood Studies may influence priorities in research with children in applied linguistics.

Having been around for decades, Childhood Studies and its associated scholarship have produced a large amount of evidence about children's active involvement in research, but Childhood Studies itself as an approach or paradigm has evolved since its beginnings. More recently, its future directions have been hotly debated.

At the early stages, inspired by the then new Convention on the Rights of the Child (1989), child-centred scholarship put a strong emphasis on rights. Viewing children as rights-based citizens elevated them to a new height and new status in society. Promoting the concept of children as active agents and recommending that participatory methods should be used to explore children's lived experiences led to the incorporation of children's insights into policy making. Listening to children was based on the conviction that children had important things to tell us, insights that adults did not have. A sharp dichotomy between traditional views and new alternative views about children was emphasised with the message that the new alternative views were 'better', more ethical and more respectful of children in research. This dichotomy, however, has increasingly come under criticism, and many scholars have started arguing that we must move beyond the simple 'celebration' of children's voices. More and more studies with participatory approaches with and by children have come under scrutiny, and scholars have begun to discuss the difficulties and the challenges inherent in these approaches, with some voices beginning to claim that the so-called voice-based and participatory approaches are not better or more effective per se, and that not all children are interested in such approaches or make for good researchers (Canosa & Graham, 2020).

Spyrou (2011) emphasised the context-specific characteristics of power dynamics and argued that participatory research did not overcome power differences between adults and children. Hammersley (2017) questioned the value of children's research and the assumption that adults cannot gain an understanding of children, while general concerns have also been raised about the fact that there appeared to be little consensus across the board about ethical guidelines and frameworks, and complexities appeared to be more difficult to untangle than previously believed. Prout (2019) raised concerns about the compartmentalisation of Childhood Studies and called for strengthening interdisciplinary collaborations. Stalford and Lundy (2020) also highlighted the importance of interdisciplinarity but noted that little has been achieved because methodological traditions in different disciplines appear to be obstacles. This is why in applied linguistics it is important to persevere with building bridges with other disciplines that are interested in children and the study of their experiences.

Early Childhood Studies scholars set out to capture children's authentic voices, but such an undertaking is now seen as simply futile since voice can never be disentangled from its context. Rather than searching for authentic voices, researchers have shifted to 'examining the assemblages of the research encounter' (Mayes, 2016, p. 14). Plows (2012, p. 288) argued that a relational and contextual approach to conceptualising agency is needed in studying interaction between children and adults.

In the future, rather than focussing on children as either actors or being acted upon (i.e. active participants or passive participants in research), it is important to engage more critically with the messiness and complexity of children's lives and to analyse the co-production of knowledge with a focus on the dynamic relationships of children with others (Spyrou, 2019). This suggests that in applied linguistics research as well, the focus should not just be on 'listening to children's voices' but on exploring and understanding the collaborative research processes when adults and children work together in unique and complex processes.

8.6.2 The Unpredictability of the Future

While it is hard to predict the future, one thing is for sure: our work with children needs to be constantly adjusted to new challenges that we face in the world, our communities, schools and classrooms. Adults

8.6 Future Directions and Challenges

need to adjust approaches and tools and explore new ways of engaging children in research that seem appropriate and effective. With the development of technology, for example, new ways of working will present themselves with children as expert users of these new technologies. But at the same time, new technologies always bring new challenges with them. This places a new responsibility on the adults in their roles as protectors of children's best interests and well-being without destroying opportunities for children to exercise their agency.

New legislation will be needed to protect children from harm on the Internet, such as on social networking sites. Children's privacy and their increasing digital footprint is a growing concern because of their parents' actions. Kravchuk (2021, pp. 116–117) argues that 'sharenting' (i.e. parents' frequent practice of sharing information about their children on the Internet) is a one of the biggest threats which needs urgent attention:

> Parents are presumed to play a key role in the protection of their children's rights since they are ideally positioned to assess and address the particular 'best interests' of their child. Measures developed to protect the privacy of the child are consequently framed within a paradigm of rendering support to parents, and not in the context of their obligation not to disclose information about their child. However, it is important not only to empower parents, but to provide for legal measures to limit the activities of those parents who choose to ignore the right of their children to privacy.

Alongside rapid technological development, climate change presents one of the other greatest threats for this generation of children, although other threats have also caught us unaware, such as the recent COVID-19 pandemic and the shocking outbreak of war in Europe.

Research has started to document the negative effects of the pandemic on children, although even in these difficult times, Lomax et al. (2022) and others have demonstrated that research with children could continue despite the heavy restrictions imposed on schools, families and children themselves. Rousell et al. (2021), for example, describe how they co-developed a climate change app with children and young people as co-researchers fully online. This project and similar ones attest to the great potential of undertaking research 'with' children in active roles in a virtual environment, although we must acknowledge the very real problems of lack of equity and the potential digital and social exclusion of some children from projects like these.

In the next few decades of the twenty-first century, new realities will mean that children's rights will need to be constantly reconsidered in light of new challenges emerging (Stalford & Lundy, 2020).

8.6.3 The Need to Embrace Critical Approaches

On the one hand childhoods have become globalised and mediated by technology to emphasise similarities of experiences, while on the other hand childhoods still continue to be vastly different across the globe. For example, as López-Gopar (2016) suggests, in indigenous communities, in Mexico for example, children work on market stalls, sweep floors, pick fruit, help with the running of shops or look after younger siblings and other family members after school. Working with children in research needs to embrace such local realities and embed any project firmly in children's priorities and lived experiences. It is also important to think about those children who are not in school due to a disability or other issues as these children can be left out inadvertently (Pincock & Jones, 2020).

A critical understanding of childhood is called upon to inform those who work with children and for children, suggesting that more targeted research in difficult contexts with marginalised communities of children will be needed in the future to counterbalance the usual focus on developed middle-class urban contexts. Thomas (2019, p. 325) talks about poverty, injustice and displacement in childhood as 'elephants in the room'. Stryker et al. (2019) also discuss generational injustice in an unequal world where children and young people suffer a disproportionate impact in contexts with extreme hardship and conflict.

Stalford and Lundy (2020) stress the importance of 'decolonising' the field and embracing approaches, epistemologies and views originating in other contexts as opposed to a Eurocentric tradition. The field needs more balanced approaches, not just Western-led ideas and Western empirical work. Faulkner and Nyamutata (2020) and Hanson and Peleg (2020) both point to the need to revisit and rethink the field of study referred to as children's rights and point out that promoting the Convention uncritically, for example, can come across as (unwittingly) colonial and ignorant of alternative world views. What do children's rights mean and what might children's active participation in research mean in different contexts in different parts of the world? Researchers need to explore these questions and take a bottom-up approach by considering the opportunities and challenges in the local realities. The important message is not to follow the Convention document to the letter but to raise both children's and adults' awareness about it and get them to think about which messages apply to them and why. Of course, it must be acknowledged that in some parts of the world any emphasis on children's rights and their voices will be met with outright rejection, and in such contexts the ideas discussed in this book will remain just abstract potentials. However, as Schostak et al. (2020, p. 192) suggest, even small 'pockets of resistance' on the margins by groups of learners and teachers taking small steps forward are worthwhile because they will be able to reap the benefits despite the very real obstacles in their contexts.

With regard to critical approaches in applied linguistics and child second language education, learning English rather than other second or foreign languages is particularly relevant as a topic for examination. 'Learning English is seen as "essential and as an "economic imperative" for a country's' *employment opportunities, economic development, modernization, internationalization, participation in the global economy* and to become an *economic global player*' (Sayer, 2015, p. 50, emphasis in original). However, due to the large and increasing gap between those who can afford high-quality English tuition and those who cannot, English ends up the 'preserve of the elites with access to private schooling, and, as such, it demarcates and divides social groups by reinforcing an unequal distribution of wealth, resources, and knowledge within and between nations' (Sayer, 2015, pp. 42–43).

In many contexts where teaching English in state schools to young children is mandated by government policy, teachers and researchers rightly question the intended benefits. Despite arguments that children do not necessarily benefit from English education, English is taught to children all over the world through educational policies and following parental demands. Yet, the lived experiences and identities of teachers and learners stand in stark contrast to the prescribed curriculum. Instead, a more inclusive pedagogy, which is often multilingual and multicultural rather than focussed on promoting English only as an L2, emerges as more meaningful and suitable. These proactively critical and transformative pedagogical approaches that aim to bolster learners' confidence and focus language teaching on their local realities often employ practices that invite children to take active roles in the everyday teaching and learning processes. These active roles would fit well with active roles in research, too.

8.7 What Is Needed in Our Field Now?

(1) We need to make children (and adults) aware that children have rights and familiarise them with the basic messages of the Convention document or its updated or locally adopted versions, creating spaces to think about what those messages mean to them in their own communities and to children in other parts of the

world. We need to explore opportunities in L2 classrooms and in schools regarding how children's rights may be implemented into everyday routines and activities including research but also other activities (e.g. Thelander, 2016). We need to encourage school-based projects where children can take active roles. In highly structured hierarchical spaces where learners' day-to-day functioning is fully prescribed, this will be challenging, but even small steps, such as informing the whole school about an ongoing project with children's active participation, can help the project to be owned by all and to succeed.

(2) We need to incorporate the extended framework for working with children and young people in research in applied linguistics into teacher education programmes, both pre-service and in-service. We need to promote networks and other initiatives that bring together interested teachers and academics who wish to implement projects that involve children in active roles in research. We need to encourage projects that can promote diverse partnerships in research (child–academic; teacher–child–academic, teams of teachers in networks, child-led projects that are sustainable). These different types of partnership allow for different dynamics and a variety of benefits for all involved.

(3) We need more studies following the examples presented in Chapter 6. These include studies that explore children's views and perspectives about various aspects of their language learning experiences, those that encourage children to take active roles, from consultants to co-researchers or researchers, and finally, those where traditional studies 'on' children are supplemented with new angles, such as insights from the participating children. We need more insights into how children experience research of all kinds, including research where they take active roles, since this can be a process that sharpens their developing understanding about research and helps them become increasingly informed about research, thus facilitating their participation in future projects (Pinter & Zandian, 2015; Zandian, 2021). There is a real need for documenting children's development over longer periods of time as active participants or developing researchers. In particular, more longitudinal studies with teachers' involvement are needed. Currently, there are very few studies that document children's development over time as they take on more roles in research. In fact, sustained involvement of children in research is rare: 'There is too little research, and particularly too little large-scale and sustainable models of research that involve children as

researchers or other deep levels of involvement' (Tisdall, 2012, p. 188). We also need more research with diverse groups of children, diverse in terms of different contexts, backgrounds, but also in terms of ages. Most research targets 10–12-year-olds or slightly older learners (13–15), and younger children are rarely included. This seems to be the case both in the wider literature outside and in applied linguistics (McNamee & Seymour, 2013). Most studies do not mention why a certain group of children are selected, with the consequence that not all children's language learning will be understood and certainly not all voices will be heard. Sometimes children are selected because the adult researcher feels that they are old enough to engage effectively with the adult's agenda (James et al., 1998).

Naturally, not every researcher or teacher will be interested to take on projects with children as active participants. However, all must at least be familiar with the extended framework for research involving children and be aware that such possibilities exist. Those who have never tried it will likely be sceptical, so for those of us who have tried it, it is our duty to speak up and tackle scepticism because the stakes for children are potentially high.

My intention with this book has been to bring together studies to illustrate what might be possible to adopt and adapt in our field. I am aware that I have not provided answers or recipes for best practice, but I hope that this book can serve as a basis for further explorations, discussions and new ways of working with children. I am also aware that much of the discussion has been about dilemmas, paradoxes and balancing acts, but numerous examples have illustrated that such complexities can be managed successfully, and future studies will continue to help us learn about the how to deal with the challenges.

The idea that research involving children can be one of the four different types (i.e. research 'on', 'about', 'with' and 'by' children) has been introduced in this book as a springboard for discussion throughout the chapters. This allowed me to maintain a sharp focus on the roles and the status of child participants in the various studies selected from the interdisciplinary literature. However, it must be acknowledged that this categorisation has also limited the discussion by attempting to shoehorn studies into just four categories. There may well be alternative ways of conceptualising active involvement of children in research in applied linguistics, and it is my hope that this volume's open-ended approach will invite such new approaches in future work.

8.8 Conclusion

The ideas in this book have grown out of my own personal interest. And they are just that. Ideas. They are not intended as a panacea or a way forward for everyone.

The real payoff for child second language education research is the very real opportunity to capture children's unique insights about their language learning experiences and to be able to work with them and respond to their concerns and the challenges they face in the language classroom, the school and beyond.

Tapping into children's abilities as partners in research, we can bring ever new perspectives to complement adult expertise and thus expand research in fresh directions. This will be an opportunity for teacher researchers as well as academic outsiders undertaking research 'with' children and enabling child-led research. All of us in the role of facilitating research 'with' or 'by' children need to seek out training opportunities to develop our skills and knowledge to find ways of moving forward and sharing experiences.

Research 'with' and 'by' children can be made relevant in all contexts, whether these are 'elite' well-resourced and well-researched contexts or whether the context in question is a school or community of children and teachers in challenging or marginalised cirumstances. Children's active participation in research can be beneficial and empowering in all contexts.

I would like to close this volume with a quote from two inspirational scholars who summarise our mission for the future.

Our research has to be relevant. It has to respond to the challenges children face, and to the legal, political, economic, social and cultural climates in which they live... we need to remain mindful of who and what our research is for, of what it is actually achieving. We need to reflect critically on whether our established methods and frameworks are fit for purpose and seek out fresh training and perspectives to update our skills and deepen our insights. Moreover, by actively engaging children in setting (rather than just responding to) our research agendas, and by investing time in cultivating a diverse range of partnerships with academics, practitioners and policy-makers in other countries and disciplines, we can react in a timely and appropriate way to issues as they arise. (Stalford & Lundy, 2020, pp. 10–11)

Appendix of Studies

These studies have not been included in the reference list except for those that are discussed in detail in Chapter 5. The purpose of the appendix is to capture the nature and the characteristics of empirical studies involving children and provide a snapshot of published work. Readers are invited to look up and explore these studies further.

Abbreviations used:

CAF	Complexity, accuracy and fluency
FFI	Form-focussed instruction
LRE	Language-related episode
NS	Native speaker
NNS	Non-native speaker
SES	Socio-economic status
WTC	Willingness to communicate

TESOL Quarterly

Author and year	Topic /key words	Country	Approach/methods	Age	Child participant role (active or passive)
Li and Hawkins (2021, 55)	Digital storytelling	USA	Ethnography/transmodal analysis	10–12	Passive, but 'about'
Villacanas et al. (2020, 55)	Culturally sustaining pedagogy	Spain	Collaborative action research		Active but not explicit 'with'
Alguilar et al. (2020, 54)	English academic language skills of dual language learners	USA	Treatment/tests/stats	10–12	Passive, 'on'
Racheho and Hamilton (2020, 54)	Bilanguaging love; student subjectivities and sensitivities	USA	Focal students/vignettes		Passive, 'about'
Britsch (2020, 54/2)	Social semiotic analysis of sheltered science instruction	USA	Extracts from classroom discourse with focus on four learners	13–14	Passive, 'on'
Beiler (2020, 54/1)	Multilingual resources in English writing instruction	Norway	Participant observation/ linguistic ethnography interviews/drawings	13–16	Passive 'about'
Davila (2020, 54/1)	Multilingual interactions and learning in sheltered classrooms	USA	Ethnographic/participant observation/focus groups/recorded classroom interaction/ longitudinal	15–18	Passive, 'about'
Seltzer (2019, 53/4)	Critical translanguaging	USA	Ethnographic/participant observations/interviews/ student writing samples	17	Passive, 'about'

Peters (2019, 53/4)	The effect of imagery on vocabulary learning	Netherlands	Experimental/control groups/pre-post tests/stats	16	Passive, 'on'
Penton Herrera (2019, 53/4)	Literacy instruction for ESOL newcomers/personal experiences on moral/ethical education	USA	Action research	15–18	Passive, 'about'
Wagner (2019, 53/4)	Reading identity and social status	USA	Micro-ethnographic approach/longitudinal/observations/draw and talk interviews	4	Passive, 'about'
Henry (2019, 53/2)	Online media creation and motivation	Sweden	Blog posts/observation/focus group interviews	13	Passive, 'about'
Kim et al. (2019, 53/2)	English language learning performance on paper and online tests	USA	Comparative analysis of writing quality/fluency and complexity/stats	6–7	Passive, 'on'
Al-Murtadha (2019, 53/1)	Enhancing willingness to communicate	Yemen	Experimental treatment/both qualitative and quantitative data/stats/interviews	16–18	Passive, 'on'
Bernstein (2018, 52/4)	Language growth of ELL learners	USA	Ethnography/observations/recording of interactions/network analysis	Pre-kindergarten	Passive, 'on'
Villacanas et al. (2018, 52/4)	Learning English in a an underprivileged context	Spain	CAR/multimodal self-portraits/interviews/collages	10–12	Active but not explicit 'about-with'
Serrano and Huang (2018, 52/4)	Learning vocabulary through assisted repeating	Taiwan	Experimental treatments/pre-post tests/stats	16	Passive, 'on'

(*continued*)

(cont.)

Author and year	Topic/key words	Country	Approach/methods	Age	Child participant role (active or passive)
Coxhead and Boutorwick (2018, 52/4)	Comparison of NS and NNS vocabulary growth in an international school	Germany	Vocabulary tests/stats	10–11	Passive 'on'
Winke et al. (2018, 52/2)	YL tests and their demands for NS and NNS children	USA	NS and NNS children took tests/interviews	7–8	Passive, 'on-about'
Rothoni (2018, 52/2)	Home and school literacies	Greece	Ethnographic case study/documents/interviews/fieldnotes	14–15	Active 'about-with'
Hwang et al. (2017, 51/4)	Relationship between vocabulary and reading performance	USA	Vocabulary and reading tests/stats	11–12 and 13–14	Passive, 'on'
Kunitz et al. (2017, 51/3)	Task-based learning/projects	Sweden	Recording of whole class and groups/conversation analysis/artefacts/handouts	12–13	Passive, 'on'
Cannon (2017, 51/2)	Drama and vocabulary learning	USA	Participant observation/group interviews	12–14	Passive, 'about-with'
Goulash (2017, 51/1)	Climate change: religious immigrant youth	USA	Observations/fieldnotes/interviews	17–18	Passive, 'about'
Galante and Thomson (2017, 51/1)	The effectiveness of drama to develop oral competence	Brazil	Experimental programme/rating learners' speech samples according to fluency, comprehensibility, accent	13–14	Passive, 'on'

Study	Topic	Country	Method	Age	Voice/preposition
Humphrey and Macnaught (2016, 50/4)	Functional language instruction and the writing growth of ELL	Australia	Longitudinal/instructional materials/audio-recorded lessons/students' writing	12–14	Passive, 'on - about'
Azkarai and Imaz Agirre (2016, 50/4)	Negotiation of meaning on tasks: mainstream and CLIL	Spain	Transcribing performances of two tasks for both age groups/comparing meaning negotiation measures/stats	9–10 and 11–12	Passive, 'on'
Chan (2016, 50/2)	Investigation of attitudes	Hong Kong	Tests/Stats	10–12 15–17 18+	Passive, 'on'
Thai and Boers (2016, 50/2)	Repeating a monologue under increasing pressure	Vietnam	CAF measures/stats	15	Passive, 'on'
Toohey et al. (2015, 49/3)	Digital tools and literacy	Canada	Ethnographic, analysis of materiality in videos made about sustainability/social justice	9–10	Active 'about-with'
Lai et al. (2015, 49/2)	Quality of out-of-class English learning	China	Mixed methods/questionnaires/grades/interviews/stats/thematic analysis	14	Passive, 'on-about'
Luk and Lin (2015, 49/1)	Criticality	Hong Kong	Reading a popular text followed by group discussions, class presentations, themes	17	Passive, 'on'
Shintani (2015, 49/1)	Incidental grammar acquisition	Japan	Treatment/pre- and post-tests/stats/extracts from interaction	6	Passive, 'on'

(*continued*)

(*cont.*)

Author and year	Topic /key words	Country	Approach/methods	Age	Child participant role (active or passive)
Kibler et al. (2014, 48/2)	Study of transitional devices in Spanish L1 students	USA	Longitudinal (over 4 years)/ transcripts of presentations/close analysis of discourse markers	13–18	Passive, 'on'
Kormos and Csiszer (2014, 48/2)	Motivation, self-regulation and autonomy	Hungary	Questionnaires/stats	16 (secondary) 21 (university) 35 (adults)	Passive, 'on'
Musk (2014, 48/1)	Avoiding target language	Sweden	Student pairs search for information on Google/ examination of search trajectories and translation tools/ conversation analysis	16	Passive, 'on'
Reed (2013, 47/4)	Effect of explicit instruction on students with intellectual disabilities	USA	Various phonics and sight word treatments/tests/ stats	13–15	Passive, 'on'
Ardasheva and Tretter (2013, 47/2)	Individual differences and contextual variables relating to ELL reading	USA	Reading tests/proficiency test/L1 literacy/maternal education levels/ metacognitive strategies/ stats	9–18	Passive, 'on'

Kim (2013, 47/1)	Effects of pre-task modelling on attention to form and question development	South Korea	Treatment and control groups/three task performances in pairs recorded/post-tests/ think-aloud protocols/ LREs/stats	12–13	Passive, 'on'
Shintani (2013, 47/1)	The effect of FonF and FonFs on the acquisition of vocabulary	Japan	Experimental groups (FonF and FonFs groups)/ control group/stats	6	Passive, 'on'
Ma (2012, 46/2)	Advantages and disadvantages of NS and NNS teachers	Hong Kong	Semi-structured interviews	13–17	Passive, 'on-about'
Li (2012, 46/1)	Effect of instruction on beginners' acquisition of request modification	China	Quasi-experimental/tests/ stats	13–14	Passive, 'on'
Collins and White (2011, 45/1)	Intensity in learning	Canada	Two types of intensive programmes compared/ pre-tests/treatments/ comprehension and production measures/ observations/ questionnaires about students' attitudes/stats	11–12	Passive, 'on'

43

Language Teaching Research

Author and year	Topic /key words	Country	Approach/methods	Age	Child participant role (active or passive)
Sato and Dussual Lam (2021, 25/6)	Metacognitive instruction: WTC, L2 use and metacognition of oral communication	Chile	Experimental and control groups/pre-post design/ questionnaire/L2 production during group work/WTC pyramids drawn before and after intervention/ post-intervention interviews/stats	8–9	Passive, 'on'
Fung and Macaro (2021, 25/4)	Relationship between strategy use and linguistic knowledge (listening to the teacher)	Hong Kong	Questionnaire on listening to the teacher/interviews/test of linguistic knowledge/stats	14	Passive, 'on'
Hidalgo and García Mayo (2021, 25/4)	Effect of repetition on collaborative writing	Spain	Analysis of LREs/ comparison of two types of repetition treatments/ exact same task versus same task type with new content/stats	11–12	Passive, 'on'

Bai and Guo (2021, 25/3)	Individual differences in students' motivation, strategy use and English writing competence	Hong Kong	Motivation questionnaire on writing/writing proficiency test/questionnaire on strategy use/stats	9–10	Passive, 'on'
Frashi and Tavakoli (2021, 25/3)	Language aptitude and learning collocations	Iran	Quasi-experimental intervention: pre-post test and delayed post-test design/three different methods of presenting input with collocations/various tests/stats	14–18	Passive, 'on'
D'Warte (2021, 25/1)	Working with culturally and linguistically diverse young people	Australia	Visual methodologies/language mapping/revisiting data from two classes from a larger study/linguistic ethnography/design research/observations/field notes and recorded lesson segments/student-produced language maps/focus group interviews;	10–12	Active 'about-with'
Choi and Slaughter (2021, 25/1)	Multilingualism through language trajectory grids	Australia	EAL learners/grids/plotting trajectories; asked to plot their reading and writing journeys/events and experiences/individual conversations	15–16	Active about-with 'child-friendly tool'

(*continued*)

(cont.)

Author and year	Topic /key words	Country	Approach/methods	Age	Child participant role (active or passive)
			based on the grid/a questionnaire about resources/ thematic analysis		
Zhang and Graham (2020, 24/6)	Vocabulary learning through listening	China	Vocabulary and listening tests/intervention/four groups compared with different types of teacher explanation/stats	15–16	Passive, 'on'
Li and Tong (2020, 24/6)	Effects of two types of visual-verbal cognitive Chinese vocabulary learning approaches (with Chinese L1 learners)	USA	Pre-test, post-tests design/ vocabulary tests/ motivation survey	9–10 and 10–11	Passive, 'on'
Villareal and Gil-Sarratea (2020, 24/6)	The effect of collaborative writing on Basque Spanish bilingual students' English	Spain	Control and experimental groups/different treatments (producing writing collaboratively or individually)/pre-tests/recordings from some collaborating pairs/LREs/CAF measures/stats	16–17	Passive, 'on'

Nguyen and Newton (2020, 24/5)	Task-based learning/ effect of rehearsal	Vietnam	Two tasks (problem solving and debate)/LRE analysis/extracts from task performances/stats	16	Passive, 'on'
Rogers and Cheung (2020, 24/5)	Input spacing and the learning of vocabulary in classroom setting	Hong Kong	Experiment (nine weeks) two conditions: input spaced short or long/pre-tests/training sessions / post-test/stats	8–9	Passive, 'on'
Zhang and Baills with Prieto (2020, 24/5)	Learning French words with hand clapping to the rhythm	China	Experiment (clapping and non-clapping groups) pre- and post-test design/ various tests, such as memory test, musical ability test, speech imitation test/ pronunciation ratings/ stats	13–15	Passive, 'on'
Fenyvesi (2020, 24/5)	English learning motivation of primary Danish learners	Denmark	Quantitative survey/ interviews/stats plus some extracts from interviews	8–10	Passive, 'on-about'
Henry and Thorsen (2020, 24/4)	Disaffection: Re-designing activities to enable authentic self-expression	Sweden	Data drawn form a larger study on motivation/ excerpts from students' presentations/identity work and resistance	16–17	Passive, 'on-about'

(*continued*)

(cont.)

Author and year	Topic /key words	Country	Approach/methods	Age	Child participant role (active or passive)
Poehner and Leontjev (2020, 24/3)	Dynamic assessment: Mediational processes (Russian as L1 speakers)	Estonia	Two studies: one case study with one learner and one study with a group of learners/ qualitative data (extracts)/stats	16	Passive, 'on'
Pladewall-Ballester (2019, 23/6)	Longitudinal study of motivation in CLIL and non-CLIL contexts	Spain	Motivation questionnaire/ CLIL versus non-CLIL/stats	9–12	Passive, 'on'
San Isidro, Lasagabaster (2019, 23/5)	Impact of CLIL on pluriliteracy development and content learning;	Spain (rural Galicia)	L3 English and L1/L2 tests/ language and content measures throughout the two years of the study/ stats	14–15	Passive, 'on'
Van de Guchte et al. (2019, 23/3)	German as an L2: Focus on language versus content in pre-task	Netherlands	Two randomly assigned groups/focus on language and focus on content conditions/pre-post and delayed post-test design/set of tests/ stats	14–15	Passive, 'on'

Author	Topic	Country	Method	Age	
Martinez-Adrian, et al. (2019, 23/1)	Self-reported use of communication strategies in primary CLIL	Spain	Basque/Spanish bilingual learners/biographical questionnaire/ proficiency test and communication strategy questionnaire/two age groups/stats	10–11 11–12	Passive, 'on'
Meguro (2019, 23/1)	Textual enhancement, grammar, reading and tag questions	Japan	Pre-post test design/three experimental groups and a control group/stats	11–12	Passive, 'on'
Dewaele et al. (2018, 22/6)	Foreign language enjoyment and anxiety	Britain	Questionnaire/stats	12–18	Passive, 'on'
Huh and Suh (2018, 22/5)	Elementary readers as critical intercultural citizens	South Korea	Practitioner action research/afterschool literacy engagement/ recording of class sessions/thematic analysis/extracts from dialogues and student work/artefacts	11–12	Passive, 'about-with'
Rostamian et al. (2018, 22/4)	The effect of planning time on task performance (writing)	Iran	Story narrated based on six pictures/control group (no planning)/two experimental groups (one with unlimited planning and one with ten minutes of planning)/ stimulated recall interviews/CAF measurements/stats	14-17	Passive, 'on'

(*continued*)

(*cont.*)

Author and year	Topic /key words	Country	Approach/methods	Age	Child participant role (active or passive)
Kamiya (2018, 22/1)	The effect of learner age on the interpretation of nonverbal behaviours of teachers in identifying questions (L1 Japanese)	Japan	Judgements about the existence of questions in the video clip without sound (elicited in an interview)/stats	11–12 and 18–21 Comparison of children with adults	Passive, 'on'
Jamagata (2018, 22/1)	Comparison of learner-centred and teacher-centred approaches to learning basic verb meanings	Japan	Two methods of learning new verbs followed by a lexical retrieval test/questionnaire about the effectiveness of each approach focussing on motivation and noticing/stats	12	Passive, 'on'
Butler (2017, 21/6)	Motivational elements of digital games: Children's game design	Japan	Mixed method: analysis of discussions, children's final game designs/peer evaluations	11–12	Active 'with'
Tragant et al. (2017, 21/5)	Comparison of two domestic summer English programmes	Spain	Pre-test and post-test design/questionnaires, oral narrative task based on pictures/written narrative based on comic strip and a dialogue task/CAF /measures and lexical richness/stats	11–13	Passive, 'on'

Author (year)	Title	Country	Method	Age	Passive
Prosic-Santovac (2017, 21/5)	Popular video cartoons and branded toys to teach English to very young learners	Serbia	Case study/daily exposure to Peppa Pig alongside with playing with branded toys/ researcher's own daughter/daily guided play/both structured and unstructured activities/ active vocabulary test (Peabody) /observation recorded in research diary/Berkeley Puppet Interview	4	Passive, 'on-about'
Azkarai and García Mayo (2017, 21/4)	Task repetition effects in L1 use in EFL child task-based interaction	Spain	Spot the difference task/ repetition of the same task (with different content)/stats	9–10	Passive, 'on'
Lee and Pulido (2017, 21/1)	The impact of topic interest, L2 proficiency and gender on incidental vocabulary learning in reading	South Korea	Repeated measures design: students read both high-interest and low-interest topic passages/ vocabulary post-tests immediate and delayed/ stats	14–15	Passive 'on'
Dolean (2016, 20/5)	The effects of teaching songs on students' foreign language anxiety	Romania	Two experimental classes and a control class /five-week programme of teaching French through music/self-reported levels of anxiety before	14–15	Passive 'on'

(*continued*)

(*cont.*)

Author and year	Topic/key words	Country	Approach/methods	Age	Child participant role (active or passive)
			and after/questionnaire completed by experimental classes/stats		
Van de Guchte et al. (2016, 20/3)	L2 German task-based study: Focus on form through repetition	Netherlands	Experimental pre-test post-test design with delayed post-test; two interventions examining the effects of task repetition/repetition or no repetition conditions/two target structures/tests for metalinguistic knowledge, written and oral accuracy and fluency/stats	14–15	Passive 'on'
Webb and Chang (2015, 19/6)	Second language vocabulary learning through extensive reading	Taiwan	Experimental and control groups/experimental group learnt through extensive reading/vocabulary test/vocabulary learning rates measured after treatment in both groups/stats	15–16	Paassive 'on'

Heras and Lasagabaster (2015, 19/1)	The impact of CLIL on affective factors and vocabulary learning	Spain (Basque country)	Pre-test, post-test delayed post-test design/CLIL and non-CLIL/ motivation and self-esteem questionnaire/ vocabulary test/stats	16	Passive 'on'
Moonen et al. (2014, 18/4)	German as L2/effects of task type on the repetition and ease of activation of second language vocabulary	Netherlands	Quasi-experimental study/ pre-test/treatment tasks/ post-test/think aloud/ stats	9–10	Passive 'on'
Shintani and Ellis (2014, 18/4)	Incidental acquisition of two adjectives	Japan	Tracking learning behaviours in nine task-based lessons/test data/ test scores and qualitative interaction data analysis	6	Passive 'on'
Davin (2013, 17/3)	Dynamic assessment of Spanish as an L2 to promote language development	USA	Interviews, fieldnotes, audio-recordings/ twenty-nine interaction extracts focussed on questions/qualitative analysis	10–12	Passive 'on'
Gagne and Parks (2013, 17/2)	Children scaffolding each other in a cooperative task	Canada	Interactions for two groups were analysed; some stats to determine differences between the groups/data extracts/	10–11	Passive 'on'

(*continued*)

(*cont.*)

Author and year	Topic/key words	Country	Approach/methods	Age	Child participant role (active or passive)
Shintani (2012, 16/2)	Input-based tasks and the acquisition of vocabulary and grammar	Japan	Experimental and control groups/experimental group exposed to input task/target vocabulary/instructional treatments and tests/analysis of extracts/some stats	6	Passive 'on'
Graham et al. (2011, 15/4)	Listening and strategy use in L2 French	UK	Teacher and individual learner interviews/test/listening scores and listening strategy elicitation/some qualitative analysis of strategy use/extracts	16–17	Passive, 'on-about'
Ballinger and Lyster (2011, 5/3)	Oral language use in a two-way Spanish–English immersion school	USA	Classroom observations/student questionnaire/teacher interview and student focus group/extracts	5–6, 7–8 and 12–13	Passive, on-about'
Whittaker et al. (2011, 15/3)	Writing development in CLIL history classes	Spain	Writing samples/compositions collected/excerpts	12–16	Passive, 'on'

Shintani (2011, 15/2)	Input-based and production-based instruction	Japan	Input-based, and control groups/Pre-post and delayed post-test design/ six weeks' of instruction/ four types of vocabulary tests/stats	6–8	Passive, 'on'
Kim and McDonough (2011, 15/2)	Pre-task modelling to encourage collaborative learning	South Korea	Between groups design/ impact of pre-task modelling (explicit instruction and video modelling of the task)/ experimental and control groups/LREs/ stats	13–14	Passive, 'on'

Applied Linguistics

Author and year	Topic /key words	Country	Approach/methods	Age	Child participant role
Kyo (2021)	L2 self-efficacy and its effect on L2 learning	South Korea	Testing at three points for all learners at 12/13/14. Longitudinal	12–14	Passive, 'on'
Booton et al. (2021, 42)	Children's knowledge of multiple word meanings	UK	Nested multilevel design/ homonym tests and other tests/stats	5–9	Passive, 'on'
Meer et al. (2021, 42)	Attitudes of German high school students to different varieties of English	Germany	Different experimental and non-experimental language attitude research methods/ questionnaire/stats	15–19	Passive, 'on'
Routarinne and Ahlholm (2021, 42/4)	Developing requests: A case of one learner L1 Russian learning Finnish	Finland	A longitudinal case study/ 48 hours of video-recorded multilingual lessons with a focus on one key learner/ multimodal interaction analysis	9	Passive, 'on-about'
Lichtman (2021, 42/4)	Implicit versus explicit training	USA	Mini-language tests/stats	Comparing adults and children 5–7 Adult 14–15	Passive, 'on'
Northbrook and Conklin (2019, 40/5)	Textbook-derived lexical bundles	Japan	Materials: some lexical bundles/tests/language background survey/ stats		Passive, 'on'

Kormos et al. (2019, 40/5)	The role of low-level L1 skills and L2 reading: Young dyslexic learners	Slovenia	All participants diagnosed with dyslexia/sets of tests for L2 reading/special needs assessment profile/stats	11–12	Passive, 'on'
Deignan et al. (2019, 40/2)	Metaphors of climate science in research articles, educational texts and interviews with school students	UK	Corpora compared/focus group interviews with students/sketch engine analysis/qualitative analysis of the metaphors in the learner corpus	11–16	Passive, 'on'
Ganuza and Hedman (2019, 40/1)	The impact of mother tongue instruction on biliteracy development in Swedish Somali speakers	Sweden	Biliteracy operationalised as reading proficiency and vocabulary knowledge in two languages/cross-sectional, cross-linguistic and longitudinal analyses/stats	6–12	Passive, 'on'
Wisniewski (2018, 39/6)	The empirical validity of the Common European Framework of Referece vocabulary and fluency scales (Italian/German) both as L1 and L2	South Tyrol (Italy)	Student asked to complete a monologue task and discuss a topic with interviewer/rated by two raters/stats	17–18	Passive, 'on'

(continued)

(cont.)

Author and year	Topic /key words	Country	Approach/methods	Age	Child participant role
Laursen and Kostrup (2018, 39/6)	Language play: Multilingual children between real and imaginary worlds (Danish as L2)	Denmark	Legogloss activity (like dictogloss but based on individual notes of a short text)/excerpts in chronological order to demonstrate how language play develops/interaction analysis	12–13	Passive, 'on-about'
Kasprowitcz and Marsden (2018, 39/6)	Input-based practice, L2 German: Form spotting	UK	Target feature: German case marking/pre-test interventions/post-test and delayed post-test	9–11	Passive, 'on'
Hawkins (2018, 39/1)	Transmodalities and transnational encounters	USA	Video shared by children across contexts/photos/ thematic analysis	11–12	Passive, 'about-with'
Courtney et al. (2017, 38/6)	Individual differences in early learning of French	UK	Language outcomes measured at three points using two oral production tasks/ longitudinal data on attitudes and motivation via questionnaires/teacher assessment of L1 skills/ stats	11–12	Passive, 'on'

Zhang (2017, 38/6)	Derivational morphology in reading comprehension	China	Effect of morphological awareness/a set of tests/tests taken a year apart	9–10	Passive, 'on'
Henry and Cliffordson (2017, 38/5)	The impact of out-of-school factors on motivation to learn English	Sweden	Measures: ideal and current selves/attributions/self-authenticity/questionnaire/hypotheses/stats	16–17	Passive, 'on'
Roquet and Perez-Vidal (2017, 38/4)	CLIL productive skills: Writing Catalan Spanish English L3 students	Spain	Written data (composition) elicited at two data collection times/CAF, task fulfilment/grammar organisation and vocabulary use analysis/stats	12–15	Passive, 'on'
Hallin and Van Lancker Sidtis (2017, 38/1)	Formulaic language (Swedish as L1), proverbs	Sweden	Swedish proverbs and control sentences/familiarity questionnaire/tonal patterns/stats	Comparing adults and children of 11–13	Passive, 'on'
Tedick and Young (2016, 37/6)	Fifth grade two-way immersion: FFI of the past tense	USA	Audio-recorded classroom observations/fieldnotes/recorded language use prior to FFI instruction/during FFI instruction and	10–11	Passive, 'on'

(*continued*)

(cont.)

Author and year	Topic /key words	Country	Approach/methods	Age	Child participant role
			after it/both quantitative and qualitative analysis of the transcripts/stats/ excerpts		
Kinginger et al. (2016, 37/5)	Mealtime talk in Chinese home stay (US students)	China	Recording conversations/ isolating meal-related episodes/counting turns in transcribed data/excerpt analysis/ microanalysis/	17–18	Passive/on
Kerfoot et al. (2016, 37/4)	Game changers: Multilingual learners in Cape Town primary	South Africa	Observations (school and home settings)/ interviews/audio-recorded peer interactions with children/focus on translanguaging/ themes/qualitative extracts	10–13	Passive, 'on'
Trebits (2016, 37/2)	Individual difference and L2 narrative production	Hungary	Two narrative tasks in speech and writing/ level of anxiety assessed/stats	17–18	Passive, 'on'

Unsworth et al. (2015, 36/5)	Factors affecting early foreign language learning in the Netherlands	Netherlands	Two groups with early EFL and later EFL groups/low level of exposure/medium and high level/control group/longitudinal (two years)/end-of-year testing/Peabody picture vocabulary test/phonological processing and grammar tests/stats	4	Passive, 'on'
Clachar (2015, 36/5)	Processing subject relative clauses, bilingual children (Creole)	USA	Sentence combining task/patterns	13	Passive, 'on'
Nishikawa (2014, 35/4)	Near-native child L2 starters of Japanese: Age and the acquisition of relative clauses (Japanese as L2)	Japan	Audio-recorded speech samples rated by adult NS/correlations between the age of immersion into a Japanese-speaking environment and nativeness/relative clause task/analysis of errors/stats	Comparison between L2 Japanese children (aged 10 or above), NS Japanese children aged 10–12 and adult NS	Passive, 'on'
Sparrow (2014, 35/3)	Unconventional word segmentation in bilingual writing	USA	Longitudinal study/patterns in segmentation over time/stats	6–8	Passive, 'on'

(*continued*)

(cont.)

Author and year	Topic /key words	Country	Approach/methods	Age	Child participant role
Wortham and Rhodes (2013, 34/5)	Life as a chord: One migrant girl	USA	Ethnographic study/ chord metaphor/ extracts	8	Passive, 'on-about'
Toth et al. (2013, 34/3)	Explicit L2 knowledge, high school Spanish	USA	Small-group and whole-class co-constructions of the target structure/ coding of the interaction/excerpts	15–18	Passive, 'on'
Levey (2012, 33/3)	General extenders: Preadolescents in London (L1 use)	UK	Audio-recorded data in school/working-class white ethnic majority/ series of interviews in pairs/vernacular discourse features/ coding/gender and age differences/some stats	7–11	Passive, 'on'
Tambulukani and Bus (2012, 33/2)	Linguistic diversity: Contributing to reading problems	Zambia	One-to-one tests/ vocabulary and reading tests in L1 and English/stats	7–8	Passive, 'on'
Kormos et al. (2011, 32/5)	Goals, attitudes, self-related beliefs and motivation in L2 learning	Chile	Questionnaire/stats	Comparing secondary (14–15), university (21) and adult (31)	Passive, 'on'

System

Author and year	Topic /key words	Country	Approach/methods	Age	Child participant role
El Majidi et al. (2021, 101)	Effects of in-class debates on argumentation skills (written and oral)	Netherlands	Pre- and post-test quasi-experimental design/ intervention: debate task/comparison of both oral and written texts before and after/stats	15–18	Passive, 'on'
Yao et al. (2021, 101)	Language mindsets: Young EFL learners' beliefs	China	Questionnaires/measuring mindsets with a language mindset inventory/stats	12–15	Passive, 'on'
Saeedaktar et al. (2021, 101)	Impact of collaborative listening on comprehension and vocabulary learning	Iran	Target words/pre- and post-tests of vocabulary knowledge and listening comprehension/ podcasts to listen to in pairs with follow-up activities/a questionnaire to elicit experimental groups' opinion of treatment / stats	13–17	Passive, 'on'

(*continued*)

(cont.)

Author and year	Topic /key words	Country	Approach/methods	Age	Child participant role
Xu and Li (2021, 101)	Comparison of three types of FFI: Effect on difficult and easy grammar learning	China	Three groups with slightly different treatments/pre- and post-test design/a set of tests: error correction test and a grammatical judgement test/stats	12–14	Passive, 'on'
Kangasvieri and Leontjev (2021, 100)	L2 self-concepts of Finnish students: Role of grades, parents, peers and society	Finland	Survey/motivational scales and self-reported grades/variety of languages learnt/stats	15–16	Passive, 'on'
Boye et al. (2021, 100)	Makes head hurt: Children's perceptions of language classroom	Brunei	Repertory grid technique	14	Passive, 'on-about'
Bashori et al. (2021, 99)	Automatic speech recognition websites: Effects on vocabulary, anxiety and enjoyment	Indonesia	Pre- and post-test design/ placement tests/ questionnaires/ vocabulary test/web-based experiments with two experimental groups/control group: no web intervention/ interviews with students and teachers/stats /some extracts from interviews	14–17	Passive, 'on'

Cancino and Panes (2021, 98)	Impact of Google Translate (GT) on L2 writing quality measures	Chile	Proficiency test/three groups with participants using GT with instruction, without instruction and not using it/writing task comparisons/stats	16–17	Passive, 'on'
Luquin and García Mayo (2021, 98)	Use of models as written corrective feedback	Spain	Pre- and post-test/ experimental group received a model/control group self-edited their texts/picture prompt to write about/texts written in pairs/a familiarisation stage to introduce the task and the idea of a model before the study starts/ stats	11–12	Passive, 'on'
Zhang and Zhang (2021, 98)	Self-initiated error correction	China	Pre-and post-test/ treatment: reading and extending sections from a novel/frequencies of different types of errors/ stats	17	Passive, 'on'

(*continued*)

(*cont.*)

Author and year	Topic /key words	Country	Approach/methods	Age	Child participant role
Hargreaves and Elhawary (2021, 98)	Children's experiences of agency when learning English	Egypt	Teachers trained to apply pair work in their classrooms/children completing open-ended sentences about their classrooms/observations of classrooms and interviews/autonomy questionnaire verbally administered/data coding/themes/extracts;	6–8	Passive, 'on-about'
Lim et al., (2021, 97)	Interactive e-book reading versus paper book reading: Effects on comprehension	South Korea	Treatment and control groups/pre- and post-tests and a survey/six books/stats	12–15	Passive, 'on'
Razi and Grenfell (2021, 97)	Strategy instruction in reading development	Cyprus	Quasi-experimental intervention/mixed methods/intervention and control groups/ strategy instruction cycle/tests/some stats/ codes	12–13	Passive, 'on'

Molway (2021, 97)	Student perceptions of modern foreign language lessons (students of French)	UK	Student and teacher surveys/descriptive stats	12–13	Passive, 'on'
Lee et al. (2021, 97)	A study of examination scripts by adolescents	Hong Kong	A corpus of students' writing analysed investigating lexical and syntactic complexity/stats	17–18	Passive, 'on'
Li and Zhang (2021, 97)	L2 motivational self-system	Tibet (China)	Questionnaire/language achievement test/stats	16–17	Passive, 'on'
Li et al. (2021, 96)	Classroom environment and emotional intelligence: Effects on foreign language anxiety and enjoyment	China	Questionnaires/stats	Comparing secondary and university students 16 and 18	Passive, 'on'
Leona et al. (2021, 96)	Extramural English exposure in the Netherlands: explaining individual differences	Netherlands	Longitudinal for two years/questionnaires/Peabody and other tests/stats	10–12	Passive, 'on'
Bai and Wang (2021, 96)	Self-regulated learning strategy use in writing: Influence of motivational beliefs	Hong Kong	Questionnaire related to writing motivation/strategy questionnaire/writing test/stats	12–16	Passive, 'on'

(*continued*)

(*cont.*)

Author and year	Topic /key words	Country	Approach/methods	Age	Child participant role
Sadeghi and Pourhaji (2021, 96)	Working memory and pre-task instruction in L2 oral performance	Iran	All complete an operation span task/experimental and control groups/both with planning time but experimental group also received explicit instruction/stats	14–16	Passive, 'on'
Liu and Song (2021, 96)	'Flow' in young Chinese learners' online activities	China	Online English activities/ dubbing task/ questionnaire about the three stages of flow/ semi-structured interview /stats/some extracts from interviews	14–15	Passive, 'on'
Herazo (2021, 96)	Mediating spoken meaning making, metalinguistic concepts	Columbia	Genre-based instructional materials are introduced/ observations/audio-recorded focal student/interaction/discourse analysis/analysis of episodes	11	Passive, 'on'

Coyle and de Larios (2020, 95)	Young learners' engagement with models as written feedback	Spain	Comparing CLIL with non-CLIL/all pairs were asked to write a story and then re-write it following feedback in the form of a model/ collaborative dialogues and written texts were analysed/LREs, descriptive stats/extracts	9–11	Passive, 'on'
Coyle et al. (2020, 94)	YL collaboratively written narratives: Improving cohesion	Spain	Experimental and control groups of children in pairs/over several weeks experimental group received reformulated feedback, whereas control group self-edited their texts/analysis of reference cohesion in all texts/stats	11–12	Passive, 'on'
Azkarai and Kopinska (2020, 94)	Young learners and collaborative writing, interaction, engagement in LREs and task motivation	Spain	Dictogloss/motivational thermometer before and after the task/oral interaction analysed for engagement in LREs/ extracts /stats	10–11	Passive, 'on'

(continued)

(*cont.*)

Author and year	Topic/key words	Country	Approach/methods	Age	Child participant role
Serfaty and Serrano (2020, 94)	Potential of digital flashcards to facilitate independent grammar learning	Cambodia	A free app is used to create flashcards/pre- and post-test design with immediate and two delayed post-tests/stats	9–17	Passive, 'on'
Farid and Lamb (2020, 94)	L2 motivation in Indonesian schools	Indonesia	Survey/interest in religious factors in paying a role in motivation/stats	16–18	Passive, 'on'
Resnik and Dewaele (2020, 94)	Positive and negative emotions in L1 and L2 classes (L1 German and L2 English)	Austria, Germany, Switzerland and Tyrol (Italy)	Several sets of surveys/ emotional intelligence scores/stats	14 + secondary and tertiary students (oldest 52)	Passive, 'on'
Meguro (2020, 94)	Field dependence and independence and analogical reasoning in L2 instruction	Japan	Pre- and post-test design/ treatment/instruction and various tests/fill in the gap task/stats	17	Passive, 'on'
Tsang (2020, 94)	Learners' views of non-standard accents	Hong Kong	Questionnaire/stats	14–17	Passive, 'on'
Sun and Dang (2020, 93)	Learner knowledge of vocabulary in textbooks	China	Vocabulary tests/analysing the vocabulary in the textbook corpus/stats	16–18	Passive, 'on'

Bi and Jiang (2020, 91)	Syntactic complexity in young learners writing	China	Narrative essays/syntactic complexity analysis/stats	13–18	Passive, 'on'
Aka (2020, 91)	Incidental learning of grammar from reading	Japan	Pre- and post-test design/experimental and control groups/experimental reading passages/grammar tests/stats	15–16	Passive, 'on'
Castellano-Risco et al. (2020, 91)	Development of receptive vocabulary in CLIL and EFL	Spain	Three CLIL groups compared to EFL/vocabulary tests/stats	14–15	Passive, 'on'
Saeeddaktar, et al. (2020, 91)	The effects of hands-on and hands-off data-driven learning of verb-preposition collocations	Iran	Two experimental groups and a control group/two types of treatment: hands-off paper-based corpus of collocations and hands-on group searching online/both experimental groups received teacher guidance/attitude questionnaire/stats	16–18	Passive, 'on'
Kang (2020, 89)	Using model texts as a form of feedback in L2 writing	South Korea	Experimental and control groups/proficiency test/writing an argumentative essay and a model text in the experimental group/questionnaires/stats	17–18	Passive, 'on'

(*continued*)

(*cont.*)

Author and year	Topic /key words	Country	Approach/methods	Age	Child participant role
Liu and Stapleton (2020, 89)	Counter-argumentation at primary level	Hong Kong	A twelve-lesson intervention focussed on counter-argumentation/ scripts analysed for argumentative elements/ pre-and post-test design/ measurements of progress at post-test and delayed post-test stage/ no control group/pie charts and descriptive stats/examples from scripts	11	Passive, 'on'
Hu and McGeown (2020, 89)	Relationship between foreign language motivation and achievement	China	Questionnaires about motivation/teachers provided measures of achievement/stats	9–12	Passive, 'on'
Candry et al. (2020, 89)	Comparing word writing and retrieval practice	Netherlands	Pre-and post-test design/ comparing three conditions: two experimental groups and one control group/ recall tests administered afterwards as post-test and again as delayed post-tests/stats	15–18	Passive, 'on'

Author	Topic	Location	Method	Age	Voice
Wong (2020, 88)	Effect of proficiency on L2 motivational selves (ethnic minority students learning Chinese)	Hong Kong	Questionnaire about L2 selves/proficiency tests in listening, reading/learners rated their own proficiency/stats	12	Passive, 'on'
Tseng et al. (2020, 88)	Vocabulary learning in virtual environments; Interplay between autonomy and collaboration	Taiwan	Quasi-experimental design/three experimental groups and one control group: pair, individual, teacher-centred and control groups/3D virtual environment/vocabulary learning programme/target word selection/stats	9	Passive, 'on'
Netz and Fogel (2020, 87)	Corrective feedback in Torah reading tutoring sessions	Israel (American parentage)	Naturalistic/observational study/corpus of dyadic tutoring analysed for error treatment episodes/descriptive stats and qualitative microanalysis/	12	Passive, 'on'
Milla et al. (2020, 87)	Language learning strategy choice by children in CLIL: Effect of age, proficiency and gender/Spanish Basque learners of English	Spain (Basque country)	Questionnaire about learning strategies/language proficiency tests/stats	10–11 and 11–12	Passive, 'on'

(*continued*)

(cont.)

Author and year	Topic/key words	Country	Approach/methods	Age	Child participant role
Allaw and McDonough (2019, 85)	The effect of task sequencing on written lexical complexity, accuracy and fluency (French learners)	Lebanon	Pre-and post-test design/ tasks with various levels of complexity/task sequencing: from simply to complex group versus complex to simple group/dependent variables: lexical CAF/ task perception questionnaire/stats	13–14	Passive, 'on'
Yasuda (2019, 85)	Children's meaning making choices in writing	Japan	Comparison of CLIL and non-CLIL; letter writing task was assigned/ analysis of the letters/ focus on cohesive devices/examples of letters/extracts/some stats	10	Passive, 'on'
Calafato and Tang (2019, 84)	Motivational L2 selves of Emirati teenagers	UAE	Motivation questionnaire/ stats	14	Passive, 'on'

Widdington (2019, 82)	Developing primary learners' foreign language self-concept	Spain (Catalonia)	Action research framework/ foregrounding participants' perspectives/ questionnaires, small-group discussions and class observations/ grounded theory/focus on self-efficacy/ contrasting pre- and after project data/ themes/relationships	10–11 and 11–12	Passive, 'about'
Reynolds and Shih (2019, 81)	The learning effects of student-constructed word cards	Taiwan	Quasi-experimental study/ vocabulary tests/ proficiency test/vocab word card questionnaire/ experimental and control groups/ experimental group was assigned a card-making task at home after reading while the other group was not/stats	16–17	Passive, 'on'

(continued)

(cont.)

Author and year	Topic /key words	Country	Approach/methods	Age	Child participant role
Ellis et al. (2019, 80)	The effect of pre-task explicit instruction on the performance of a focussed task	China	Pre-post test design/two oral dictogloss tasks/one group with pre-task preparation and one without/CAF measures and coding of output/ target structure 'passive'/stats	14–15	Passive, 'on'
Liu and Brantmeier (2019, 80)	I know English: Self-assessment of reading and writing	China	Reading test/writing task/ self-assessment items of reading and writing abilities/stats	12–14	Passive, 'on-about'
Yung (2019, 80)	L2 selves of senior secondary students (reasons to learn English)	Hong Kong	Questionnaire/three pieces of reflective writing and six individual interviews throughout the year/ narrative analysis/some extracts from interviews/some counting of questionnaire responses	17–18	Passive, 'on-about'

García Mayo and Imaz Agirre (2019, 80)	Task modality and pair formation: LREs	Spain	Proficiency-paired, teacher-selected and self-selected groups/ outcome of two tasks analysed for LREs/some stats	11–12	Passive, 'on'
Tragant Mestres and Pellicer-Sanchez (2019, 80)	Processing multimodal input: Eye tracking	Spain	Within subject design: two types of multimodal materials: storybook with audio or video/eye tracking of learners' processing of picture and texts/vocabulary tests/stats	10–11	Passive, 'on'
Chan (2019, 80)	Acquisition of simple past: Comparison of different instruction methods	Hong Kong	Three types of instruction: processing instruction, traditional and implicit instruction/pre- and post-test design with some tasks/stats	7–8	Passive, 'on'
Bai (2018, 78)	Use of self-regulated writing strategies	Singapore	Composition writing while thinking aloud/analysis of self-regulated strategies/comparing high/low proficiency and higher and lower grade/stats	8–12	Passive, 'on'

(*continued*)

257

(*cont.*)

Author and year	Topic /key words	Country	Approach/methods	Age	Child participant role
Chan (2018, 76)	Attitudes to different Englishes and gender	Hong Kong	Questionnaire survey on attitudes/speech samples/stats	10–14 and 15–19	Passive, 'on'
Albaladejo et al. (2018, 76)	Songs, stories and vocabulary acquisition with pre-schoolers	Spain	Pre- and post-test design,/delayed post-test/three conditions: story/song/story plus song/five words for each condition/tests/video recording of the sessions/stats	2–3	Passive, 'on'
Li et al. (2018, 76)	Chinese high school students' enjoyment	China	Questionnaire (Chinese version of the foreign language enjoyment scale)/stats	16–17	Passive, 'on'
Martin-Laguna and Alcon-Soler (2018, 76)	Development of discourse pragmatic markers	Spain (Catalonia)	Each learner wrote three argumentative essays in three languages three times a year/trajectories of textual and interpersonal markers/teacher interviews and learner diaries/some stats/some extracts from learner diaries	16–20	Passive, 'on -about'

					Passive, 'on'
Portoles and Safont (2018, 75)	Children's requesting behaviour in multilingual classrooms (Romanian and Arabic speakers)	Spain (Catalonia)	Audio-visual pragmatic test (watching a video in all three languages with puppets acting out a situation, and an appropriate request had to be identified using a sticker)/spontaneous teacher–learner interactions recorded in English classes/ children's requests noted/stats	8–9	Passive, 'on'
Loh et al. (2018, 74)	Chinese orthography: Developmental trends (different ethnic groups; Chinese as L2)	Hong Kong	Series of tasks/stats	12–17	Passive, 'on'
Butler and Lee (2018, 73)	Longitudinal investigation of socio-economic status and young learners' language learning	China	Children followed for three years/each year they took Cambridge ESOL test and filled in survey/parental data: extensive surveys/stats	12–15	Passive, 'on'
Fernandez Sanjurjo (2018, 73)	Influence of socio-economic status on students' performance in CLIL	Spain	Tests: knowledge of science and a context questionnaire/stats	10–11	Passive, 'on'

(*continued*)

(cont.)

Author and year	Topic /key words	Country	Approach/methods	Age	Child participant role
Huang et al. (2018, 73)	SES, input and L2 learning outcomes	Taiwan	Students completed a storytelling task and a survey/parents' survey/ stats	15–17	Passive, 'on'
Kuchah (2018, 73)	Early English medium instruction in francophone Cameroon	Cameroon	A range of qualitative tools, case study, interviews with children and parents; two children's learning experiences and prospects/extracts	12	Passive, 'on-about'
Nikolov and Csapo (2018, 73)	L1 and L2 reading skills, inductive reasoning and SES in early English and German	Hungary	Online tests assessing L1 and L2 reading/SES/ inductive reasoning / stats	14	Passive, 'on'
Shin and So (2018, 73)	The moderating role of SES on motivation of strategy use	South Korea	Questionnaires/stats	13–14	Passive, 'on'
Wong (2018, 72)	Relationship between L2 future self-image and reading achievement	Hong Kong	Reading comprehension assessed/motivation questionnaire/stats	12	Passive, 'on'

Peltonen (2017, 70)	Fluency and problem solving in L2 dialogue	Finland	Problem solving pair task/ fluency measures/ stimulated recall /stats + some extracts for qualitative analysis	15–17	Passive, 'on'
Oliver et al. (2017, 69)	Children working it out together: Collaboration and EAL children	Australia	Analysis of transcribed dialogues/some stats and some qualitative analysis of extracts	5–8 compared to 9–12	Passive, 'on'
Thorstensson (2017, 67)	Newly arrived immigrant youth negotiate identity/ language and literacy	Sweden	Longitudinal two-year-long/interviews with teachers and students/ observations paying attention to materials/ approaches and student engagement/extracts/ qualitative	9–12	Passive, 'about'
Huang et al. (2017, 67)	English language outcomes of proficient bilingual students	USA	Comparing similarities and differences between monolingual and bilingual students/ survey/English tests on vocabulary, grammar and morphology/stats	10–14	Passive, 'on'

(continued)

(cont.)

Author and year	Topic/key words	Country	Approach/methods	Age	Child participant role
Park and Hiver (2017, 67)	Tracing motivational change in project-based learning	South Korea	Materials for the project-based lessons/ questionnaire to assess motivational factors/ reflective journal submitted by participants/some interviews/some stats and some extracts from journals and interviews	12–13	Passive, 'on'
Muñoz (2017, 67)	The role of age and proficiency levels in subtitle reading/eye-tracking study	Spain (Catalonia)	Two clips of the Simpsons/ L1 and L2 subtitles/age and movement behaviour and proficiency and movement behaviour/ stats	Comparison of 10–11 with 15 and adults	Passive, 'on'
García Mayo and Hidalgo (2017, 67)	L1 use among learners in CLIL and non-CLIL in task-supported interaction	Spain (Basque country)	Task performance twice in two academic years/ analysis of the outcome with a focus on functions of L1/stats	8–10	Passive, 'on'

Jimenez Catalan and Agustin Llach (2017, 66)	Lexical profile of CLIL and non-CLIL learners	Spain	Lexical availability task/background questionnaire/means/stats	13–14	Passive, 'on'
Buckingham and Stott Alpaslan (2017, 65)	Speaking and willingness to communicate through asynchronous computer mediated practice	Türkiye	Experimental and control groups/homework completed in speaking or writing/pre-and post-test design/speaking tests/measuring WTC/stats	9	Passive, 'on'
Vorobel and Kim (2017, 65)	Collaborative writing practices in face-to-face and online contexts	USA	Multiple case studies/ecological approach/longitudinal nine months/researcher journal/participant journals/several drafts and peer-edited checklists for writing assignments/within-case and cross-case analysis/qualitative analysis based on themes	14	Passive, 'on-about'
Song and Kim (2017, 65)	De-motivation and re-motivation	South Korea	Graph mapping changes in motivation/questionnaire and interviews/both quant and qualitative analysis	17–18	Passive, 'on'

(continued)

(cont.)

Author and year	Topic/key words	Country	Approach/methods	Age	Child participant role
Oga-Baldwin and Nakata (2017, 65)	Engagement, gender and motivation	Japan	Two surveys: one about engagement and one about motivation/stats	10–11	Passive, 'on'
Austin et al. (2017, 64)	Video-conferencing: Children's conversations of skype (L1 Urdu and Punjabi and L1 Portuguese)	UK and Portugal	Multimodal interaction analysis/weekly talk on Skype during extra-curricular hour/qualitative analysis with photos and extracts	6–7	Passive, 'on-about'
Zhou (2017, 63)	Social anxiety, autonomy and learning orientation	China	Set of hypotheses/anxiety inventory/self-regulation questionnaire/English achievement test/stats	10–11	Passive, 'on'
Tammenga-Helmantel et al. (2017, 63)	L2 German: Explicit instruction of grammar, Dutch students	Netherlands	Learning the subjunctive for reported speech/pre- and post-test design/comparing grammaticality tests/three groups: explicit inductive/explicit deductive and control groups/stats	17–18	Passive, 'on'

Chang and Liu (2016, 61)	Communication strategies: Problem-orientedness and goal-orientedness	China	Data collected from an oral task and stimulated recall interviews/ analysis of communication strategies/extracts and some descriptive stats/ mainly qualitative	13–14	Passive, 'on'
Anam and Stracke (2016, 60)	Link between learning strategies and self-efficacy beliefs	Indonesia	Self-efficacy questionnaire and strategy inventory/ stats	11	Passive, 'on'
Li and Chen (2016, 60)	Relative effectiveness of phonological and morphological training on L2 word reading	Taiwan	English proficiency test/ word reading test/ training programme/ three groups/one experimental group with phonological training/one with morphological training and a control group/ stats	11	Passive, 'on'
Leontjev et al. (2016, 59)	Word derivational knowledge and writing proficiency	Finnish, Estonian and Russian learners	Writing assignments rated by CEFR criteria/word derivational tasks/stats	15–18	Passive, 'on'

(*continued*)

(cont.)

Author and year	Topic /key words	Country	Approach/methods	Age	Child participant role
Pladevall-Ballaster and Vallbona (2016, 58)	Longitudinal study of CLIL minimal input context and the learners' receptive skills	Spain (Catalonia)	Two groups (CLIL and non-CLIL) were administered a language test four times during two academic years/stats	10–11	Passive, 'on'
Lee (2016, 58)	Enriching short stories through processes	Hong Kong	Two groups: one received instruction on functional grammar and one did not/pre-post test design/some stats and some extracts	11	Passive, 'on'
Gu and Cheung (2016, 57)	Ideal self, acculturation and Chinese learning (as an L2)	Hong Kong (ethnic minority students)	Questionnaire/stats	12–18	Passive, 'on'
Serrano et al. (2016, 57)	Examining L2 development in two short-term intensive programmes: Study abroad versus at home	Spain	Set of tests/oral narrative based on pictures/questionnaires and observations/stats	13–17	Passive, 'on'

Nix (2016, 57)	Measuring latent listening strategies	Taiwan	Listening inventory/questionnaire/stats	13–17	Passive, 'on'
Manoli et al. (2016, 56)	Immediate and delayed effects of strategy instruction in primary EFL	Greece	Quasi-experimental study/reading tests, strategy training in experimental groups/immediate and delayed effects	11–12	Passive, 'on'
Eykmans et al. (2016, 56)	The effect of imposing processing strategies on L2 learners' deliberate study of lexical items	Belgium (Flanders)	Materials for the intervention phrases with translations selected/three different learning conditions/quasi-experimental study/pre-post test design/stats	13–14	Passive, 'on'
Lee (2016, 55)	Peer feedback in L2 writing; students' perspectives	Hong Kong	Intervention/questionnaires/interviews/comparison between teacher and peer feedback/stats and some extracts (perspectives)	14–15	Passive, 'on-about'
Lin (2016, 55)	Impact of problem-based learning on English vocabulary learning and use	Taiwan	Two classes/one experimental and one control group/experimental group used problem-based learning technique/pre-post test of vocabulary knowledge/writing and self-reports/stats	11	Passive, 'on'

(*continued*)

(cont.)

Author and year	Topic /key words	Country	Approach/methods	Age	Child participant role
Lin (2016, 55)	Intercultural online communication: Analysis of learner and NS language use	Taiwan and UK	Participants interacted for twelve months on Moodle/Keynesian approach to corpus analysis/stats	13–15	Passive, 'on'
Granena et al. (2015, 55)	L1 reading factors in extensive L2 reading	Spain	Two intact classes/pre-and post-test quasi-experimental design/ reading questionnaire/ stats	10–11	Passive, 'on'
Wei et al. (2015, 55)	Student perception of teacher–student interpersonal behaviour	China	Questionnaire/English language achievement tests/stats	12–17	Passive, 'on'
Lyster (2015, 54)	Using form-focussed tasks across the immersion curriculum	Canada	Two studies with two different foci in form features/quasi-experimental study with pre-and post-tests/ instructional tasks/ summary of positive outcomes for both studies	7–8 and 10–11	Passive, 'on'

García Mayo and Lazaro Ibarolla (2015, 54)	Meaning negotiation in task-based interactions in CLIL and EFL	Spain	Interactions of dyads are recorded/picture placement task/stats	8–9 and 10–11	Passive, 'on'
Juan-Garau and Jacob (2015, 54)	Developing transcultural skills through content- and task-based lessons	Spain and Poland	A task-based unit of work about the African continent/voicing own thoughts/co-construction of shared knowledge/third space/pre-task/principal task and post-task activities/content analysis/some stats	14–16	Passive, 'on-about'
Llinares and Dalton-Puffer (2015, 54)	Role of different tasks in CLIL students' use of evaluative language	Austria, Finland and Spain	Analysis of evaluative language in five tasks: discussion, group talk, role play, interview and presentation/stats	12–16	Passive, 'on'
Perez-Vidal and Roquet (2015, 54)	The linguistic impact of the CLIL science programme	Spain (Catalonia)	Experimental (formal instruction + CLIL) and control groups (formal instruction only)/pre-test and post-test design/ tests in all domains: a range of receptive and productive tasks/stats	12–13, 13–14, and 14–15	Passive, 'on'

(*continued*)

(cont.)

Author and year	Topic /key words	Country	Approach/methods	Age	Child participant role
Butler (2015, 54)	The use of computer games as foreign language learning tasks	Japan	Children worked in groups designing vocabulary games/ children identified game elements in discussion	11–12	Active 'with'
Bai (2015, 53)	The effects of strategy-based writing instruction	Singapore	Experimental and control classes/pre-and post-test design/questionnaires/ delayed tests/target strategies/student interviews/stats and some qualitative analysis	10–11	Passive, 'on'
Lee et al. (2015, 52)	The effects of extensive reading and translation on grammar knowledge and attitudes to EFL	South Korea	Pre-and post-test design; comparison of two types of reading instructions for two semesters (extensive reading or translation instruction)/linguistic tests and attitude survey/stats	13–14	Passive, 'on'

Canovas Guirao et al. (2015, 52)	The use of models as written feedback	Spain	Sets of proficiency matched pairs/learners' collaborative dialogue and written notes/experimental and control groups/LREs, descriptive stats	10–11	Passive, 'on'
Yang and Lin (2015, 52)	Online collaborative note-taking strategies	Taiwan	Experimental group online and control group paper based/stats	15–16	Passive, 'on'
Eguchi and Sugiura (2015, 25)	Processability theory; early syntactic and morphological development	Japan	Four communication tasks used as elicitation tools/target structures to focus on/stats	12–15	Passive, 'on'
Chang and Miller (2015, 52)	Audio-assisted extensive reading	Taiwan	Two groups: silent reading and audio-assisted reading for twenty-six weeks/pre-and post-test design plus delayed post-test/stats	15	Passive, 'on'
Sundqvist and Wikstrom (2015, 51)	Out-of-school digital game play and in-school L2 vocabulary	Sweden	Non-gamers/moderate gamers and frequent gamers/questionnaire/diaries/vocab tests/essays and grades/stats	15–16	Passive, 'on'

(*continued*)

(*cont.*)

Author and year	Topic /key words	Country	Approach/methods	Age	Child participant role
Maxwell-Reid (2015, 49)	The role of clausal embedding in argumentative writing	Spain	30-minute writing/ examination of clauses in the texts/comparison of CLIL/EFL and L1 English (visiting students from the UK)/ counting and examining clauses	14	Passive, 'on'
Alcon-Soler (2015, 48)	Pragmatic learning and study abroad	Spanish students in the UK	Experimental groups: explicit instruction on requests/pre-and post-test design with delayed post-test/stats plus example email requests	17–19 (average 18)	Passive, 'on'
Lorenzo and Rodriguez (2014, 47)	L2 cognitive academic language proficiency in CLIL	Spain	Narrative writing/ examination of syntax and cohesion/stats	13–17	Passive, 'on'
Sardegna et al. (2014, 47)	Development and validation of learner attitudes and motivation to pronunciation inventory	South Korea	Questionnaire/stats	14–19	Passive, 'on'

Kim and Kim (2014, 46)	Perceptual learning styles, ideal L2 self, motivated behaviour and English proficiency	South Korea	Questionnaire/correlation among variables/stats	9–18		Passive, 'on'
Dolean (2014, 45)	Keyword method: Classroom application	Romania (Italian as L2)	Experimental and control groups/range of tests/stats	9–10		Passive, 'on'
Iwaniec (2014, 45)	Motivation of pupils form Southern Poland	Poland	Motivational questionnaire and some interviews/stats plus extracts from interviews	15–16		Passive, 'on'
Tammenga-Helmantel et al. (2014, 45)	The effectiveness of different grammar instruction approaches	Netherlands (German, English and Spanish as L2s)	Experimental and control groups/four experimental groups with various grammar instruction treatments/pre- and post-test design/hypotheses/stats	12–15		Passive, 'on'
Gunning and Oxford (2014, 43)	Effects of learning strategy instruction	Canada	Two intact groups as experimental and control groups/pre- and post-test design/questionnaires/videorecording/fieldnotes/some interviews/strategy log/some stats/qualitative analysis	11		Passive, 'on-about'

(*continued*)

(cont.)

Author and year	Topic /key words	Country	Approach/methods	Age	Child participant role
Ashton (2014, 42)	Using self-assessment to compare learners' reading proficiency (German, Japanese and Urdu L2s)	UK	Self-assessment survey (can do statements)/language tests/background information and teacher assessment/stats	12–15	Passive, 'on'
Campfield and Murphy (2014, 42)	Elicited imitation: The influence of linguistic rhythm on child L2 acquisition	Poland	Experimental and control groups/experimental group exposed to salient linguistic rhythm/stats	8	Passive, 'on'
Yon Yim (2014, 42)	An anxiety model for young learners: Path analysis	South Korea	Two questionnaires/the possible relationship between three anxiety models and five variables was analysed/stats	10–12	Passive, 'on'
Hakki Eren and Burden (2014, 42)	The relationship between academic self-concept, attributions and L2 achievement	Türkiye	Questionnaire (myself as a learner)/set of tests to measure achievement/stats	12–13	Passive, 'on'

Dabarera et al. (2014, 42)	The impact of metacognitive scaffolding and monitoring on reading comprehension	Singapore	Experimental and control groups/intervention with metacognitive strategies using the reciprocal teaching approach/pre-and post-tests/stats plus some interview data	12–15	Passive, 'on'
Zhang and Koda (2013, 41/4)	Morphological awareness and reading comprehension	China	Questionnaire about learners' backgrounds/ morphological segmentation and other tasks/grammar and vocab tests/reading comprehension/stats	12	Passive, 'on'
Jean and Simard (2013, 41/3)	Deductive versus inductive grammar instruction: Relationships between gains, preferences and learning styles	Canada	Pre- and post-test design/ deductive versus inductive grammar instruction /treatment appraisal and preference questionnaires/learning style survey/stats	12–14	Passive, 'on'
Trofimovich et al. (2013, 41)	Are certain types of instruction better for some learners?	Canada	Experimental/control groups/pre-and post-test design/comprehension-based and traditional L2 programmes/links between learner variables and type of instruction/stats	8–9	Passive, 'on'

(*continued*)

(cont.)

Author and year	Topic /key words	Country	Approach/methods	Age	Child participant role
Liyanage and Bartlett (2013, 41/3)	Personality types and language learning strategies	Sri Lanka	Personality questionnaire/ language learning strategy inventory/ examining relationships/stats	16–18	Passive, 'on'
Matsuzaki Carreira et al. (2013, 41/3)	Motivational model of English learning among elementary learners in Japan	Japan	Questionnaires/exploring developmental differences across age groups/correlations/stats	8–9, 9–10 and 10–11	Passive, 'on'
Kim and Tracy-Ventura (2013, 41/3)	The role of task repetition in L2 performance development	South Korea	Pre-and post-test design/ task repetition/coding for CAF/three information exchange collaborative tasks/ comparison of two different types of repetition (same procedure or same content)/post background questionnaire/coding and stats	13–14	Passive, 'on'

Izwan Abdullad et al. (2013, 41/2)	Validation of a productive vocabulary test below the 2,000-word level	Malaysia	Validation procedures/vocabulary tests/stats	17–18	Passive, 'on'
Kormos and Kiddle (2013, 41/2)	The role of socio-economic factors in motivation to learn English	Chile	Motivation and social class/questionnaire/analysis of relationship/stats	15–16	Passive, 'on'
Tragant et al. (2013, 41/2)	Understanding foreign language strategies: Validation study	Spain (Catalonia)	Questionnaire/stats	12–15 and 16–17	Passive, 'on'
MacIntyre and Blackie (2012, 40/4)	Predictors of intention to continue learning French	Canada (French as an L2)	Questionnaire for motivation strategies/attitude motivation test battery/correlations/stats	14–19	Passive, 'on'
Koizumi and In'nami (2012, 40/4)	Effects of text length of lexical diversity measures	Japan	Speaking tests /eliciting one minute of spontaneous speaking without planning/analysis of transcribed data/correlations/stats	14–18	Passive, 'on'
Kamiya (2012, 40/3)	Proactive and reactive focus on form and gestures	Japan	Teacher–learner interaction recorded/focus on form episodes identified/gestures coded/stats plus short extracts	17	Passive, 'on'

(*continued*)

(cont.)

Author and year	Topic /key words	Country	Approach/methods	Age	Child participant role
Llanes (2012, 40/2)	The short- and long-term effects of a short study abroad experience	Spain (Catalan Spanish bilinguals)	Pre-and post-test design with delayed post-test/ study abroad versus at home groups/written and oral tests/ questionnaires/stats	11	Passive, 'on'
Matsuzaki Carreira (2012, 40/2)	Motivational orientations and psychological needs in EFL learning	Japan	Motivation questionnaire/ hypotheses/correlation analysis/stats	11–12	Passive, 'on'
Dixon et al (2012, 40/2)	Dialectal influence on spelling of English words	Singapore	Tests such as dictation and letter-word identification, patterns of spelling/descriptive stats	6	Passive, 'on'
Unlu and Hatipglu (2012, 40/2)	The acquisition of the copula 'be' in present simple tense	Russia	Questionnaire about background/tests/ comparison of age groups/stats	8–10, 11–12 and 14–15	Passive, 'on'
Zietek and Roehr (2011, 39/4)	Metalinguistic knowledge and cognitive style	Poland	Tests of metacognitive knowledge and cognitive style/ correlations/stats	18	Passive, 'on'

De Costa (2011, 39/3)	Learner beliefs: The case of a Chinese immigrant in Singapore	Singapore	Year-long ethnographic study/case study/observation/use of artefacts/interview/excerpts/qualitative	16	Passive, 'on-about'
Huang (2011, 39/2)	Motivating lessons: A classroom investigation of effects of content-based instruction on motivation and verbal interaction	Taiwan	Observation scheme/recording of lessons/both qualitative and quantitative analysis/descriptive stats	6–12	Passive, 'on'
Matsuzaki Carreira (2011, 39/1)	Relationships between motivation for learning EFL and intrinsic motivation for learning in general	Japan	Motivation and attitude questionnaires/effects of grade and gender on variables of motivation/stats	8–9, 9–10, 10–11 and 11–12	Passive, 'on'

The Language Learning Journal

Author and year	Topic /key words	Country	Approach/methods	Age	Child participant role
Jaekel et al. (2021, no volume yet)	Transition from elementary to secondary school	Germany	Investigating the perception of transition two months after they switched school/ language proficiency assessed/stats	10–11	Passive, 'on'
Akyildiz and Celik 2021 (no volume yet)	Using WhatsApp to support EFL reading	Türkiye	Pre-and post-test quasi-experimental design/ experimental and control groups/experimental groups used WhatsApp for receiving reading texts and answers to comprehension questions/ some interviews/pre-test English achievement test/ treatment eight weeks/ stats plus extracts from interviews	11–12	Passive, 'on'
Young (2021, no volume number yet)	Bilingual Polish adolescents negotiate the position of linguistic expert	UK	Narrative enquiry: observations, group interview, pair and individual interviews/all data transcribed and analysed/thematic approach/data presented as case studies of learners/	11–16	Passive, 'about'

Study	Title	Country	Method	Age	Preposition
Hoxha and Sumner (2021, February, no volume number yet)	Children with English as an L1 or L2: Exploring reading	UK	Comparing EAL and monolingual children on measures of reading, literacy-related abilities, motivation and environmental factors/a set of tests/background questionnaire about home environment/stats	7–10	Passive, 'on'
Normann (2021, 49/6)	Students' perceptions of language learning experiences in short Erasmus+ mobilities	Norway	Qualitative case study/observations/reflection logs/interviews/qualitative analysis using constant comparative method	17	Passive, 'about-with'
Haukas et al. (2021, 49/4)	Developing and validating a questionnaire on young learners/multilingualism and multilingual identity	Norway	Correlating variables such as open-mindedness with multilingual identity	Lower secondary (exact age not given)	Passive, 'on'
Owen and Thomas (2021, 49/3)	The carousel-style lesson: An effective intervention to enhance motivation and the learning of foreign languages in primary French	UK	Case study/observation and questionnaires of pupil perceptions	11	Passive, 'about'
Yu and Liu (2021, 49/1)	Reading aloud in ELT in China	China	Interview-based investigation/extracts	12–15 and 15–18	Passive, 'about'

(*continued*)

(*cont.*)

Author and year	Topic /key words	Country	Approach/methods	Age	Child participant role
San Isidro and Lasagabaster (2020, no volume number yet)	Students' and families' attitudes to motivation, language learning and CLIL	Spain (Spanish Galician bilinguals)	Longitudinal/CLIL and non-CLIL groups/experimental and control groups/set of L1 and L2 tests/attitude and motivation battery test/parents' questionnaire/ questionnaires administered three times in the year/stats	14 (at the start)	Passive, 'on'
MacFarlane et al. (2020, no volume yet)	Core Academic Language Skills	South Africa	Piloting a version of an instrument developed in the USA (CALS: Core Academic Language Skills)/results compared and correlated with US results/stats	11	Passive, 'on'
Goris et al. (2020, no volume yet)	Determinants of success in CLIL (comparisons of four countries)	Hungary, Italy, Germany and Netherlands	Sets of tests at the beginning and end of year/ questionnaire at the beginning/growth over the year in CLIL/stats	12–15	Passive, 'on'

Paraz Canado (2020, 48/1)	CLIL and elitism	Spain	Large-scale study with thousands of learners/ verbal intelligence tests/ motivation/English language level/SES/type of schools/urban and rural/ stats	11–12 and 15–16	Passive, 'on'
Navarro-Pablo and López Gándara (2020, 48/1)	The effects of CLIL on L1 competence	Spain	End-of-year Spanish results of CLIL and non-CLIL students/interviews with teachers and students/stats and some extracts	11 and 15	Passive, 'on'
Lahuerta (2020, 48/ 2)	Accuracy of writing in EFL and CLIL: Impact of grade and gender	Spain	Four groups of students/ composition writing/texts analysed for measures of accuracy/stats	13 and 15	Passive, 'on'
Costley et al. (2020, 48/5)	Multilingual and monolingual children in primary language classrooms (learning of French as an L2)	UK	Background and attitude questionnaire for children/ individual interviews with children and teacher/ observed classes/test of metalinguistic awareness/ test of French proficiency/ memory test/comparisons between EAL and monolingual children/ correlations/some stats	8–9	Passive, 'on-about'

(*continued*)

(cont.)

Author and year	Topic /key words	Country	Approach/methods	Age	Child participant role
Porter (2020 48/5)	Early start to foreign language literacy in English primary schools (French as an L2)	UK	Integrated literacy programme as treatment for twenty-three weeks/ pre- and post-test design/a range of tests/stats plus qualitative: children in groups ranked activities/ questionnaire about children's confidence levels/	9–11	Passive, 'about-with'
Molway and Mutton (2020, 48/5)	Mindsets intervention (German as L2)	UK	Student questionnaires/ intervention/correlation/ descriptive stats	13	Passive, 'on'
Iwaniec (2020, 48/4)	The effects of parental education level and school location on motivation	Poland	Questionnaire/correlation analysis/stats	15–16	Passive, 'on'
Osborne et al. (2020, 48/4)	Introducing Chinese characters to beginners	Ireland	Action research/four groups and four different approaches to teaching the characters/translation exercises/completing re-ordering sentences/ descriptive stats	14–16	Passive, 'on'

284

Groff and Bellamy (2020, 48/3)	Biliteracy development in Mexico (Spanish and P'urchepecha)	Mexico	Written essay produced by students in two languages/ analysis of orthography, lexicon, sentence structure, analysing connections between the languages/qualitative with extracts	9	Passive, 'on'
Aldekoa et al. (2020, 48/3)	A trilingual teaching sequence for oral presentations	Spain (Basque country)	Trilingual learners/ multilingual oral presentations/teaching sequence/comparison of initial and final presentations/textual analysis/discourse analysis/extracts	16	Passive, 'on'
Deckner (2019, 47/5)	Motivational dip in year 7 (German or French as L2)	UK	Two questionnaires/stats	11–12	Passive, 'on'
Bower (2019, 47/5)	Explaining motivation in language learning (CLIL French and German)	UK	Questionnaire-based on the 'process motivation' model/focus groups/ interview/qualitative extracts	12–14	Passive, 'on-about'
Pujadas and Muñoz, (2019, 47/4)	Extensive viewing of captioned and subtitled TV series: Vocabulary learning	Spain (Catalonia)	Four groups/four experimental conditions; captioned and focussed instruction, captioned non-focussed instruction, subtitles-focussed and	13–14	Passive, 'on'

(*continued*)

(cont.)

Author and year	Topic /key words	Country	Approach/methods	Age	Child participant role
			non-subtitles-focussed instruction/'Fresh off the boat' series selected/pre- and post-test design/ intervention a year long/ proficiency and vocabulary tests before and after/questionnaire after/stats		
Azkarai and Oliver (2019, 47/3)	Negative feedback on task repetition ESL and EFL settings	Spain and Australia	Children worked in pairs on a 'spot the differences' task/T1 and T2 testing times/transcription, coding and stats	7–8	Passive, 'on'
Kalogirou et al. (2019, 47/3)	Vocabulary acquisition via drama, Welsh as an L2	UK	Pedagogy is task-based and communicative comprising pre-drama, drama and post-drama activities/two experimental drama groups and one control group/pre-test post-test design/three test of vocabulary/stats	9–10	Passive, 'on'

Goris et al. (2019, 47/2)	Contribution of CLIL to learners' international orientation and confidence	Netherlands, Germany and Italy	International orientation and confidence in EFL questionnaires repeated after 1–2 years/stats	12–15	Passive, 'on'
Walters (2019, 47/2)	Learning to read Hebrew in a Jewish community school	UK	Observations and interviews/ longitudinal/over a year/ interviews with headteacher and parents/ qual analysis/extracts	5–13	Passive, 'about'
Millonig et al. (2019, 47/2)	Young pupils' perceptions of their foreign language learning lessons; use of drawings	Austria	Qualitative ethnographic case study of eighteen months/forty-eight drawings collected in two primary schools/ interviews: learners' commentary on the drawings/analysis of the drawings in both classrooms/extracts and drawings	7–8	Passive, 'about'
Al-Hroub et al. (2019, 47/2)	The impact of the writers' workshop approach on L2 writing	Lebanon	Intervention based action research/pre-test post-test design/eight weeks of intervention with writers' workshop approach/ participants had to write an opinion-based essay before and after/no control group/writing samples were scored/stats	10–11	Passive, 'on'

(*continued*)

(*cont.*)

Author and year	Topic /key words	Country	Approach/methods	Age	Child participant role
Chambers (2019, 47/1)	Pupils' perceptions of Key Stage 2 to 3 transition in modern foreign languages	UK	The same cohort of pupils interviewed a year apart (last year of primary and first year of secondary)/ qualitative analysis/themes	10–11 and 11–12	Passive, 'about-with'
Hofer and Jessner (2019, 47/1)	How does multilingual education affect young learners' metalinguistic awareness and proficiency in L1 (Italian), L2 (German) and L3 (English)?	Italy	All participants completed a metalinguistic awareness test (L1) and a German and English test/ traditional and multilingual education subjects compared/ experimental and control groups/correlation analysis and stats	9	Passive, 'on'
Lanvers et al. (2019, 47/1)	Changing students' attitudes to language learning through teaching linguistics	UK	Pre-post questionnaire and intervention: a teaching pack plus qualitative student feedback/stats plus extracts from feedback	12–13	Passive, 'on'
Papdopoulou et al. (2018, 46/5)	The Strategy Inventory for Language Learning revisited	Greece	Questionnaire/stats	9–16	Passive, 'on'

Mitits et al. (2018, 46/5)	Does the language you speak at home affect the size of your L2 vocabulary? (Turkish minority language users)	Greece	Vocabulary size test in Greek and Turkish/language and social background questionnaire/ correlations, gender effects/stats	10–16	Passive, 'on'
Wyra and Lawson (2018, 46/5)	Vocabulary learning: Using the keyword method, strategy and meta-strategy knowledge (Spanish as L2)	Australia	Two groups of learners/ experimental group: slightly different treatment/questionnaire about students' strategies and meta-strategy knowledge/stats	11–12	Passive, 'on'
Llaner et al. (2018, 46/2)	Role of learning contexts and individual differences in L2 writing performance on an intensive study abroad programme	UK (Spanish Catalonian students)	Three-week study abroad experience/pre-and post-test design/picture-based writing (one of the tests)/ questionnaire about background and motivation and attitude/ FAC examined in the writing/stats	12–17	Passive, 'on'
Foster (2018, 46/2)	Attitudes to ancient Greek in three schools	UK	Attitude questionnaires given to both teachers and students in three secondary schools/some interviews/main themes discussed qualitatively	12–18	Passive, 'about'

(*continued*)

(cont.)

Author and year	Topic /key words	Country	Approach/methods	Age	Child participant role
Lanes and Serrano (2017, 47/4)	At home versus study abroad for learners of English (primary, secondary and university)	Spain (Catalonia)	Several tests before and after to explore oral and writing skills (CAF)/written composition and an oral picture elicited narrative task/interview/ questionnaire about their background/pre-post test design/comparisons/stats	10–11, 12–15 and 19 +	Passive, 'on'
Gruber and Tonkyn (2017, 45/3)	Writing in French in English and German secondary schools	UK and Germany	All students were given a battery of tasks/ questionnaire/semi-structured interviews/ comparisons/descriptive stats	14–16	Passive, 'on'
Kirsch and Bes Izuel (2017, 47/2)	Learning language with the iPad app iTeo (German and French as L2s)	Luxembourg	Longitudinal qualitative research study/video-recordings of the children's collaboration in iTeo, using various languages and working on various types of texts/ interviews with children, teacher and parents/ thematic analysis/ discourse analysis/excepts	6–7	Passive, 'on – about'

Birketveit and Rimmereide (2017, 45/1)	Using authentic picture books and illustrated books to improve L2 writing	Norway	Case study/logbooks, a questionnaire (about enjoyment and perceived language progress)/ individual interviews and learners' written texts before and after the reading project/both quantitative and qualitative analysis/five weeks: choosing as many books to read as possible/ writing on first day and last day based on pictures/ interviews on the last day/ discussion of themes	11	Passive, 'on-about'
Campfield and Murphy (2017, 45/1)	The influence of prosodic input on word order acquisition	Poland	Three groups/experimental materials/teaching interventions/pre- and post-tests/stats	8–9	Passive, 'on'
Montero et al. (2017, 45/1)	The influence of context and age on the use of L2 communicative strategies	Spain (Catalonia)	Comparison of age and context (study abroad and at home instruction); pre-post test design/an oral narrative both before and after the treatment/stats	10–11 and adults (university students)	Passive, 'on'

(continued)

(*cont.*)

Author and year	Topic /key words	Country	Approach/methods	Age	Child participant role
Ashton, (2016, 47/1)	Reading approach and strategy use across languages in assessment (CEFR A1 and A2)	England	Three languages: (German, Japanese and Urdu)/paired think-aloud protocol for uncovering strategies used while reading/interviews conducted after think-aloud/summary of the strategies/some stats and some extracts	13–15	Passive, 'on'
García Mayo and Imaz Agirre (2016, 44/4)	Task repetition and negotiation of meaning in pairs	Spain	Experimental and control groups/placement tests/ self-selected pairs worked on 'spot the differences' task at times 1 and 2 (two months apart); one group repeated the same task and one group a similar task (procedural repetition)/ coding/stats	8–9 and 9–10	Passive, 'on'
Gagne and Parks, (2016, 44/2)	Cooperative learning tasks: Turn-taking and participation (English as an L2)	Canada	Participation patterns of two heterogenous groups of grade 6 students/a set of collaborative tasks /two teams of four students/ both high and low achievers/video-taped recordings of the task	11–12	Passive, 'on'

Porter (2016, 44/2)	Teaching French vocabulary with gesture	UK	Pre-test/post-test and delayed post-test design/ story told with pictures and gestures/story told with pictures only/video recording by teacher researchers/stats	5–7	Passive, 'on'
Agustin Llach (2016, 44/2)	Does L1 make a difference? Vocabulary of German and Spanish EFL learners	Spain and Germany comparison	General language proficiency tests (to establish comparability of the groups)/two vocabulary tests/stats	9–10	Passive, 'on'
Kirsch, (2016, 44/1)	Using storytelling to teach vocabulary (primary MFL class) German as L2	UK	Ethnographic/observations, interviews and post-tests/ following six children-what vocabulary they learnt/asking the children to retell the story and recall any new words they learnt/interviews in pairs/ children's oral participation during storytelling recorded/ evidence of vocabulary learning analysed qualitatively	10–11	Passive, 'on-about'

(*continued*)

(cont.)

Author and year	Topic /key words	Country	Approach/methods	Age	Child participant role
Gene-Gil et al. (2015, 43/3)	Development of EFL writing over three years in CLIL and non-CLIL	Spain (Catalonia)	Longitudinal study; timed composition/measures taken at T1, 2, 3 and 4/ CAF measures/stats	13 (at the start)	Passive, 'on'
Ruiz de Zarobe and Zentoz (2015, 43/3)	Reading strategies and CLIL: Training in formal instruction	Spain (Basque country)	Experimental and control groups/pre-post-test design/both groups completed the same tests and questionnaires/the experimental group had the training intervention/ stats	10–11	Passive, 'on'
Doiz et al. (2014, 42/2)	CLIL and motivation	Spain (Basque Country)	Two year groups and within each one CLIL and one non-CLIL group/ questionnaire/stats	12–13 and 14–15	Passive, 'on'
Nayak and Sylva (2013, 41/1)	The effects of a guided reading intervention on reading comprehension (Chinese learners of English)	Hong Kong	Three groups/guided reading book, e-reading book and control group/reading comprehension pre-tests/ eight-week treatment/ post-tests/stats	9–10	Passive, 'on'

Mearns, (2012, 40/2)	Using CLIL to enhance pupils' experience of learning and raise attainment in German (L2)	UK	Action research project/teacher research questionnaire/unit of work development/evaluation and assessment/summative survey/some descriptive stats	13–14		Passive, 'about'
Liyanaga and Bartlett (2012, 40/2)	Gender and language learning strategy use	Sri Lanka	Questionnaire/stats	16–18		Passive, 'on'
Hamid and Baldauf (2011, 39/2)	Learner voices form rural Bangladesh	Bangladesh	Interviews/themes generated after transcribing the data/qualitative/some extracts	16+		Passive, 'about'
Pennington et al. (2011, 39/2)	London English by Chinese and Bangladeshi adolescents	UK	Conversations and interviews in same gender pairs recorded/analysis of linguistic features in the data/extracts	13–18		Passive, 'on-about'
Polat (2011, 39/1)	Gender differences in motivation and L2 accent attainment (Kurdish learners of Turkish as L2)	Türkiye	Background questionnaire/reading aloud samples/NS judges scored accents/questionnaire to measure motivation/interviews and filed notes/comparisons between genders/stats plus some qualitative analysis excerpts	13–18		Passive, 'on'
59						TOTAL 324 (in all five journals)

References

AARE (1993). *Code of Ethics*. Australian Association for Research in Education.
Abebe, T., & Bessell, S. (2014). Advancing ethical research with children: Critical reflections on ethical guidelines, *Children's Geographies*, 12(1), 126–133. https://doi.org10.1080/14733285.2013.856077
AERA (2011). *Code of Ethics*. American Educational Research Association.
Ahearn, L. M. (2001). Language and agency. *Annual Review of Anthropology*, 30 (1), 109–137. https://doi.org/10.1146/annurev.anthro.30.1.109
Alderson, P. (1995). *Listening to Children: Children, Social Research and Ethics*. Barnardo's.
Alderson, P. (2001). Research by children: Rights and methods. *International Journal of Social Research Methodology*, 4(2), 139–153. https://doi.org/10.1080/13645570120003
Alderson, P. (2008). Children as researchers: Participation rights and research methods. In P. Christensen & A. James (eds), *Research with Children* (pp. 276–290). Routledge. https://doi.org/10.4324/9780203964576-21
Alderson, P. (2014). Ethics. In A. Clark, R. Flewitt, M. Hammersley, & M. Robb (eds), *Understanding Research with Children and Young People* (pp. 85–102). Open University Press.
Alderson, P., & Morrow, V. (2004). *Ethics, Social Research and Consulting with Children and Young People*. Barnardo's.
Alderson, P., & Morrow, V. (2020). *The Ethics of Research with Children and Young People (A Practical Handbook)*, 2nd ed. SAGE.
Alerby, E., & Kostenius, C. (2011). 'Dammed taxi cab' – how silent communication in questionnaires can be understood and used to give voice to children's experiences. *International Journal of Research & Method in Education*, 34(2), 117–130. https://doi.org/10.1080/1743727X.2011.578821
Andrews, J. (2021). 'I don't want to talk any more': Reflecting on research into young children's perspectives on their multilingual lives. In A. Pinter & K. Kuchah (eds), *Ethical and Methodological Issues in Researching Young Learners in School Contexts* (pp. 147–164). Multilingual Matters. https://doi.org/10.21832/9781800411432
Andrews, P. (2010). Hope and the many discourses of education. *Cambridge Journal of Education*, 40(4), 323–326. https://doi.org/10.1080/0305764X.2010.533898
Appadurai, A. (2013). The future as cultural fact: Essays on the global condition. *Rassegna Italiana di Sociologia* 54(4) 649–650.

APS (2017). *Ethical Principles of Psychologists and Code of Conduct.* American Psychological Society.
Archard, D. (2013). Children's rights. In H. LaFolette (ed.), *The International Encyclopedia of Ethics,* (pp. 756–764). Wiley-Blackwell.
Aries, P. (1986). *Centuries of Childhood: A Social History of Family Life.* Penguin.
Arnold, W., Bradshaw C., & Gregson, K. (2019) Language learning through projects. In S. Garton & F. Copland (eds), *Routledge Handbook of Teaching English to Young Learners* (pp. 288–302). Routledge.
Aro, M. (2012). Effects of authority: Voicescapes in children's beliefs about the learning of English. *International Journal of Applied Linguistics,* 22(3), 331–346. https://doi.org/10.1111/j.1473-4192.2012.00314.x
Assor, A., Kaplan, H., & Roth, G. (2002). Choice is good, but relevance is excellent: Autonomy-enhancing and suppressing teaching behaviours predicting students' engagement in schoolwork. *British Journal of Educational Psychology,* 27, 261–278. https://doi.org/10.1348/000709902158883
Azkarai, A., & García Mayo, M. P. (2016). Task repetition effects of L1 use in EFL child task-based interaction. *Language Teaching Research,* 21(4), 480–495. https://doi.org/10.1177/1362168816654169
Azkarai, A. & Imaz Agirre, A. (2016), Negotiation of meaning strategies in child EFL mainstream and CLIL settings. *TESOL Quarterly,* 50(4), 844–870. https://doi.org/10.1002/tesq.249
BAAL (2016). *Recommendations on Good Practice in Applied Linguistics.* British Association of Applied Linguistics.
Bailey, A. L., & Carroll, P. E. (2015). Assessment of English language learners in the era of new academic content standards. *Review of Research in Education,* 39(1), 253–294. https://doi.org/10.3102/0091732X14556074
Bandura, A. (1997) *Self-Efficacy.* W. H. Freeman.
Barker, J., & Weller, S. (2003). Geography of methodological issues in research with children. *Qualitative Research,* 3(2), 207–227. https://doi.org/10.1177/14687941030032004
Barrett, K. C., & Morgan, G. A. (2018). Mastery motivation: Retrospect, present, and future directions. In A. J. Elliot (ed.), *Advances in Motivation Science,* vol. 5 (pp. 1–39). Elsevier.
Barratt Hacking, E., & Barratt, R. (2009). Children researching their urban environment: Developing a methodology. *Education 3–13,* 37(4), 371–383. https://doi.org/10.1080/03004270903099884
Barrios, E., & Acosta-Manzano, I. (2020). Primary students' satisfaction with CLIL and perceived CLIL linguistic difficulty. *Journal of Multilingual and Multicultural Development,* 43(7), 665–678. https://doi.org/10.1080/01434632.2020.1759610
Beane, J. A., & Apple, M. (2007) The case for democratic schools. In M. W. Apple & J. A. Beane (eds), *Democratic Schools: Lessons in Powerful Education* (pp. 5–8). Heinemann.
Beauchamp, T., & Childress, J. (1979). *Principles of Biomedical Ethics.* Oxford University Press.

Beckett, G. H., & Slater, T. (2005). The project framework: A tool for language, content, and skills integration. *ELT Journal, 59*(2), 108–116. https://doi.org/10.1093/eltj/cci024

Benson, P. (2007). Autonomy in language teaching and learning. *Language Teaching 40*(1), 21–40. https://doi.org/10.1017/S0261444806003958

BERA (2011). *Ethical Guidelines for Educational Research.* British Educational Research Association.

Bergum, V., & Dossetor, J. B. (2005). *Relational Ethics: The Full Meaning of Respect.* University Publishing Group.

Berko, J. (1958). The child's learning of English morphology. *Word, 14*(2–3), 150–177. https://doi.org/10.1080/00437956.1958.11659661

Bialystok, E. (2001). *Bilingualism in Development: Language, Literacy, and Cognition.* Cambridge University Press.

Binkley, M., Erstad, O., Herman, H., Raizen, S., Ripley, M., Miller-Ricci, M., & Rumble, M. (2012). Defining twenty-first century skills. In P. Griffin, B. McGaw, & E. Care (eds), *Assessment and Teaching of 21st Century Skills.* Springer. https://doi.org/10.1007/978-94-007-2324-5_2

BIPS (2018). *Code of Ethics and Conduct.* The British Psychological Society.

Blaisdell, C., Arnott, L., Wall, K., & Robinson, C. (2019). Look who's talking: Using creative, playful arts-based methods in research with young children. *Journal of Early Childhood Research, 17*(1), 14–31. https://doi.org/10.1177/1476718X18808816

Bland, J. (ed.) (2016). *Teaching English to Young Learners: Critical Issues in Language Teaching with 3–12 Year Olds.* Bloomsbury.

Bradbury-Jones, C., & Taylor, J. (2015). Engaging with children as co-researchers: Challenges, counter-challenges and solutions. *International Journal of Social Research Methodology, 18*(2), 161–173. https://doi.org/10.1080/13645579.2013.864589

Braun, V., & Clarke, V. (2006). Using thematic analysis in psychology. *Qualitative Research in Psychology, 3*(2), 77–101.

Brough, C. J. (2012). Implementing the democratic principles and practices of student-centred curriculum integration in primary schools. *The Curriculum Journal, 23*(3), 345–369. https://doi.org/10.1080/09585176.2012.703498

Brown, P., & Lauder, H. (2012). The great transformation in the global labour market. *Soundings: A Journal of Politics and Culture, 51,* 41–53.

Bruner, J. (1983). *Child's Talk: Learning to Use Language.* W. W. Norton.

Bucknall, S. (2012). *Children as Researchers in Primary Schools: Choice, Voice and Participation.* Routledge.

Bucknall, S. (2014). Doing qualitative research with children and young people. In A. Clark, R. Flewitt, & M. Hammersley (eds), *Understanding Research with Children and Young People* (pp. 69–84). SAGE. https://doi.org/10.4135/9781526435637

Budd, J. (2013). Informational education: Creating an understanding of justice. *Education, Citizenship and Social Justice, 8,* 17–28. https://doi.org/10.1177/1746197912448710

Burke, C. (2008). Play in focus: Children's visual voice in participative research. In P. Thompson (ed.), *Doing Visual Research with Children* (pp. 23–36). Routledge. https://doi.org/10.4324/9780203870525

Butler, Y. G. (2015). English language education among young learners in East Asia: A review of current research (2004–2014). *Language Teaching*, *48*(3), 303–342. https://doi.org/10.1017/S0261444815000105

Butler, Y. G. (2017a). The dynamics of motivation development among young learners of English in China. In J. Enever & E. Lindgren, (eds), *Early Language Learning: Complexity and Mixed Methods* (pp. 167–185). Multilingual Matters. https://doi.org/10.21832/9781783098323-012

Butler, Y. G. (2017b). Motivational elements of digital instructional games: A study of young L2 learners' game designs. *Language Teaching Research*, *21*(6), 735–750. https://doi.org/10.1177/1362168816683560

Butler, Y. G. (2019). Gaming and young learners In S. Garton & F. Copland (eds), *Routledge Handbook of Teaching English to Young Learners*. (pp. 305–319). Routledge.

Butler, Y. G. (2022). Considerations for research methods to study child second language development, In Butler, Y. G. & Huang, B. H. (eds), *Research Methods for Understanding Child Second Language Development* (pp. 187–201). Routledge.

Butler, Y. G., Peng, X., & Lee, J. (2021). Young learners' voices: Towards a learner-centred approach to understanding language assessment literacy. *Language Testing*, *38*(3):429–455. https://doi.org/10.1177/0265532221992274

Butler, Y. G., & Zeng, W. (2014). Young foreign language learners' interactions during task-based paired assessments. *Language Assessment Quarterly*, *11*(1), 45–75. https://doi.org/10.1080/15434303.2013.869814

Cagliari, P., Castegnetti, M., Giudici, C., Rinaldi, C., Vecchi, V., & Moss, P. (eds) (2016). *Loris Malaguzzi and the Schools of Reggio Emilia: A Selection of His Writings and Speeches 1945–1993*. Routledge.

Cameron, L. (2001). *Teaching Languages to Young Learners*. Cambridge University Press. https://doi.org/10.1017/CBO9780511733109

Canosa, A., & Graham, A. (2020). Tracing the contribution of childhood studies: Maintaining momentum while navigating tensions. *Childhood*, *27*(1) 25–47 https://doi.org/10.1177/0907568219886619

Carnevale, F. A. (2009). A conceptual and moral analysis of suffering. *Nursing Ethics*, *16*(2), 174–183. https://doi.org/10.1177/0969733008100076

Carnevale, F. A. (2020). A 'thick' conception of children's voices: A hermeneutical framework for childhood research. *International Journal of Qualitative Methods*. *19*, 1–9. https://doi.org/10.1177/1609406920933767

Carreira, J. M. (2012). Motivational orientations and psychological needs in EFL learning among elementary school students in Japan. *System*, *40*(2), 191–202. https://doi.org/10.1016/j.system.2012.02.001

Carter, B., & Coyne, I. (2018). Participatory research: Does it genuinely extend the sphere of children's and young people's participation? In I. Coyne & B. Carter (eds), *Being Participatory: Researching with Children and Young People* (pp. 171–178). Springer. https://doi.org/10.1007/978-3-319-71228-4_9

Chik, A. (2018). Beliefs and practices of foreign language learning: A visual analysis. *Applied Linguistics Review*, *9*(2–3), 307–331. https://doi.org/10.1515/applirev-2016-1068

Christensen, P., & Prout, A. (2002). Working with ethical symmetry in social research with children. *Childhood*, 9(40), 477–497. https://doi.org/10.1177/0907568202009004007

Clark, A. (2001). How to listen to very young children: The mosaic approach. *Child Care in Practice*, 7(4), 333–341. https://doi.org/10.1080/13575270108415344

Clark, A. (2010). Young children as protagonists and the role of participatory, visual methods in engaging multiple perspectives. *American Journal of Community Psychology*, 46(1–2), 115–123. https://doi.org/10.1007/s10464-010-9332-y

Clark, A., & Moss, P. (2005). *Spaces to Play: More Listening to Young Children Using the Mosaic Approach*. National Children's Bureau.

Clark, A., & Moss, P. (2011). *Listening to Young Children: The Mosaic Approach*. Jessica Kingsley.

Coad, J., & Evans, R. (2008). Reflections on practical approaches to involving children and young people in the data analysis process. *Children & Society*, 22(1), 41–52. https://doi.org/10.1111/j.1099-0860.2006.00062.x

Collins, L., & Muñoz, C. (2016). The foreign language classroom: Current perspectives and future considerations. *The Modern Language Journal*, 100, 133–147. https://doi.org/10.1111/modl.12305.

Conteh, J., & Brock, A. (2011). 'Safe spaces'? Sites of bilingualism for young learners in home, school and community. *International Journal of Bilingual Education and Bilingualism*, 14(3), 347–360. https://doi.org/10.1080/13670050.2010.486850

Cook, T., & Hess, E. (2007). What the camera sees and from whose perspective: Fun methodologies for engaging children in enlightening adults. *Childhood*, 14(1), 29–45. https://doi.org/10.1177/0907568207068562

Copland, F., & Garton, S. (2014). Key themes and future directions in teaching English to young learners: Introduction to the Special Issue. *ELT Journal*, 68(3), 223–230. https://doi.org/10.1093/elt/ccu030

Copland, F., Garton, S., & Burns, A. (2014). Challenges in teaching English to young learners: Global perspectives and local realities. *TESOL Quarterly*, 48(4), 738–762. https://doi.org/10.1002/tesq.148

Copland, F., & Yonetsugi, E. (2016). Teaching English to young learners: Supporting the case for the bilingual native English speaker teacher. *Classroom Discourse*, 7(3), 221–238. https://doi.org/10.1080/19463014.2016.1192050

Coppock, V. (2011). Children as peer researchers: Reflections on a journey of mutual discovery. *Children & Society*, 25, 435–446. https://doi.org/10.1111/j.1099-0860.2010.00296.x

Coyne, I. (2010). Research with children and young people: The issue of parental (proxy) consent. *Children & Society*, 24, 227–237. https://doi.org/10.1111/j.1099-0860.2009.00216.x

Crookes, G. (2005). Resources for incorporating action research as critique into applied linguistics graduate education *Modern Languages Journal* 89, 467–475.

Csikszentmihalyi, M. (1990). *Flow: The Psychology of Optimal Experience*. Harper & Row.
Csikszentmihalyi, M. (2003). *Flow: The Classic Work on How to achieve Happiness*. Rider.
Cummins, J. (2000). Language, power and pedagogy. In *Language, Power and Pedagogy*. Multilingual Matters www.multilingual-matters.com/page/detail/Language-Power-and-Pedagogy/?k=9781853594731
Cutter-Mackenzie, A., & Rousell, D. (2019). Education for what? Shaping the field of climate change education with children and young people as co-researchers, *Children's Geographies*, 17(1), 90–104, https://doi.org/10.1080/14733285.2018.1467556
Dahlberg, G., & Moss, P. (2005). *Ethics and Politics in Early Childhood Education*. Routledge Falmer.
Dam, L. (1995). *Learner Autonomy*. Authentik.
Darian-Smith, K., & Henningham, N. (2014). Social research and the privacy and participation of children: Reflections on researching Australian children's playlore. *Children & Society*, 28 (4), 327–338. https://doi.org/10.1111/j.1099-0860.2012.00475.x
David, M., Edwards, R., & Alldred, P. (2001). Children and school-based research: 'Informed consent' or 'educated consent'? *British Educational Research Journal*, 27 (3), 347–365. https://doi.org/10.1080/01411920120048340
Davis, J. (2009). Involving children. In K. Tisdall, J. Davis, & M. Gallagher (eds), *Research with Children and Young People: Research Design, Methods and Analysis* (pp. 154–193). SAGE.
Deci, E. L., & Ryan, R. M. (2012). Self-determination theory. In P. A. M. Van Lange, A. W. Kruglanski, & E. T. Higgins (eds), *Handbook of Theories of Social Psychology*, vol. 1 (pp. 416–436). SAGE. https://doi.org/10.4135/9781446249215.n21
Declaration of Helsinki (1964). https://www.wma.net/policies-post/wma-declaration-of-helsinki-ethical-principles-for-medical-research-involving-human-subjects/
DeKeyser, R. (2012). Interactions between individual differences, treatments, and structures in SLA. *Language Learning*, 62, 189–200. https://doi.org/10.1111/j.1467-9922.2012.00712.x
Deleuze, G., & Guattari, S. (2004). *A Thousand Plateaus: Capitalism and Schizophrenia*. Continuum.
DiCarlo, C. F., Baumgartner, J. J., Ota, C., & Geary, K. (2016). Child sustained attention in preschool-age children. *Journal of Research in Childhood Education*, 30(2), 143–152. https://doi.org/10.1080/02568543.2016.1143416
Dobson, A. (2003). *Citizenship and the Environment*. Oxford University Press. https://doi.org/10.1093/0199258449.001.0001
Dobson, A. (2007). Environmental citizenship: Towards sustainable development. *Sustainable Development*, 15, 276–285. https://doi.org/10.1002/sd.344
Donaldson, M. (1986). *Children's Minds*. Fontana.
Dourda, K., Bratitsis, T., Griva, E., & Papadopoulou, P. (2014). Content and language integrated learning through an online game in primary school: A case study. *Electronic Journal of e-Learning*, 12(3), 243–258.

Driessnack, M., & Furukawa, R. (2012). Arts-based data collection techniques used in child research. *Journal for Specialists in Pediatric Nursing, 17(*1), 3–9. https://doi.org/10.1111/j.1744-6155.2011.00304.x

Dulay, H., & Burt, M. (1972). Goofing: An indicator of children's second language learning strategies. *Language Learning, 22* (2), 235–252. https://doi.org/10.1111/j.1467-1770.1972.tb00085.x

Dulay, H., & Burt, M. (1974). Natural sequences in child second language acquisition. *Language Learning, 24*(1), 37–53. https://doi.org/10.1111/j.1467-1770.1974.tb00234.x

D'Warte, J. (2021). Facilitating agency and engagement: Visual methodologies and pedagogical interventions for working with culturally and linguistically diverse young people. *Language Teaching Research, 25*(1), 12–38. https://doi.org/10.1177/1362168820938826

Dweck, C. S. (2006). *Mindset: The New Psychology of Success*. Random House.

Edwards, C., Gandini, L., & Foreman, G. (eds) (1998). *The Hundred Languages of Children.* Greenwood Publishing Group.

EECERA (2015). European Early Childhood Education Research Association Ethical Code. www.eecera.org/wp-content/uploads/2016/07/EECERA-Ethical-Code.pdf

Einarsdottir, J. (2014). Children's perspectives on play. In L. Brooker, M. Blaise, & S. Edwards (eds), *The SAGE Handbook of Play and Learning in Early Childhood* (pp. 319–329). SAGE. https://doi.org/10.4135/9781473907850

Ellis, G. (2014). 'Young learners': Clarifying our terms. *ELT Journal, 68*(1), 75–78. https://doi.org/10.1093/elt/cct062

Ellis, G., & Knagg, J. (2013). British Council signature event: Global Issues in primary English. In T. Pattison (ed.), *IATEFL 2012 Glasgow Conference Selections* (pp. 20–21). IATEFL Publications.

Ellison, M. (2019). CLIL in the primary school context In S. Garton & F. Copland (eds), *Routledge Handbook of Teaching English to Young Learners* (pp. 247–268). Routledge.

Emery, H. (2012). A global study of primary English teachers' qualifications, training and career development: ELT Research Papers, 12-08. British Council.

Enever, J. (ed.) (2011). *ELLiE, Early Language Learning in Europe*. British Council.

Enever, J. (2014). Primary English teacher education in Europe. *ELT Journal, 68*(3), 231–242. https://doi.org/10.1093/elt/cct079

Enever, J. (2018). *Policy and Politics in Global Primary English*. Oxford University Press.

Enever, J., & Lindgren, E. (eds) (2017). *Early Language Learning: Complexity and Mixed Methods*. Multilingual Matters.

Ennew, J. (2009). *The Right to Be Properly Researched: How to Do Rights-Based Scientific Research with Children.* Norwegian Centre for Child Research and World Vision International.

ERIC (2016) The International Charter and Guidelines for Ethical Research Involving Children. https://childethics.com

Facca, D., Gladstone, B., & Teachman, G. (2020). Working the limits of 'giving voice' to children: A critical conceptual review. *International Journal of Qualitative Methods, 19*, 1–10. https://doi.org/10.1177/1609406920933391

Faulkner, E. A., & Nyamutata, C. (2020). The decolonisation of children's rights and the colonial contours of the convention on the rights of the child, *The International Journal of Children's Rights, 28*(1), 66–88. https://doi.org/10.1163/15718182-02801009

Feinberg, J. (2007) The child's right to an open future. In R. R. Curren (ed.), *Philosophy of Education: An Anthology* (pp. 112–123). Wiley-Blackwell.

Fielding, M. (2001). Beyond the rhetoric of student voice: New departures and new constraints in the transformation of 21st century schooling. *Forum, 43*(2), 100–112. https://doi.org/10.2304/forum.2001.43.2.1

Fielding, M. (2011). Patterns of partnership: Student voice, intergenerational learning and democratic fellowship. In: N. Mockler & J. Sachs (eds), *Rethinking Educational Practice through Reflexive Inquiry* (pp. 61–75). Springer. https://doi.org/10.1007/978-94-007-0805-1_5

Fielding, M., & Bragg, S. (2003). *Students as Researchers: Making a Difference*. Pearson.

Fielding, M., & Moss, P. (2011). *Radical Education and the Common School: A Democratic Alternative*. Routledge.

Flutter, J., & Rudduck, J. (2004) *Consulting Pupils: What's in it for Schools?* Routledge.

Franks, M. (2011). Pockets of participation: Revisiting child-centred participation research. *Children & Society, 25*(1), 15–25. https://doi.org/10.1111/j.1099-0860.2009.00258.x

Fraser, S., Flewitt, R., & Hammersley, M. (2014) What is research with children and young people? In A. Clark, R. Flewitt, M., Hammersley, & M. Robb, (eds), *Understanding Research with Children and Young People*. (pp. 34–50). Open University Press.

Freeman, M. (2011) Children's rights and human rights: Reading the UNCRC. In J. Qvortrup, W. A. Corsaro, & M-S. Honig (eds), *The Palgrave Handbook of Childhood Studies* (pp. 377–393). Palgrave Macmillan.

Freire, P. (1970). *Pedagogy of the Oppressed*. Seabury Press.

Freire, P. (1973). *Education for Critical Consciousness*. Seabury Press.

Gallagher, M. (2008). Power is not an evil: Rethinking power in participatory methods. *Children's Geographies, 6*(2), 137–150. https://doi.org/10.1080/14733280801963045

Gallagher, M, Haywood, S. L., Jones, M. W., & Milne, S. (2010). Negotiating informed consent with children in school-based research: A critical overview *Children & Society, 24*, 471–482. https://doi.org/10.1111/j.1099-0860.2009.00240.x

Gao, X. (2013). Reflexive and reflective thinking: A crucial link between agency and autonomy. *Innovation in Language Learning and Teaching, 7*(3), 226–237. https://doi.org/10.1080/17501229.2013.836204

García Mayo, M. P. (ed.) (2017). *Learning Foreign Languages in Primary School: Research Insights*. Multilingual Matters.

García Mayo, M. P. (2021). 'Are you coming back? It was fun': Turning ethical and methodological challenges into opportunities in task-based research with children. In A. Pinter & K. Kuchah (eds), *Ethical and Methodological Issues in Researching Young Learners in School Contexts* (pp 68–86). Multilingual Matters.

García Mayo, M. P., & Lázaro Ibarrola, A. (2015). Do children negotiate meaning in task-based interaction? Evidence from CLIL and EFL settings. *System*, 54, 40–54. https://doi.org/10.1016/j.system.2014.12.001

Garton, S., & Copland, F. (eds) (2019). *The Routledge Handbook of Teaching English to Young Learners*. Routledge. https://doi.org/10.4324/9781315623672

Geertz, C. (1973). Thick description: Toward an interpretive theory of culture. In C. Geertz (ed.), *The Interpretation of Cultures: Selected Essays* (pp. 3–30). Basic Books.

Genesee, F. (2016). North America. Rethinking early childhood education for English language learners: The role of language. in V. Murphy & M. Evangelou (eds), *Early Childhood Education in English for Speakers of Other Languages* (pp. 21–42). British Council.

Giddens A (1984) *The Constitution of Society: Outline of the Theory of Structuration*. University of California Press.

Gillett-Swan, J. K., & Sargeant, J. (2018). Voice inclusive practice, digital literacy and children's participatory rights. *Children & Society*, 32(1), 38–49. https://doi.org/10.1111/chso.12230

Gilligan, C. (1982). *In a Different Voice: Psychological Theory and Women's Development*. Harvard University Press.

Gittins, D. (2009). The historical construction of childhood In M. J. Kehily (ed.), *An Introduction to Childhood Studies* (pp. 35–49). Open University.

Graham, A., Powell, M. A., & Taylor, L. (2015). Ethical research involving children: Encouraging reflexive engagement in research with children and young people *Children & Society*, 29, 331-343. https://doi.org/10.1111/chso.12089

Graham, A., Powell, M. A., & Truscott, J. (2016). Exploring the nexus between participatory methods and ethics in early childhood research. *Australasian Journal of Early Childhood*, 41(1), 82–89. https://doi.org/10.1177/183693911604100111

Granena, G., & Long, M. (eds). (2013). *Sensitive Periods, Language Aptitude, and Ultimate L2 Attainment*. John Benjamins Pulishing. https://doi.org/10.1075/lllt.35

Graue, M. E., & Walsh, D. J. (1998). *Studying Children in Context: Theories, Methods and Ethics*. SAGE.

Gray, C., & Winter, E. (2011). The ethics of participatory research involving young children with special needs. In D. Harcourt, B. Perry, & T. Walker (eds), *Researching Young Children's Perspectives* (pp. 26–37). Taylor and Francis.

Greene, S., & Hill, M. (2005). Researching children's experiences: Methods and methodological issues. In S. Greene & D. Hogan (eds), *Researching Children's Experiences: Methods and Approaches* (pp. 1–21). SAGE.

Greenfield, C. (2011). Personal reflection on research process and tools: Effectiveness, highlights and challenges in using the Mosaic approach. *Australasian Journal of Early Childhood*, 36(3), 109–116. https://doi.org/10.1177/183693911103600314

Griffin, K. M. (2019). Participatory research interviewing practices with children. In A. Eckhoff (ed.), *Participatory Research with Young Children. Educating the Young Child* (pp. 55–71). Springer. https://doi.org/10.1007/978-3-030-19365-2_4

Groundwater-Smith, S., Dockett, S., & Bottrell, D. (2015). Ethical questions in relation to participatory research with children and young people. In S. Groundwater-Smith, S. Dockett, & D. Bottrell (eds), *Participatory Research with Children and Young People* (pp. 37–54). SAGE. https://doi.org/10.4135/9781473910751

Groundwater-Smith, S., & Mockler, N. (2016). From data source to co-researchers? Tracing the shift from 'student voice' to student–teacher partnerships in Educational Action Research. *Educational Action Research*, 24(2), 159–176. https://doi.org/10.1080/09650792.2015.1053507

Hakuta, K. (1976). A case study of a Japanese child learning English. *Language Learning*, 26, 321–351. https://doi.org/10.1111/j.1467-1770.1976.tb00280.x

Hammersley, M. (2015). Research ethics and the concept of children's rights. *Children & Society*, 29, 569–582. https://doi.org/10.1111/chso.12077

Hammersley, M. (2017). Childhood Studies: A sustainable paradigm? *Childhood*, 24(1), 113–127. https://doi.org/10.1177/0907568216631399

Hanson, K., & Peleg, N. (2020). Waiting for children's rights theory. *The International Journal of Children's Rights*, 28(1), 11–35. http://dx.doi.org/10.2139/ssrn.3501733

Harcourt, D., & Hägglund, S. (2013). Turning the UNCRC upside down: A bottom-up perspective on children's rights *International Journal of Early Years Education*, 21(4), 286–299. https://doi.org/10.1080/09669760.2013.867167

Hardman, C. (1973). Can there be an anthropology of children? *Journal of the Anthropology Society of Oxford*, 4(1), 85–99.

Hart, R. (1992). Children's Participation: From Tokenism to Citizenship. Innocenti Essays. UNICEF International Child Development Centre.

Harwood, D. (2010). Finding a voice for child participants within doctoral research: Experiences from the field. *Australasian Journal of Early Childhood*, 35(4), 4–13. https://doi.org/10.1177/183693911003500402

Hasselgreen, A. (2005). Assessing the language of young learners. *Language Testing*, 22(3), 337–354. https://doi.org/10.1191/0265532205lt312oa

Hatch, M. (2014). *The Maker Movement Manifesto: Rules for Innovation in the New World of Crafters, Hackers, and Tinkerers*. McGraw-Hill Education.

Hayes, D (2000) Factors Influencing Success in Teaching English in State Primary Schools. British Council. www.teachingenglish.org.uk/sites/teacheng/files/pub_E324_Factors_influencing_success_in_teaching_English_in_state_primary_schools_FINAL%20v3_WEB.pdf

Heath, S., Brooks, R., Cleaver, E., & Ireland, E. (2009). *Researching Young People's Lives*. SAGE. https://dx.doi.org/10.4135/9781446249420

Held, V. (2006). *The Ethics of Care: Personal, Political, and Global.* Oxford University Press. https://doi.org/10.1093/0195180992.001.0001

Herring, J. (2013). Forging a relational approach: Best interests or human rights? *Medical Law International, 13*(1), 32–54. https://doi.org/10.1177/0968533213486542

Hohti, R., & Karlsson, L. (2014). Lollipop stories: Listening to children's voices in the classroom and narrative ethnographical research. *Childhood, 21*(4), 548–562. https://doi.org/10.1177/0907568213496655

Holec, H. (1981). *Autonomy and Foreign Language Learning.* Pergamon.

Holm, M. (2011). Project-based instruction: A review of the literature on effectiveness in prekindergarten. *River Academic Journal, 7*(2), 1–13.

Holmberg, A., & Alvinius, A. (2020). Children's protest in relation to the climate emergency: A qualitative study on a new form of resistance promoting political and social change. *Childhood, 27*(1), 78–92. https://doi.org/10.1177/0907568219879970

Huang, B. H. (2016). A synthesis of empirical research on the linguistic outcomes of early foreign language instruction. *International Journal of Multilingualism, 13*(3), 257–273. https://doi.org/10.1080/14790718.2015.1066792

Ibrahim, N. (2021). Artefactual narratives of multilingual identity: Methodological and ethical considerations in researching children. In A. Pinter & K. Kuchah (eds), *Ethical and Methodological Issues in Researching Young Language Learners in School Contexts* (pp. 126–146). Multilingual Matters. https://doi.org/10.21832/9781800411432-008

Ioannou-Georgiu, S., & Pavlou, P. (eds) (2011). *Guidelines for CLIL Implementation in Primary and Pre-Primary Education.* European Commission.

Jaekel, N., Schurig, M., Florian, M. & Ritter, M. (2017). From early starters to late finishers? A longitudinal study of early foreign language learning in school. *Language Learning, 67,* 631–664. https://doi.org/10.1111/lang.12242

James, A., Jenks, C., & Prout, A. (1998). *Theorising Childhood.* Polity Press.

James, A., & Prout, A. (eds) (1990). *Constructing and Re-constructing Childhood.* Routledge. https://doi.org/10.4324/9781315745008

James A., & Prout, A. (eds). (2004). *Constructing Childhood: Theory, Policy and Social Practice.* Palgrave Macmillan.

Jarrold, C., Mackett, N., & Hall, D. (2014). Individual differences in processing speed mediate a relationship between working memory and children's classroom behaviour. *Learning and Individual Differences, 30,* 92–97. https://doi.org/10.1016/j.lindif.2013.10.016

Jia, G., & Aaronson, D. (2003). A longitudinal study of Chinese children and adolescents learning English in the United States. *Applied Psycholinguistics, 24*(1), 131–161. https://doi.org/10.1017/S0142716403000079

Jia, G., & Fuse, A. (2007). Acquisition of English grammatical morphology by native Mandarin-speaking children and adolescents: Age-related differences. *Journal of Speech, Language and Hearing Research, 50*(5), 1280–1299. https://doi.org/10.1044/1092-4388(2007/090)

Johnson, K. (2008). Teaching children to use visual research methods. In Thompson, P. (ed.) *Doing Visual Research with Children and Young People* (pp. 77–94). Routledge.

Johnstone, R. (2019). Languages policy and English for young learners in early education. In S. Garton & F. Copland (eds), *Routledge Handbook of Teaching English to Young Learners* (pp. 13–29). Routledge.
Jones, A. (2004). Involving children and young people as researchers. In S. Fraser, V. Lewis, S. Ding, M. Kellett, & C. Robinson (eds), *Doing Research with Children and Young People* (pp. 113–130). SAGE.
Jónsdóttir, S. R. (2017). Innovation and entrepreneurial education and makerspaces. In J. Marsh, K. Kumpulainen, B. Nisha, A. Velicu, A. Blum-Ross, D. Hyatt, S Jónsdóttir, R Levy, S. Little, G. Marusteru, M. Ólafsdóttir, K Sandvik, F. Scott, K. Thestrup, H. C. Arnseth, K. Dýrfjörð, A. Jornet, S. H. Kjartansdóttir, K. Pahl, & G. Thorsteinsson (eds), *Makerspaces in the Early Years: A Literature Review* (pp. 21–26). University of Sheffield. http://makeyproject.eu/wp-content/uploads/2017/02/Makey_Literature_Review.pdf
Jónsdóttir, S. R., & Macdonald, A. (2013). Settings and pedagogy in innovation education. In L. V. Shavinina (ed.), *The Routledge International Handbook of Innovation Education* (pp. 273–287). Routledge.
Kahila, J., Tedre, M., Kahila, S., Vartiainen, H., Valtonen, T., & Mäkitalo, K. (2021). Children's gaming involves much more than the gaming itself: A study of the metagame among 12- to 15-year-old children. *Convergence*, 27(3), 768–786. https://doi.org/10.1177/1354856520979482
Kanat-Maymon, Y., & Assor, A. (2010). *Teachers' Support for Students' Explorations of Values and Goals: Effects on Perceived Autonomy, Engagement and Grades.* Ben Gurion University.
Kehily, M. J. (2009). *Childhood Studies: An Introduction*, 2nd ed. Open University Press.
Kellett, M. (2005). *How to Develop Children as Researchers: A Step-by-Step Guide to Teaching the Research Process.* SAGE. https://dx.doi.org/10.4135/9781446212288
Kellett, M. (2006). Pupils as active researchers: Using engagement with research process to enhance creativity and thinking skills in 10–12 year-olds. [Paper presentation]. British Educational Research Association Annual Conference 6–9 September 2006. University of Warwick. http://oro.open.ac.uk/25779/
Kellett, M. (2010a). *Rethinking Children and Research: Attitudes in Contemporary Society.* Continuum.
Kellett, M. (2010b), Small shoes, big steps! Empowering children as active researchers. *American Journal of Community Psychology*, 46, 195–203. https://doi.org/10.1007/s10464-010-9324-y
Kellett, M. (2014). Images of childhood and their influence on research. In A. Clark, R. Flewitt, M. Hammersley & M. Robb (eds), *Understanding Research with Children and Young People* (pp. 15–33). SAGE Books. https://dx.doi.org/10.4135/9781526435637.n2
Kellett, M., Forrest, R., Dent, N., & Ward, S. (2004). 'Just teach us the skills please, we'll do the rest': Empowering ten-year-olds as active researchers. *Children & Society*, 18, 329–343. https://doi.org/10.1002/chi.807
Kinash, S., & Hoffman, M. (2008). Child as researcher: Within and beyond the classroom. *Australian Journal of Teacher Education*, 33(6), 76–93. http://dx.doi.org/10.14221/ajte.2008v33n6.6

Kirova, A., & Emme, M. (2008). Fotonovela as a research tool in image-based participatory research with immigrant children. *International Journal of Qualitative Methods*, 7(2), 35–57. https://doi.org/10.1177/160940690800700203

Kim, C-Y. (2016). Why research by children? Rethinking the assumptions underlying the facilitation of children as researchers. *Children & Society*, 30, 230–240. https://doi.org/10.1111/chso.12133

Komulainen, S. (2007). The ambiguity of the child's 'voice' in social research. *Childhood*, 14(1), 11–28. https://doi.org/10.1177/0907568207068561

Kormos, J., Brunfaut, T., & Michel, M. (2020). Motivational factors in computer-administered integrated skills tasks: A study of young learners. *Language Assessment Quarterly*, 17(1), 43–59. https://doi.org/10.1080/15434303.2019.1664551

Kravchuk, N. (2021). Privacy as a new component of the 'best interest' of the child in the new digital environment *The International Journal of Children's Rights*, 29(1), 99–121. https://doi.org/10.1163/15718182-29010006.

Kress, G., & van Leeuwen, T. (1990). *Reading Images*. Deakin University Press.

Kuchah, K. (2013) *Context-Appropriate ELT Pedagogy: An Investigation in Cameroonian Primary Schools*. Doctoral Dissertation, University of Warwick.

Kuchah, K., & Milligan, L. (2021). Navigating cultural and methodological complexities in research with children in a sub-Saharan African context. In A. Pinter & K. Kuchah (eds), *Ethical and Methodological Issues in Researching Young Learners in School Contexts* (pp. 165–183). Multilingual Matters. https://doi.org/10.21832/9781800411432

Kuchah, K., & Pinter, A. (2012). 'Was this an interview?' Breaking the power barrier in adult-child interviews in an African context. *Issues in Educational Research*, 22(3), 283–297.

Kumpulainen, K. (2017) Makerspaces: Why they are important for digital literacy education. In J. Marsh, K. Kumpulainen, B. Nisha, A. Velicu, A. Blum-Ross, D. Hyatt, S Jónsdóttir, R Levy, S. Little, G. Marusteru, M. Ólafsdóttir, K Sandvik, F. Scott, K. Thestrup, H. C. Arnseth, K. Dýrfjörð, A. Jornet, S. H. Kjartansdóttir, K. Pahl, & G. Thorsteinsson (eds), *Makerspaces in the Early Years: A Literature Review*, (pp. 12–16). University of Sheffield. http://makeyproject.eu/wp-content/uploads/2017/02/Makey_Literature_Review.pdf

Kumpulainen, K., Lipponen, L., Hilppo, J., & Mikkola, A. (2014). Building on the positives in children's lives: A co-participatory study on the social construction of children's sense of agency. *Early Childhood Development and Care*, 184(2) 211–229. https://doi.org/10.1080/03004430.2013.778253

Kumpulainen, K., & Ouakrim-Soivio, N. (2019). My treasure box: Pedagogical documentation, digital portfolios and children's agency in Finnish early years education. In A. Eckhoff (ed.), *Participatory Research with Young Children* (pp. 105–126). Springer International.

Lamb, M. (2011). Future selves, motivation and autonomy in long-term EFL learning trajectories. In G. Murray, X. Gao, & T. Lamb (eds), *Identity, Motivation and Autonomy in Language Learning* (pp. 177–194). Multilingual Matters.

Lamb, M., & Budiyanto (2013). Cultural challenges, identity and motivation in state school EFL. In E. Ushioda (ed.), *International Perspectives on Motivation: Language Learning and Professional Challenges* (pp. 18–34). Palgrave Macmillan.

Lambelet, A., & Bethele, R. (2015). *Age and foreign Language Learning in School* Palgrave Macmillan.

Lansdown, G. (2005). Can you hear me? The right of young children to participate in decisions affecting them. Working papers in early childhood development, No. 36. Bernard van Leer Foundation. https://bibalex.org/baifa/Attachment/Documents/114976.pdf

Larkins, C., & Young Researchers (2014). Essential ingredients in child- and young-person-led research. In: J. Westwood, C. Larkins, D. Moxon, Y. Perry, N Thomas (eds), *Participation, Citizenship and Intergenerational Relations in Children and Young People's Lives: Children and Adults in Conversation* (pp. 109–116). Palgrave Pivot. https://doi.org/10.1057/9781137379702_11

Legenhausen, L. (2001). Discourse behaviour in an autonomous learning environment. *AILA Review* 15, 65–69.

Lenneberg, E. H. (1967). The biological foundations of language. *Hospital Practice*, 2(12), 59–67. https://doi.org/10.1080/21548331.1967.11707799

Leith, R. (2008). Creatively researching children's narratives through images and drawings. In P. Thomson (ed.), *Doing Visual Research* (pp. 37–58). Routledge.

Leonard, M. (2016). *The Sociology of Children, Childhood and Generation.* SAGE. https://doi.org/10.4135/9781529714494

Leonet, O., Cenoz, J., & Gorter, D. (2017). Challenging minority language isolation: Translanguaging in a trilingual school in the Basque Country. *Journal of Language, Identity & Education*, 16(4), 216–227. https://doi.org/10.1080/15348458.2017.1328281

Lewis, A. (2010), Silence in the context of 'child voice'. *Children & Society*, 24, 14–23. https://doi.org/10.1111/j.1099-0860.2008.00200.x

Li, Y., Han Y., & Gao, X. (2019) Young learners' motivation for learning English. In S. Garton & F. Copland (eds,) *Routledge Handbook of Teaching English to Young Learners* (pp. 60–72). Routledge.

Liebenberg, L., Jamal, A., & Ikeda, J. (2020). Extending youth voices in a participatory thematic analysis approach. *International Journal of Qualitative Methods*, 19, 1–13. https://doi.org/10.1177/1609406920934614

Lightbown, P. M., & Spada, N. (1990). Focus-on-form and corrective feedback in communicative language teaching: Effects on second language learning. *Studies in Second Language Acquisition*, 12(4), 429–448. http://dx.doi.org/10.1017/S0272263100009517

Lin, A. M. Y., & Wu, Y. 2015. 'May I speak Cantonese?' Co-constructing a scientific proof in an EFL junior secondary science classroom. *International Journal of Bilingual Education and Bilingualism* 18, 289–305. https://doi.org/10.1080/13670050.2014.988113

Lipponen, S., Rajala, A., Hilppö, J., & Paananen, M. (2016) Exploring the foundations of visual methods used in research with children, *European*

Early Childhood Education Research Journal, 24(6), 936–946. https://doi.org/10.1080/1350293X.2015.1062663

Little, D. (2011). *The European language portfolio: A guide to the planning, implementation and evaluation of whole-school projects.* Council of Europe.

Little, D. (2022). Language learner autonomy: Rethinking language teaching. *Language Teaching, 55*(1), 64–73. https://doi.org/10.1017/S0261444820000488

Little, D., Dam, L., & Legenhausen, L. (2017). *Language Learner Autonomy: Theory, Practice and Research.* Multilingual Matters.

Lloyd-Smith, M., & Tarr, J. (2000). Researching children's perspectives: A sociological dimension. In A. Lewis, & G. Lindsey (eds), *Researching Children's Perspectives* (pp. 59–70). Open University Press.

Lomax, H. (2012). Contested voices? Methodological tensions in creative visual research with children. *International Journal of Social Research Methodology, 15*(2), 105–117. https://doi.org/10.1080/13645579.2012.649408

Lomax, H., Smith, K., McEvoy, J., Brickwood, E., Jensen, K., & Walsh, B. (2022). Creating online participatory research spaces: Insights from creative, digitally mediated research with children during the COVID-19 pandemic. *Families, Relationships and Societies, 11*(1), 19–37. https://doi.org/10.1332/204674321X16274828934070

López-Gopar, M. E. (2016). *Decolonizing Primary English Language Teaching.* Multilingual Matters.

López-Gopar, M. E. (2019). Introducing international critical pedagogies in ELT. In M. E. López-Gopar (ed.), *International Perspectives on Critical Pedagogies in ELT* (pp 1–15). Palgrave Macmillan. https://doi.org/10.1007/978-3-319-95621-3_1

López-Gopar, M. E., & Sughrua, W. (2014). Social class in English language education in Oaxaca, Mexico, *Journal of Language, Identity & Education, 13*(2), 104–110. https://doi.org/10.1080/15348458.2014.901822

Lowden, J. (2002). Children's rights: A decade of dispute. *Journal of Advanced Nursing, 37*(1), 100–107. https://doi.org/10.1046/j.1365-2648.2002.02049.x

Lundy, L. (2007). 'Voice' is not enough: Conceptualising Article 12 of the United Nations convention on the rights of the child. *British Educational Research Journal, 33*(6), 927–942. https://doi.org/10.1080/01411920701657033

Lundy, L. (2018). In defence of tokenism? Implementing children's right to participate in collective decision-making. *Childhood, 25*(3), 340–354. https://doi.org/10.1177/0907568218777292

Lundy, L., & McEvoy, L. (2012). Childhood, the United Nations Convention on the Rights of the Child, and research: What constitutes a 'rights-based' approach? In M. Freeman (ed.), *Law and Childhood Studies: Current Legal Issues 14* pp. 75–91. Oxford University Press. https://doi.org/10.1093/acprof:oso/9780199652501.003.0006

Lundy, L., McEvoy, L., & Byrne, B. (2011). Working with young children as co-researchers: An approach informed by the United Nations Convention on the Rights of the Child. *Early Education & Development, 22*(5), 714–736. https://doi.org/10.1080/10409289.2011.596463

Lyster, R., & Ranta, L. (1997). Corrective feedback and learner uptake: Negotiation of form in communicative classroom. *Studies in Second Language Acquisition*, 19(1), 37–66. https://doi.org/10.1017/S027226319 7001034

Mackey, A., Kanganas, A. P., & Oliver, R. (2007). Task familiarity and interactional feedback in child ESL classrooms. *TESOL Quarterly*, 41(2), 285–312. https://doi.org/10.1002/j.1545-7249.2007.tb00060.x

Mackey, A., Oliver, R., & Leeman, J. (2003). Interactional input and the incorporation of feedback: An exploration of NS–NNS and NNS–NNS adult and child dyads. *Language Learning*, 53(1), 35–66. https://doi.org/10.1111/1467-9922.00210

Mandell, N. (1988). The least-adult role in studying children. *Journal of Contemporary Ethnography*, 16, (4), 433–467. https://doi.org/10.1177/0891241688164002

Marsh, J. (2017). Introduction. In J. Marsh, K. Kumpulainen, B. Nisha, A. Velicu, A. Blum-Ross, D. Hyatt, S. Jónsdóttir, R. Levy, S. Little, G. Marusteru, M. Ólafsdóttir, K. Sandvik, F. Scott, K. Thestrup, H. C. Arnseth, K. Dýrfjörð, A. Jornet, S. H. Kjartansdóttir, K. Pahl, & G. Thorsteinsson (eds), *Makerspaces in the Early Years: A Literature Review*, (pp. 6–11). University of Sheffield. http://makeyproject.eu/wp-content/uploads/2017/02/Makey_Literature_Review.pdf

Mathew, R., & Pinter, A. (2021). Children and teachers as co-researchers in Indian classrooms: Some ethical issues. In A. Pinter & K. Kuchah (eds), *Ethical and Methodological Issues in Researching Young Language Learners in School Contexts* (pp. 206–222). Multilingual Matters. https://doi.org/10.21832/9781800411432-012

Mayall, B. (2002). *Towards a Sociology of Childhood: Thinking from Children's Lives*. Open University Press.

Mayes, E. (2016). Shifting research methods with a becoming-child ontology: Co-theorising puppet production with high school students. *Childhood*, 23(1), 105–122. https://doi.org/10.1177/0907568215576526

Mayne, F., & Howitt, C. (2015). How far have we come in respecting young children in our research?: A meta-analysis of reported early childhood research practice from 2009 to 2012. *Australasian Journal of Early Childhood*, 40(4), 30–38. https://doi.org/10.1177/183693911504000405

Mazzei, L. A. (2003). Inhabited silences: In pursuit of a muffled subtext. *Qualitative Inquiry*, 9(3), 355–368. https://doi.org/10.1177/1077800403009 003002

McKay, P. (2006). *Assessing Young Language Learners*. Cambridge University Press.

McNamee, S., & Seymour, J. (2013). Towards a sociology of 10–12 year olds? Emerging methodological issues in the 'new' social studies of childhood. *Childhood*, 20(2), 156–168. https://doi.org/10.1177/0907568212461037

Mead, M. (1934). The use of primitive material in the study of personality. *Character & Personality; A Quarterly for Psychodiagnostic & Allied Studies*, 3, 1–16.

Mercer, S. (2012). The complexity of learner agency. *Journal of Applied Language Studies*, 6(2), 41–59. https://apples.journal.fi/article/view/97838

Mercer, S. (2019). Language learner engagement: Setting the scene. In X. Gao (ed.), *Second Handbook of English Language Teaching* (pp. 643–660). https://doi.org/10.1007/978-3-319-58542-0_40-1

Miliander, J., & Trebbi, T. (eds) (2008). *Policies and Language Learning Autonomy in Schools*. Authentik.

Millonig, D. M., Stickler U., & Coleman J. (2019) Young pupils' perceptions of their foreign language learning lessons: The innovative use of drawings as a research tool. *The Language Learning Journal*, 47(2), 229–245. https://doi.org/10.1080/09571736.2016.1270348

Moon, J. (2000). *Children Learning English*. Macmillan Education.

Montreuil, M., Bogossian, A., Laberge-Perrault, E., & Racine, E. A. (2021). Review of approaches, strategies and ethical considerations in participatory research with children. *International Journal of Qualitative Methods*, 20. https://doi.org/10.1177/1609406920987962

Moriarty, M. (2017). Developing resources for translanguaging in minority language contexts: A case study of rapping in an Irish primary school. *Language, Culture and Curriculum*, 30(1), 76–90. https://doi.org/10.1080/07908318.2016.1230623

Morrow, V., & Richards, M. (1996). The ethics of social research with children: An overview. *Children & Society*, 10(2), 90–105. https://doi.org/10.1111/j.1099-0860.1996.tb00461.x

Mortari, L., & Harcourt, D. (2012). 'Living' ethical dilemmas for researchers when researching with children. *International Journal of Early Years Education*, 20(3), 234–243. https://doi.org/10.1080/09669760.2012.715409

Moss, P. (2014). *Transformative Change and Real Utopias in Early Childhood Education: A Story of Democracy, Experimentation and Potentiality*. Routledge.

Moss, P. (2019). Alternative Narratives in early childhood, or why contest early childhood. *Innovations in Early Education*, 12–20. www.reggioalliance.org/wp-content/uploads/2019/04/NAR19_Innovations_261_PeterMoss.pdf

Mourão, S. (2021). The ethical practices of collecting informed consent from child participants in action research projects. In A. Pinter & K. Kuchah (eds), *Ethical and Methodological Issues in Researching Young Learners in School Contexts* (pp. 223–242). Multilingual Matters.

Mourão, S., & Lourenço, M. (eds) (2015). *Early Years Second Language Education: International Perspectives on Theory and Practice*. Routledge. https://doi.org/10.4324/9781315889948

Mukhurjee, K. (2015). Investigating the impact of project-based learning in an Indian ESL classroom. In C. N. Giannikas, L. McLaughlin, G. Fanning, & N. Deutsch Muller (eds), *Children Learning English: From Research to Practice*. IATEFL/Garnet Education.

Muñoz, C. (2006). The effects of age on foreign language learning: The BAF project. In C. Muñoz (ed.), *Age and the Rate of Foreign Language Learning* (pp. 1–40). Multilingual Matters.

Muñoz, C. (2008). Symmetries and asymmetries of age effects in naturalistic and instructed L2 learning. *Applied Linguistics*, 29(4), 578–596. https://doi.org/10.1093/applin/amm056

Muñoz, C. (2014). Contrasting effects of starting age and input on the oral performance of foreign language learners. *Applied Linguistics*, 35(4), 463–482. https://doi.org/10.1093/applin/amu024

Muñoz, C., & Singleton, D. (2011). A critical review of age-related research on L2 ultimate attainment. *Language Teaching*, 44(1), 1–35. https://doi.org/10.1017/S0261444810000327

Murphy, V. A. (2014). *Second language Learning in the Early School Years: Trends and Contexts*. Oxford University Press.

Murphy, V. A. (2021). Social justice and questions of marginalization in research with linguistically diverse children. In A. Pinter & K. Kuchah (eds), *Ethical and Methodological Issues in Researching Young Learners in School Contexts* (pp. 87–105). Multilingual Matters.

Murphy, V., & Evangelou, M. (eds) (2016). *Early Childhood Education in English for Speakers of Other Languages*. British Council. www.teachingenglish.org.uk/sites/teacheng/files/pub_F240%20Early%20Childhood%20Education%20inners%20FINAL%20web.pdf

Myers, J. P. (2006). Rethinking the social studies curriculum in the context of globalization: Education for global citizenship in the U.S. *Theory and Research in Social Education*, 34(3), 370–394. https://doi.org/10.1080/00933104.2006.10473313

Newmann, F. M., King, M. B., & Carmichael, D. L. (2007). Authentic instruction and assessment: Common standards for rigor and relevance in teaching academic subjects. Iowa Department of Education. http://psdsped.pbworks.com/w/file/fetch/67042713/Authentic-Instruction-Assessment-Blue Book.pdf

Niemi R., Kumpulainen, K., & Lipponen, L. (2015). Pupils' documentation enlightening teachers' practical theory and pedagogical actions. *Educational Action Research*, 23(4), 599–614, https://doi.org/10.1080/09650792.2014.942334

Nikolov, M. (1999). 'Why do you learn English?' 'Because the teacher is short.' A study of Hungarian children's foreign language learning motivation. *Language Teaching Research*, 3(1), 33–56. https://doi.org/10.1177/136216889900300103

Nikolov, M. (ed.) (2016). *Assessing Young Learners of English: Global and Local Perspectives*. Springer International.

Nikolov, M., & Lugossy, R. (2021). A critical overview of research methods used in studies on early foreign language education in pre-schools. In M. Schwartz (ed.), *Handbook of Early Language Education*. (pp. 1–37) Springer. https://doi.org/10.1007/978-3-030-47073-9_9-1

Nikolov, M., & Mihaljevič Djigunovič J. (2011). All shades of every colour: An overview of early teaching and learning of foreign languages. *Annual Review of Applied Linguistics*, 31, 95–119. https://doi.org/10.1017/S0267190511000183

Nikolov, M., & Timpe-Laughlin, V. (2021). Assessing young learners' foreign language abilities. *Language Teaching*, *54*(1), 1–37. https://doi.org/10.1017/S0261444820000294

Noddings, N. (1984). *Caring: A Feminine Approach to Ethics and Moral Education*. University of California Press.

Noddings, N. (2003). *Happiness and Education*. Cambridge University Press. https://doi.org/10.1017/CBO9780511499920

Noyes, A. (2008). Using video diaries to investigate learner trajectories: Researching the 'unknown unknowns'. In P. Thompson (ed.), *Doing Visual Research with Children and Young People* (pp. 132–145). Routledge. https://doi.org/10.4324/9780203870525

Nuremberg Code (1947). https://research.wayne.edu/irb/pdf/2-2-the-nuremberg-code.pdf

Nutbrown, C. (ed.) (1996). *Respectful Educators – Capable Learners: Children's Rights and Early Education*. SAGE. https://dx.doi.org/10.4135/9781446219003

O'Donnell, H. (2017). UFA young researchers and evaluators impact report. Children's University. www.childrensuniversity.co.uk/media/1094/ufa-report-final.pdf

O'Kane, C. (2008). The development of participatory techniques: Facilitating children's views about decisions which affect them. In P. Christensen & A. James (eds), *Research with Children: Perspectives and Practices*, 2nd ed., (pp. 125–155). Routledge. https://doi.org/10.4324/9780203964576

Oliver, R. (2000). Age differences in negotiation of feedback in classroom and pairwork. *Language Learning*, *50*(1), 119–151. https://doi.org/10.1111/0023-8333.00113

Oliver, R. (2002). The patterns of negotiation for in child interactions. *The Modern Language Journal*, *86*(1), 97–111. https://doi.org/10.1111/1540-4781.00138

Oliver, R. (2009). How young is too young: Investigating negotiation of meaning and corrective feedback in children aged five to seven years. In A. Mackey & C. Polio (eds), *Multiple Perspectives on Interaction: Second Language Research in Honor of Susan M. Gass* (pp. 135–156). Routledge. https://doi.org/10.4324/9780203880852

Oliver, R., & Azkarai, A. (2017). Review of child second language acquisition (SLA): Examining theories and research. *Annual Review of Applied Linguistics*, *37*, 62–76. https://doi.org/10.1017/S0267190517000058

Oliver, R., Nguyen, B., & Sato, M. (2017). Child ISLA. In S. Loewen & M. Sato (eds), *The Routledge Handbook of Instructed Second Language Acquisition* (pp. 468–487). Routledge.

Ortega, L. (2005). Methodology, epistemology, and ethics in instructed SLA research: An introduction. *The Modern Language Journal*, *89*(3), 317–327. https://doi.org/10.1111/j.1540-4781.2005.00307.x

Otwinowska, A., & Foryś, M. (2017). They learn the CLIL way, but do they like it? Affectivity and cognition in upper-primary CLIL classes. *International Journal of Bilingual Education and Bilingualism*, *20*(5), 457–480. https://doi.org/10.1080/13670050.2015.1051944

Papp, S. (2019). Assessment of English language learners. In S. Garton and F. Copland (eds), *Routledge Handbook of Teaching English to Young Learners* (pp 389–408). Routledge.

Paradis, J. (2007). Second language acquisition in childhood. In E. Hoff & M. Shatz (eds), *Blackwell Handbook of Language Development* (pp. 387–405). Blackwell. https://doi.org/10.1002/9780470757833.ch19

Pascal, C., & Bertram, T. (2009). Listening to young citizens: The struggle to make real a participatory paradigm in research with young children, *European Early Childhood Education Research Journal*, 17(2), 249–262. https://doi.org/10.1080/13502930902951486

Patkowski, M. (1994). The critical age hypothesis and interlanguage phonology. In M. Yavas (ed.), *First and second Language Phonology* (pp. 205–221). Singular Publishing Group Inc.

Partnership for 21st Century Skills, (2009). Learning environments: A 21st Century skills implementation guide. https://skupnost.sio.si/pluginfile.php/464207/mod_resource/content/0/Gradivo/21st_century_learning_environments.pdf

Parry, B. (2015). Arts-based approaches to research with children: Living with mess. In E. Stirling & D. Yamada-Rice (eds), *Visual Methods with Children and Young People. Studies in Childhood and Youth* (pp. 89–99). Palgrave Macmillan. https://doi.org/10.1057/9781137402295_6

Parsons, S., Sherwood, G., & Abbott, C. (2016). Informed consent with children and young people in social research: Is there scope for innovation? *Children & Society*, 30, 132–145. https://doi.org/10.1111/chso.12117

Pellerin, M. (2014). Language tasks using touch screen and mobile technologies: Reconceptualizing task-based CALL for young language learners. *Canadian Journal of Learning and Technology*, 40(1).

Pfenninger, S. E., & Singleton, D. (2016). The age factor in the foreign language class: What do learners think. *Theory and Practice of Second Language Acquisition*, 2(1), 7–23. www.journals.us.edu.pl/index.php/TAPSLA/article/view/3930

Pfenninger, S. E., & Singleton, D. (2017). *Beyond Age Effects in Instructional L2 Learning: Revisiting the Age Factor*. Multilingual Matters.

Phillips, L. G. (2016). Educating children and young people on the UNCRC: Actions, avoidance and awakenings. In J. Gillet-Swan & V. Coppock (eds), *Children's Rights, Educational Research and the UNCRC Past, Present and Future* (pp. 39–59). Symposium Books. https://doi.org/10.15730/books.98

Phillips, M. (2010). The perceived value of videoconferencing with primary pupils learning to speak a modern language. *The Language Learning Journal*, 38(2), 221–238. https://doi.org/10.1080/09571731003790532

Philp, J., Borowczyk, M., & Mackey, A. (2017). Exploring the uniqueness of child Second Language Acquisition (SLA): Learning, teaching, assessment, and practice. *Annual Review of Applied Linguistics*, 37, 1–13. https://doi.org/10.1017/S0267190517000174

Philp, J., Oliver, R., & Mackey, A. (eds) (2008). *Second Language Acquisition and the Younger Learner: Child's Play?* John Benjamins.

Pincock, K., & Jones, N. (2020). Challenging power dynamics and eliciting marginalized adolescent voices through qualitative methods. *International Journal of Qualitative Methods, 19*, 1–11 https://doi.org/10.1177/1609406920958895

Plows, V. (2012). Conflict and coexistence: Challenging interactions, expressions of agency and ways of relating in work with young people in the Minority World. *Children's Geographies, 10*(3), 279–291. https://doi.org/10.1080/14733285.2012.693378

Piaget, J. (1923). *The Language and the Thought of the Child* Harcourt Brace and World.

Pinter A. (2006). Verbal evidence of task-related strategies: Child versus adult interactions. *System, 34*(4), 615–630. https://doi.org/10.1016/j.system.2006.09.005

Pinter, A. (2007). Some benefits of peer–peer interaction: 10-year-old children practising with a communication task. *Language Teaching Research, 11*(2), 189–207. https://doi.org/10.1177/1362168807074604

Pinter, A. (2011). *Children Learning Second Languages*. Palgrave Macmillan.

Pinter, A. (2014). Child participant roles in applied linguistics research. *Applied Linguistics, 35*(2), 168–183. https://doi.org/10.1093/applin/amt008

Pinter, A. (2017) *Teaching Young Language Learners*. Oxford University Press.

Pinter, A. (2019). Learning to become researchers: towards participation? In A. Eckhoff (ed.), *Participatory Research with Young Children* (pp. 177–194). Springer. https://doi.org/10.1007/978-3-030-19365-2_11

Pinter, A. (2022). Child-centred ethics in second language education: Navigating the ethical maze when working with child participants in research. *Language Teaching for Young Learners, 4*(1), 4–29. https://doi.org/10.1075/ltyl.21019.pin

Pinter, A., Mathew, R., & Smith, R. (2016). *Children and Teachers as Co-Researchers in Indian Primary English Classrooms*, ELT research papers 16.03. British Council.

Pinter, A., & Zandian, S. (2015). 'I thought it would be tiny little one phrase that we said, in a huge big pile of papers': Children's reflections on their involvement in participatory research. *Qualitative Research, 15*(2), 235–250. https://doi.org/10.1177/1468794112465637

Pladevall-Ballester, E. (2019). A longitudinal study of primary school EFL learning motivation in CLIL and non-CLIL settings. *Language Teaching Research, 23*(6), 765–786. https://doi.org/10.1177/1362168818765877

Poehner, M.E. (2007), Beyond the test: L2 dynamic assessment and the transcendence of mediated learning. *The Modern Language Journal, 91*(3), 323–340. https://doi.org/10.1111/j.1540-4781.2007.00583.x

Porto, M. (2016). Ecological and intercultural citizenship in the primary English as a foreign language (EFL) classroom: An online project in Argentina. *Cambridge Journal of Education, 46*(4), 395–415. https://doi.org/10.1080/0305764X.2015.1064094

Powell, M. A., Fitzgerald, R. M., Taylor, N., & Graham, A. (2012). International literature review: Ethical issues in undertaking research with children and young people. Southern Cross University, Centre for Children and Young

People/University of Otago, Centre for Research on Children and Families. https://researchportal.scu.edu.au/esploro/outputs/report/International-literature-review-ethical-issues-in/991012821664802368#file-0

Powell, M. A., Graham, A., & Truscott, J. (2016). Ethical research involving children: facilitating reflexive engagement *Qualitative Research Journal*, 16(2), 197–208. https://doi.org/10.1108/QRJ-07-2015-0056

Prasad, G. (2013). Children as co-ethnographers of their plurilingual literacy practices: An exploratory case study. *Language and Literacy*, 15(3), 4–30. https://doi.org/10.20360/G2901N

Prasad, G. (2014). Portraits of plurilingualism in a French international school in Toronto: Exploring the role of visual methods to access students' representations of their linguistically diverse identities. *Canadian Journal of Applied Linguistics*, 17(1), 51–77.

Prasad, G. (2015). Beyond the mirror towards a plurilingual prism: Exploring the creation of plurilingual 'identity texts' in English and French classrooms in Toronto and Montpellier. *Intercultural Education*, 26(6), 497–514. https://doi.org/10.1080/14675986.2015.1109775

Prasad, G. (2018). 'But do monolingual people really exist?' Analysing elementary students' contrasting representations of plurilingualism through sequential reflexive drawing. *Language and Intercultural Communication*, 18(3), 315–334. https://doi.org/10.1080/14708477.2018.1425412

Prasad, G. (2020) 'How does it look and feel to be plurilingual?': analysing children's representations of plurilingualism through collage. *International Journal of Bilingual Education and Bilingualism*, 23(8), 902–924. https://doi.org/10.1080/13670050.2017.1420033

Prasad, G. (2021). Reframing expertise: Learning with and from children as co-investigators of their plurilingual practices and experiences. In A. Pinter & K. Kuchah (eds), *Ethical and Methodological Issues in Researching Young Language Learners in School Contexts* (pp. 106–125). Multilingual Matters. https://doi.org/10.21832/9781800411432-007

Probst, B., & Berenson, L. (2014). The double arrow: How qualitative social work researchers use reflexivity. *Qualitative Social Work*, 13(6), 813–827. https://doi.org/10.1177/1473325013506248

Prout, A. (2019). In defence of interdisciplinary childhood studies. *Children & Society*, 33(4), 309–315. https://doi.org/10.1111/chso.12298

Prošić-Santovac, D., & Rixon, S. (2019) *Integrating Assessment into early Language Learning and Teaching*. Multilingual Matters.

Punch, S. (2002). Research with children: The same or different from research with adults? *Childhood*, 9(3), 321–341. https://doi.org/10.1177/0907568202009003005

Purdy, L. (1994). Why children shouldn't have equal rights. *International Journal of Children's Rights*, 1(3), 223–241.

Rich, S. (ed.) (2014). *International Perspectives on Teaching English to Young Learners*. Palgrave Macmillan.

Qvortrup, J. (ed.) (1994). *Childhood Matters: Social Theory, Practice and Politics*. Avebury Press.

Quennerstedt, A., & Moody, Z. (2020). Educational children's rights research 1989–2019: Achievements, gaps and future prospects, *The International Journal of Children's Rights*, 28(1), 183–208. https://doi.org/10.1163/15718182-02801003

Reeve, J. (2006). Teachers as facilitators: What autonomy-supportive teachers do and why their students benefit. *The Elementary School Journal*, 106(3), 225–236. https://doi.org/10.1086/501484

Reeve, J., & Assor, A. (2011). Do social institutions necessarily suppress individuals' need for autonomy? The possibility of schools as autonomy-promoting contexts across the globe. In V. I. Chirkov, R. M. Ryan, & K. M. Sheldon (eds), *Human Autonomy in Cross-Cultural Context: Perspectives on the Psychology of Agency, Freedom, and Well-Being* (pp. 111–132). Springer. https://doi.org/10.1007/978-90-481-9667-8_6

Rich, S. (ed.) (2014). *International Perspectives on Teaching English to Young Learners*. Palgrave Macmillan.

Rinaldi, C. (2001). The image of the child and the child's environment as fundamental principle. In L. Gandini & C. P. Edwards (eds), *Bambini: The Italian Approach to Infant Toddler Care* (pp. 45–53). Teachers College Press.

Rinaldi, C. (2005). *In Dialogue with Reggio Emilia: Listening, Researching and Learning*. Routledge. https://doi.org/10.4324/9780203317730

Ritterbusch, A. E., Boothby, N., Mugumya, F., Wanican, J., Bangirana, C., Nyende, N., Ampumuza, D., Apota, J., Mbabazi, C., Nabukenya, C., Kayongo, A., Ssembatya, F., & Meyer, S. R. (2020). Pushing the limits of child participation in research: Reflections from a youth-driven participatory action research (YPAR) initiative in Uganda. *International Journal of Qualitative Methods*. 19. https://doi.org/10.1177/1609406920958962

Rixon, S. (2013). *British Council Survey of Policy and Practice in Primary English Language Teaching Worldwide*. British Council.

Robinson, C., & Taylor, C. (2013). Student voice as a contested practice: Power and participation in two student voice projects. *Improving Schools*, 16(1), 32–46. https://doi.org/10.1177/1365480212469713

Rogers, M., & Boyd, W. (2020). Meddling with Mosaic: Reflections and adaptations, *European Early Childhood Education Research Journal*, 28(5), 642–658. https://doi.org/10.1080/1350293X.2020.1817236

Rousell, D., Wijesinghe,T., Cutter-Mackenzie-Knowles, A., & Osborn, M. (2021). Digital media, political affect, and a youth to come: Rethinking climate change education through Deleuzian dramatization. *Educational Review*, 75(1), 33–53 https://doi.org/10.1080/00131911.2021.1965959

Rout, A. (2017). Designing a feedback questionnaire. In A. Pinter, & R Mathew (eds), *Children and Teachers as Co-Researchers: a Handbook of Activities*, ELT Research Papers 16.03 (pp 74–75). British Council.

Rouvali, A., & Riga, V. (2019) Redefining the importance of children's voices in personal social emotional development curriculum using the Mosaic approach, *Education 3–13*, 47(8), 998–1013. https://doi.org/10.1080/03004279.2018.1553990

Ryan, R. M., & Deci, E. L. (2020). Intrinsic and extrinsic motivation from a self-determination theory perspective: Definitions, theory, practices, and future directions. *Contemporary Educational Psychology, 61*, 101860. https://doi.org/10.1016/j.cedpsych.2020.101860

Sandoval, M., & Messiou, K. (2022) Students as researchers for promoting school improvement and inclusion: A review of studies, *International Journal of Inclusive Education, 26*(8), 780–795. https://doi.org/10.1080/13603116.2020.1730456

Sargeant, J., & Gillett-Swan, J. K. (2015). Empowering the disempowered through voice-inclusive practice: Children's views on adult-centric educational provision. *European Educational Research Journal, 14*(2), 177–191. https://doi.org/10.1177/1474904115571800

Sayer, P. (2015). 'More & earlier': Neoliberalism and primary English education in Mexican public schools. *L2 Journal, 7*(3) 40–56. http://dx.doi.org/10.5070/L27323602

Schäfer, N., & Yarwood, R. (2008). Involving young people as researchers: Uncovering multiple power relations among youths, *Children's Geographies, 6*(2), 121–135. https://doi.org/10.1080/14733280801963003

Schneider, W., & Ornstein, P. A. (2015). The development of children's memory. *Child Development Perspectives, 9*(3), 190–195. https://doi.org/10.1111/cdep.12129

Schostak, J., Clarke, M., & Hammersley-Fletcher, L. (2020). Conclusion. In J. Schostak, M. Clarke, & L. Hammersley-Fletcher (eds), *Paradoxes of Democracy, Leadership and Education* (pp. 190–195). Routledge.

Schweisfurth, M. (2013). *Learner-Centred Education in international Perspective: Whose Pedagogy for Whose Development?* Routledge.

Scott, W. A., & Ytreberg, L. H. (1990). *Teaching English*. Longman.

Segers, E., & Verhoeven, L. (2002). Multimedia support of early literacy learning. *Computers & Education, 39*(3), 207–221. https://doi.org/10.1016/S0360-1315(02)00034-9

Shamim, F., & Qureshi, R. (2013). Informed consent in educational research in the South: Tensions and accommodations. *Compare: A Journal of Comparative and International Education, 43*(4), 464–482. https://doi.org/10.1080/03057925.2013.797729

Shernoff, D. J. (2013). *Optimal Learning Environments to Promote Student Engagement*. Springer Science. https://doi.org/10.1007/978-1-4614-7089-2

Shier, H. (2001). Pathways to participation: Openings, opportunities and obligations. *Children & Society, 15*(2), 107–117. https://doi.org/10.1002/chi.617

Shin, H., & Ryan, A. M. (2014). Early adolescent friendships and academic adjustment: Examining selection and influence processes with longitudinal social network analysis. *Developmental Psychology, 50*(11), 2462–2472. https://doi.org/10.1037/a0037922

Shin, J. K., & Crandall, J. A. (2014). *Teaching Young Learners English: From Theory to Practice*. National Geographic Learning/Cengage Learning.

Shintani, N. (2015). The incidental grammar acquisition in focus on form and focus on forms instruction for young beginner learners. *TESOL Quarterly, 49*(1), 115–140. https://doi.org/10.1002/tesq.166

Simon, T. W. (2000). United Nations convention on wrongs to the child. *The International Journal of Children's Rights*, 8(1), 1–13. https://doi.org/10.1163/15718180020494497

Slattery, M. & Willis, J. (2001). *English for Primary Teachers*. Oxford University Press.

Skelton, T. (2008). Research with children and young people: Exploring the tensions between ethics, competence and participation. *Children's Geographies*, 6(1), 21–36. https://doi.org/10.1080/14733280701791876

Skinner, E. A., & Pitzer, J. R. (2012). Developmental dynamics of student engagement, coping, and everyday resilience. In S. Christenson, A. Reschly, & C. Wylie (eds), *Handbook of Research on Student Engagement* (pp. 21–44). Springer. https://doi.org/10.1007/978-1-4614-2018-7_2

Skinner, E. A., Kindermann, T. A., Connell, J. P., & Wellborn, J. G. (2009). Engagement and disaffection as organizational constructs in the dynamics of motivational development. In K. Wentzel & A. Wigfield (eds), *Handbook of Motivation at School* (pp. 223–245). Routledge.

Smit, B. H. J. (2013). Young people as co-researchers: Enabling student participation in educational practice. *Professional Development in Education*, 39(4), 550–573. https://doi.org/10.1080/19415257.2013.796297

Spriggs, M., & Gillam, L. (2019). Ethical complexities in child co-research. *Research Ethics*, 15(1), 1–16. https://doi.org/10.1177/1747016117750207

Spyrou, S. (2011). The limits of children's voices: From authenticity to critical reflexive representation. *Childhood*, 18(2),151–165. https://doi.org/10.1177/0907568210387834

Spyrou, S. (2016) Researching children's silences: Exploring the fullness of voice in childhood research. *Childhood*, 23(1), 7–21. https://doi.org/10.1177/0907568215571618

Spyrou, S. (2018). *Disclosing Childhoods*. Palgrave Macmillan. https://doi.org/10.1057/978-1-137-47904-4_1

Spyrou, S. (2019). An ontological turn for childhood studies? *Children & Society*, 33(4), 316–323. https://doi.org/10.1111/chso.12292

Stalford, H., & Lundy, L. (2020). The field of children's rights; taking stock, travelling forward. *The International Journal of Children's Rights*, 28(1), 1–13. https://doi.org/10.1163/15718182-02801010.

Stryker, H., Boddy, J., Bragg S, & Sims-Schouten, W. (2019). The future of childhood studies and *Children and Society. Children & Society*, 33(4), 301–308. https://doi.org/10.1111/chso.12345

Sung, H., & Padilla, A. M. (1998). Student motivation, parental attitudes, and involvement in the learning of Asian languages in elementary and secondary schools. *The Modern Language Journal*, 82(2), 205–216. https://doi.org/10.1111/j.1540-4781.1998.tb01193.x

Sylvén, L., & Sundqvist, P. (2012). Gaming as extramural English L2 learning and L2 proficiency among young learners. *ReCALL*, 24(3), 302–321. https://doi.org/10.1017/S095834401200016X

Tabali, P. (2017) *Learning English as a Foreign Language: Eliciting Young Chilean Children's Views*. Unpublished Doctoral Dissertation, University of Warwick.

Tai, K. W. H. & W., Li. (2020). Bringing the outside in: Connecting students' out-of-school knowledge and experience through translanguaging in Hong Kong English medium instruction mathematics classes. *System 95*, 102364. https://doi.org/10.1016/j.system.2020.102364

Tisdall, E. K. M. (2012). The challenge and challenging of childhood studies: Learning from disability studies and research with disabled children. *Children & Society*, 26(3), 181–191. https://doi.org/10.1111/j.1099-0860.2012.00431.x

Thelander, N. (2016). Human rights education: Teaching children's human rights – a matter of why, what and how. In J. Gillet-Swan & V. Coppock (eds), *Children's Rights, Educational Research and the UNCRC Past, Present and Future* (pp. 61–79). Symposium Books. https://doi.org/10.1111/chso.12405

Thomas, N. (2007). Towards a theory of children's participation. *The International Journal of Children's Rights*, 15(2), 199–218. https://doi.org/10.1163/092755607X206489

Thomas, N. P. (2017). Turning the tables: Children as researchers In P. Christensen & A. James (eds), *Research with Children: Perspectives and Practices*, 3rd ed. Routledge. https://doi.org/10.4324/9781315657349

Thomas, N. P. (2019) What is the point of studying childhood as a social phenomenon? *Children & Society*, 33(4), 324–332. https://doi.org/10.1111/chso.12297

Thomas, N. P. (2021). Child-led research, children's rights and childhood studies: A defence. *Childhood*, 28(2), 186–199. https://doi.org/10.1177/0907568221996743

Thomas, N., & O'Kane, C. (1998). The ethics of participatory research with children. *Children & Society*, 12, 336–348. https://doi.org/10.1111/j.1099-0860.1998.tb00090.x

Thomson, P. (ed.) (2008). *Doing Visual Research with Children and Young People*. Routledge. https://doi.org/10.4324/9780203870525

Thomson, P., & Gunter, H. (2007). The methodology of students-as-researchers: Valuing and using experience and expertise to develop methods. *Discourse: Studies in the Cultural Politics of Education*, 28(3), 327–342. https://doi.org/10.1080/01596300701458863

Thomson, P., & Gunter, H. (2009). Students' participation in school change: Action research on the ground. In S. E. Noffke & B. Somekh (eds), *The SAGE Handbook of Educational Action Research* (pp. 409–419). SAGE.

Tragant, E., Serrano, R., & Llanes, À. (2017). Learning English during the summer: A comparison of two domestic programs for pre-adolescents. *Language Teaching Research*, 21(5), 546–567. https://doi.org/10.1177/1362168816639757

Treseder, P. (1997). *Empowering Children and Young People*. Save the Children Fund.

Truscott, J., Graham, A., & Powell, M.A. (2019). Ethical considerations in participatory research with young children. In A. Eckhoff (ed.), *Participatory Research with Young Children. Educating the Young Child* (pp 21–38). Springer. https://doi.org/10.1007/978-3-030-19365-2_2

United Nations (1989). *United Nations Conventions on the Rights of the Child.* United Nations.

UNICEF (2002). *State of the World's Children 2002.* UNICEF.

Urbach, J., & Banerjee, R. (2019). Participatory research with young children from special populations: Issues and recommendations. In A. Eckhoff (ed.), *Participatory Research with Young Children. Educating the Young Child* (pp. 127–144). Springer. https://doi.org/10.1007/978-3-030-19365-2_8

Ushioda, E. (2021) *Language Learning Motivation: An Ethical Agenda for Research.* Oxford University Press.

Vacchelli, E. (2018). *Embodied Research in Migration Studies: Using Creative and Participatory Approaches.* Bristol University Press. https://doi.org/10.2307/j.ctv301ddv

Valentine, G. (1999). Being seen and heard? The ethical complexities of working with children and young people at home and at school. *Ethics, Place & Environment,* 2(2), 141–155. https://doi.org/10.1080/1366879X.1999.11644243

Valli, C. (2021). Participatory dissemination: Bridging in-depth interviews, participation, and creative visual methods through Interview-Based Zine-Making (IBZM). *Fennia – International Journal of Geography,* 199(1), 25–45. https://doi.org/10.11143/fennia.99197

Van den Branden, K. (2000). Does negotiation of meaning promote reading comprehension? A study of multilingual primary school classes. *Reading Research Quarterly,* 35, 426–443. https://doi.org/10.1598/RRQ.35.3.6

Veerman, P. (1992). *The Rights of the Child and the Changing Image of Childhood.* Martinus Nijhoff.

Villacañas de Castro, L. S., Cano Bodi, V., Hortelano Montejano, A., Giner Real, C., Gómez Pons, I., Mesas Tomás, B., Sanz Martínez, C., & Tortosa Gozálvez, C. (2021), Matter, literacy, and English language teaching in an underprivileged school in Spain. *TESOL Quarterly,* 55(1), 54–79. https://doi.org/10.1002/tesq.572

Vygotsky, L. (1978). *Mind and Society. The Development of Higher Mental Processes.* Harvard University Press.

Walkerdine, V. (2009). Developmental psychology and the study of childhood. In M. J. Kehily (ed.), *An Introduction to Childhood Studies* (pp. 112–123). Open University Press.

Warin, J. (2011) Ethical mindfulness and reflexivity: Managing a research relationship with children and young people in a 14-year qualitative longitudinal research. *Qualitative Inquiry,* 17(9), 805–814. https://doi.org/10.1177/1077800411423196

Water, T. (2018). Ethical issues in participatory research with children and young people. In I. Coyne & B. Carter (eds), *Being Participatory: Researching with Children and Young People* (pp 37–56). Springer. https://doi.org/10.1007/978-3-319-71228-4_3

Webb, D. (2010). Paulo Freire and 'the need for a kind of education in hope'. *Cambridge Journal of Education,* 40(4), 327–339. https://doi.org/10.1080/0305764X.2010.526591

Wei, R., & Feng, J. (2015). Implementing CLIL for young learners in an EFL context beyond Europe: Grassroots support and language policy in China. *English Today*, *31*(1), 55–60. https://doi.org/10.1017/S0266078414000558

Wilkinson, C., & Wilkinson, S. (2018). Principles of participatory research. In I. Coyne & B. Carter (eds), *Being Participatory: Researching with Children and Young People* (pp. 15–35). Springer. https://doi.org/10.1007/978-3-319-71228-4_2

Winke, P., Lee, S., Ahn, J. I., Choi, I., Cui, Y., & Yoon, H. J. (2018). The cognitive validity of child English language tests: What young language learners and their native-speaking peers can reveal. *TESOL Quarterly*, *52*(2), 274–303. https://doi.org/10.1002/tesq.396

Woodhead, M. (2005). Early childhood development: A question of rights. *International Journal of Early Childhood*, *37*(3), 79–98.

Wright, S., Shelley, B., Fitzallen, N., & Lang, M. (2019). Inspiring the next generation of scientists: Children as researchers and storytellers. *Teaching Science*, *65*(4), 11–25.

Wyness, M. (2015). *Childhood*. John Wiley & Sons.

Wyness, M. (2018). Children's participation: Definitions, narratives and disputes. In C. Baraldi & T. Cockburn (eds), *Theorising Childhood. Studies in Childhood and Youth* (pp. 53–72). Palgrave Macmillan. https://doi.org/10.1007/978-3-319-72673-1_3

Wyness, M. (2019). *Childhood and Society*, 3rd ed. Bloomsbury.

Yates, L. (2005). Introducing new researchers to qualitative research: Some current options for textbooks. *The Modern Language Journal*, *89*(3), 475–482. http://www.jstor.org/stable/3588673

Zandian, S (2015). *Children's Perceptions of Intercultural Issues: An Exploration into an Iranian Context*. Unpublished Doctoral Dissertation, University of Warwick.

Zandian, S. (2021). Constructing joint understanding of research with children. In A. Pinter & K. Kuchah (eds), *Ethical and Methodological Issues in Researching Young Language Learners in School Contexts* (pp. 48–67). Multilingual Matters. https://doi.org/10.21832/9781800411432-004

Zhang, Q. (2015). The voice of the child in early childhood education research in Australia and New Zealand: A systematic review. *Australasian Journal of Early Childhood*, *40*(3), 97–104. https://doi.org/10.1177/183693911504000313

Index

action research, 151, 156, 193, 196
active child roles in research, 149–164
   child-led research, 164–170
   eliciting views, 129–149
adult conception of childhood, 4, 18–21, 26, 39, 99
adult–child relationships
   dialogue, 38, 60, 64, 78, 88, 92, 96, 186, 190
   power gap, 45, 74, 95
   reflexivity, 183, 200
autonomy-promoting schools, 88–90

Bucknall, 39, 45, 63, 64, 70

child development theories, 103–107
child second language education research
   age of participants, 114–115
   child roles, 116–117
   contexts, 115–116
   topic areas in, 109–110
child-centredness
   in applied linguistics, 80–82
   definition of, 9
   in education, 76
Childhood Studies
   emergence of, 23–28
   future of, 209–210
   recent developments, 32–34
codes of ethical practice, 183–185
   BAAL, 179
   BERA, 179
   EECERA, **185–200**
   ERIC, 180–183
consent
   challenges with, 196
   child active roles, 198–200
   child assent, 36, 174, 197
   debate about, 187–188
   parental consent, 174, 181, 188, 191, 194–196
critical period hypothesis, 19, 109, 111

decomratic schools, 95–97
definition of childhood, 12, 18, 113
developmental psychology, 22–23
diamond ranking activity, 139

education as happiness, 84
ethics of care, 185
extended framework of reseach
   in applied linguistics, 34–41
   key components of, 97–101
   relevance of, 201–204

frameworks of participation
   Hart's ladder, 48
   Lundy's model, 51–53
   Shier's pathways, 49–51

Gillick competence, 188
growth mindset, 82

Hart, 48, 53, 93

International Baccalaureate schools, 90
interview
   child conferencing, 143
   focus group, 123
   mobile, 137, 143
   participatory, 54, 62, 138, 145, 152, 159, 164
   peer, 67, 144, 153, 162
   semi-structured, 121, 134
   traditional, 104

James and Prout, 10, 25, 32, 43, 46

Kellett, 6, 11, 16, 31, 32, 34, 37, 38, 46, 63, 65, 69, 71, 114, 153, 175, 192, 199

learner consultation, 92–93
Lundy, 51

maker space, 90–92, 162
mosaic approach, 142–143, 145

on-about-with-by continuum, 5–6, 40, 128–129
Open University Child Research Centre, 63

participatory tools
  art-based, 54, 163
  artefact, 57, 138
  collage, 57, 164
  doll, 54
  drawing, 56, 138
  friendship circle, 145, 146
  mapping, 59, 124, 143, 147, 159
  mask, 54
  my favourite things, 145
  photo, 55, 56–57, 148, 152
  puppet, 54
  story, 59, 124, 149
  video, 57–59
Piaget, 23, 104

questionnaire, 65, 136, 150, 151, 157, 164, 166

Reggio Emilia schools, 3, 78, 143
relationship between research with and by children, 68–74

research by children, 37, 63–68
research ethics
  origins of, 173
  privacy and confidentiality, 197–198
research on and about children, 36–40, 117–122
research training, 62, 63, 64, 70, 90, 100, 125, 128, 153, 157, 159, 161, 162, 165, 166
research with children, 36–37, 60–63, 198–199
research with children, 122–126

school councils, 31
Self-Determination Theory, 15
Shier, 49
social child, 7, 24–26, 33, 38, 39
Spyrou, 32, 42, 43, 44, 45, 74, 210
study of childhood
  historical overview, 21–23

tokenism, 48, 52
twenty-first century skills, 84

UN Convention on the Rights of the Child
  articles of, 174–176
  debate about, 29–30, 176–178
  interpretaions of, 29
  rights, 7, 95, 213
UNICEF schools, 94–95

Voice
  authenticity of, 43
  silence, 45
  situated, 44
Vygotsky, 105

Printed in the USA
CPSIA information can be obtained
at www.ICGtesting.com
LVHW012131060224
771159LV00001B/52